FAMOUS AMERICAN SHIPS

BEING AN HISTORICAL SKETCH OF THE
UNITED STATES AS TOLD THROUGH
ITS MARITIME LIFE

BY

FRANK O. BRAYNARD

Illustrated by the Author

REVISED AND ENLARGED

HASTINGS HOUSE, PUBLISHERS, NEW YORK

COPYRIGHT ACKNOWLEDGMENTS

The author wishes to thank the following authors and publishers for permission to make short quotations from their works:

> HOUGHTON MIFFLIN CO., *The Maritime History of Massachusetts,* by S. E. Morison

> KENNEBECK JOURNAL PRESS, *The Sewall Ships of Steel,* by Mark W. Hennessy

> McBRIDE COMPANY, *Commodore Vanderbilt, An Epic of American Achievement,* by A. D. H. Smith

> PEABODY MUSEUM, *Mary Celeste, The Odyssey of an American Ship,* by C. E. Fay

> UNIVERSITY OF CALIFORNIA PRESS, *The Panama Route,* by John H. Kemble

> VIKING PRESS, *Steamboats Come True,* by James T. Flexner

> W. W. NORTON & CO., *Roll and Go,* by Joanna Colcord

Library of Congress Cataloging in Publication Data

Braynard, Frank Osborn, 1916-
    Famous American ships.

    Bibliography: p.
    Includes index.
    1. Ships—History. 2. Navigation—United States—History. 3. Merchant marine—United States—History. I. Title.
    VM23.B7 1978   387.2'0973   78-8748
    ISBN 0-8038-2377-0

Published simultaneously in Canada by
Saunders of Toronto, Ltd., Don Mills, Ontario

Printed in the United States of America

To Mother S ——

Ella Clayton Shelland

FOREWORD TO ORIGINAL EDITION

It is good to find a book with a new perspective. It is especially gratifying to find one which revives an old and vital, but long neglected viewpoint. A maritime history of the United States has been long overdue. Here it is, and an excellent one at that. Our energies, thoughts and culture have faced West for a century. We have been preoccupied for even longer with wilderness frontiers. Today our future is the world. Our boundaries are not our coastlines, but the oceans of the globe.

We are no longer self sufficient. Essential elements of our daily needs must come across these oceans from abroad. We are coming to realize that there must be at least a minimum ocean merchant marine flying the American flag to insure that these imports are not halted. The same is true, perhaps even more evident in regard to exports. Our present surplus production levels require an uninterrupted flow of sales overseas. The continuity of this trade can only be assured by the existence of a strong American Merchant Marine.

Mr. Braynard's book should help revive America's long dormant interest in things maritime. The book will doubtless be highly popular in the schools of America. However, the story is not didactic. There is no preaching. Ships did help make America and there was never a dull moment in the making. No other phase of our American epic is more exciting, has more drama or appeal to every red-blooded American. Without ships our rivers would have remained streams, our continent would never have been joined politically. We might well have become another Europe, torn by rivalries, peopled by a dozen different nations, speaking different languages, raising customs walls and other barriers between one another.

It is obvious that the sixty-one excellent pen-and-ink sketches by the author were a labor of love. They add much to making the book a continuous whole, aside from their own merit. They have remarkable motion and give zest to the text. Combined with the book's personalized ship histories, they make for a rounded and worthy addition to every man's bookshelf of Americana.

John Marshall Butler
Ranking Minority Member, Merchant Marine Subcommittee
Committee on Interstate and Foreign Commerce
United States Senate

by Senator Daniel K. Inouye, Chairman,
Subcommittee on Merchant Marine and Tourism

"Sign on, young man, and sail with me. The stature of our homeland is no more than the measure of ourselves. Our job is to keep her free. Our will is to keep the torch of freedom burning for all. To this solemn purpose we call on the young, the brave, the strong, and the free. Heed my call. Come sail with me."

JOHN PAUL JONES

SHIPS AND SHIPPING were among the most important tools of the earliest colonists in their battle to turn a new Continent into what is today the United States. Water was the easiest, most reliable and often the only means of travel to open up the North American continent for development of its vast agricultural and industrial resources.

With the cessation of the Revolutionary War and the establishment of the nation, the first Congress looked immediately to strengthening the nation's important merchant marine industry. Significantly, one-third of the 27 laws passed during the first year of the First Congress were maritime laws.

The early years of the nineteenth century saw American vessels carrying a large part of the country's imports and exports. This was the golden age of clipper ships, when American bottoms were not only carrying American cargoes but offering stiff competition for world and British Empire trade.

Our government's modern day commitment to the American merchant marine is embodied in the Merchant Marine Act of 1936, as amended.

That Act is designed to establish and maintain a strong merchant fleet, built by Americans, owned by American citizens, operated by American crews, and fully capable of serving our international economic, military and political commitments under all foreseeable circumstances.

It recognizes that even in times of peace, economic and political tensions and other unforeseen contingencies may seriously disrupt or distort traditional patterns of commercial intercourse on international trade routes.

As such, the Act reflects the realization that an international power such as the United States cannot be dependent upon ocean transportation media owing allegiance to alien flags without threatening its national security.

Regrettably, and to our peril, we seem to have lost sight of the reasons for this commitment and its importance. I believe it is in our national interest to reaffirm that commitment, and our chances for doing so are infinitely better if there is a general understanding and appreciation of the history of our merchant marine.

I therefore especially welcome the new edition of "Famous American Ships" by Frank O. Braynard. By according our maritime heritage the historical importance he does, Mr. Braynard states the case for a strong and viable merchant marine in the strongest possible terms. Wider public understanding will, I believe, encourage a revitalization of this essential national asset. The new edition of "Famous American Ships" can help in this respect, and I commend it to everyone.

Daniel K. Inouye, Chairman
Subcommittee on Merchant Marine and
      Tourism
United States Senator

TABLE OF CONTENTS

Foreword to Original Edition, vi

Foreword by Sen. Daniel K. Inouye, vii

Introduction, xiii

SHIPS helped make America. How they did it and continue to do it is the theme of this book.

The book is prejudiced, we admit. For us ships are about the most wonderful things man has ever made. We have a feeling that most people share in our fascination for ships, boats, clippers and liners. It's hard to explain, but to many of us ships have an almost human appeal. What other inanimate object is so universally referred to as "she"? Is there a child in our country who has not had a toy boat, be it a fancy factory job or a stick of wood? And yet has a book ever been written to show just how great has been the contribution ships have made to America of today?

It's a big order, we know. We don't always stick to our text either. There are doubtless many other famous American ships which should have been included. Perhaps we bent over backwards a bit to pick ships with exciting "lives" for our story.

We chose our sixty famous ships more or less in chronological order. Our first is not strictly a single ship at all, but rather a type of ship—the Viking ship. We firmly believe that much remains to be unearthed about the Viking visits to America. Our history books of today give them far too little credit. More runic markings, mooring rocks and perhaps even a buried Viking ship or two will probably be found on our Continent in the years to come.

Four pre-Revolutionary ships round out our rather sketchy coverage of the era from 1000 A.D. to 1776. A purist might say these weren't really American ships, but rather ships of the 13 British colonies, but we will stick with calling them American.

The remaining fifty-five ships were selected by several different yardsticks. We wanted interesting ships. We looked for a fair geographical distribution. We tried to vary the ships being described, alternating where we could between coastal and deep-sea, side-wheeler and sail, lake and liner. No warships are included, although many of the craft described saw heroic service as auxiliaries in our various wars.

It may be that we have overstressed the role played by steam. It is certainly true that sail played a great part longer under the American flag perhaps than under any other. And yet this was our weakness, with apologies to our sailing men, not our strength. It was with steam that we built much of what is America today, along our coasts, on the Great Lakes and on our great inland waterways.

We would be the last to regard the following pages as more than a beginning. The importance of ships to America will take many studies. Within the past quarter century the interest in our maritime past has quadrupled. There has been formed, for example, the Steamship Historical Society of America. In less than 20 years this group has grown from 7 members to over 1,000. New marine museums on all our coasts have been established. More old ships are being preserved. A maritime Williamsburg is rising at Mystic, Conn. More and more marine books are being written.

Reprints and other publications of the Steamship Historical Society have proved of great help in the preparation of this book. Many friends in the organization have contributed time and ideas. I would like particularly to thank C. Bradford Mitchell, William King Covell, Roger W. McAdam, Donald Ringwald, William H. Ewen, E. K. Hale, Kenneth Haviland, Freeman Hathaway, Capt. Frederick Way, Jr., Alexander C. Brown, and Harlan Scott.

Many associates in the field of steamship operations and public relations have also helped. These include W. Z. Gardner and his son Bill, of Esso Shipping Co.; George Killion and Eugene Hoffman, of American President Lines; Cyrus F. Judson and Paul Knapp, of Alcoa Steamship Co.; John Gehan and Allison Graham, of American Export Lines; Randolph Sevier, Hugh Gallagher and Bernard Clayton, Jr., of Matson Navigation Co.; Walter Jones, of United States Lines; James F. Roche and Clinton Hodder, of Moore-McCormack Lines; James A. Farrell, Jr., and Walter McCormick, of Farrell Lines; Henry F. McCarthy and David M. Brush, of Seatrain Lines; Frederic P. Sands, of Grace Lines; Harry Kelly and G. E. McCaskey, of Delta Line; Capt. William Anderson, of the American Tramp Shipowners Association, and Marge Meyer, Kay and Nancy Reil and especially Eleanor Liebich Jacobick, of the American Merchant Marine Institute.

Other friends to whom we are indebted include William M. Williamson, curator of the Marine Museum of the City of New York; Charles H. P. Copeland, curator of maritime history of the Peabody Museum; John L. Lockhead, librarian of the Mariners' Museum; Paul E. R. Scarceriaux, of the Belgian Nautical Research Association; Frederick Pohl, of the Brooklyn Ship Lore and Model Club, and William Bell Clark.

When all is said and done, it was Doris, my wife, whose help and encouragement in a thousand ways made the book possible.

FRANK O. BRAYNARD

Sea Cliff, L. I.
Dec. 2, 1955

Famous
American
Ships

The Viking ship, whose exploits are still only partly known. Vikings reached as far inland as Minnesota

The Pre-Revolutionary Period

Ever since the earth's crust shriveled and sank making the Atlantic and Pacific oceans, it was ordained that ships would play a leading part in the development of North America. We know relatively little about the countless thousands of Indian canoes and war craft that first dotted our rivers, lakes and coastlines. We are only now learning about the early Viking visitors to our shores. Part One will deal with these ships and with others that sailed from our ports before the shots at Lexington and Concord that were heard around the world. . . .

VIKING SHIPS

I T WAS clear and sunny. The waters of Follins Pond were choppy. The sands of Cape Cod were not far off, set in the deep blue frame of the Atlantic.

A middle-aged couple obviously bent on some errand of keen interest was moving out into the pond in a small, flat-bottomed rowboat. The wind blew stronger, the waves rose and finally Frederick Pohl, teacher, author, explorer, determined that caution was the best part of bravery. He would return Mrs. Pohl to watch from the beach, while he set out alone to search for something he knew must be there, hoped against hope he would find. With Mrs. Pohl safely ensconced on a log, he set out again. The pair had spent days walking, crawling, poking their way through brambles, underbrush and thickets on the edge of the pond, in search of a very special rock. And now they were approaching their problem from the water side. Follins Pond was linked with the Atlantic by Bass River.

The going was heavy, but suddenly Mr. Pohl stopped. While the northern half of the lake's surface was rough, the water near the southern shore was smooth. The high ground above this shore gave shelter against the prevailing southwest winds. But more interesting than that, there were boulders under the high bank, and springs. Most thought-provoking, however, was a tiny rock islet. No such islet or skerry had been indicated on the geological survey map of the area. This is it, he thought, changing course and pulling for the pile of rock.

In a matter of minutes he was gliding up to the twenty-foot-long islet. It was about fifteen feet wide, eight high. A level spot about two feet above the water beckoned like a doorstep on the shoreward side. The other three sides were precipitous. Anchoring his craft and leaping onto the rock was the task of but a moment. Once there it was only a matter of seconds before his eager eyes saw the object of his search, evidence that he was standing on what might well be one of the first landing points of the Vikings in America, the mooring rock of Leif Ericson!

The evidence, and there of course are those who dispute it, was a five-inch hole in the rock. The hole was an inch in diameter. It was a perfect mooring hole, typical of those used by the ancient Norse sailors to hold a ship's stern into the shore. Such mooring holes, expertly drilled with hammer and chisel in a matter of minutes, were ideal to hold peg or bolt fast. They were made slanting shoreward to hold tenaciously against any pull from seaward, but to be flipped out at will by a jerk of the hawser from shipboard when time came to sail.

The discovery of this site and the many further pieces of corroborative evidence since put together in this fascinating historic puzzle will doubtless add new chapters to the history books of the future. Many pieces of the jigsaw picture are still missing, but the general outlines are relatively clear. The Vikings discovered North America some 500 years before Columbus. Their first voyages of exploration were accidental, but these were followed by purposeful missions seeking lumber, sources of food and land for colonization. The story goes something like this:

Thorvald, son of Asvald, had killed a man. He was driven into exile from his home in Norway. He found a refuge in Iceland in the last half of the tenth century. There, his son Eric the Red, by coincidence of fate, also committed manslaughter and was forced to flee. He had heard that there was still another island far west of Iceland, and in 982 he set out to find it. He discovered Greenland, which he so named to make it sound enticing to prospective colonists he hoped would follow him to his new home. The name was deceiving, for except for a thin strip of open land at the southern end, Greenland was a mammoth island of ice.

In 986, the same year in which triumphant Eric led 1,000 eager colonists from Iceland to his "greenland," another Norseman, named Bjarni, set out on what was to become the first more-or-less recorded voyage to the North American Continent. Bjarni intended to go to Greenland. His father had sailed there with Eric as a colonist. But he had only the flimsiest notion of how to reach the new colony. Nothing daunted, he set sail only to be blown far south. He sighted three different lands, or islands, as he thought them, before finally reaching Greenland in a voyage reminiscent of "wrong-way Corrigan" in our own age. Modern navigators and scholars believe he first was blown as far south as Cape Cod, then turned north and sighted Nova Scotia and Newfoundland. His voyage is basically important because it spurred on Leif, son of Eric the Red, to further voyages of discovery which Fred Pohl has devoted such time and energy to documenting, nearly 1,000 years later.

There was good reason for the Norse to strike out first to Iceland, then Greenland and finally to North America. Their homeland is about as big as New Mexico. All but ten per cent is either boggy or mountainous. Only part of the remainder, which is the size of Maryland, was usable for agriculture. The extent of their colonizing is only now being fully understood. Few realize how large and cultured was the Greenland colony. Even less known are their Polar voyages. Some Viking explorations got as far as the 79th parallel in their search for new lands to draw supplies and food from.

Leif Ericson's voyage to North America in 1003 began with a retracing of the route of Bjarni. He established a camp on Cape Cod and made extensive exploration and fishing visits. His brother Thorvald followed in 1005 and did further exploration as far south as Long Island Sound. A second voyage traced the coastline to Maine, where Thorvald was killed by Indians. Five years later another Norse explorer sailed for Wineland, or Vineland as it is more frequently called. He brought his wife, five other women and sixty men. Other visits were made in the eleventh, twelfth and thirteenth centuries.

The most successful of the many voyages that followed in the wake of Bjarni and Leif took place in 1355. Paul Knutson, a nobleman of the combined kingdom of Norway-Sweden, led this historic expedition. He had been assigned by King Magnus to the task of bringing back to Christianity the westernmost settlement in Greenland. Word had reached Magnus that the colonists of this settlement had left their homes and churches to the Eskimos and moved to parts unknown. It was thought they had moved to Vineland, and this, therefore, became the destination of the Knutson expedition. A wide variety of references to this expedition exists in song and legend. Written records, some first-hand, also substantiate the voyage. One outstanding piece of evidence is a sixteenth century copy of the letter by King Magnus to Knutson outlining the importance of the venture and authorizing Knutson to pick his men from the King's own guard. Another is the celebrated Kensington Stone.

Kensington is a town in Minnesota, one thousand miles from salt water. The stone which has made this town's name famous was discovered in 1898. Now lodged in the Smithsonian Institution in Washington, it is generally accepted today as a true relic. Its runic markings describe how a Norse expedition "from Vineland to the West" reached this spot in 1362. It tells how, while eighteen of the men were on a fishing trip, Indians massacred the ten who remained at camp. Another ten had been left by the sea "fourteen-days journey from this island." The story of this stone's history, how it first had wide acceptance only to be denounced as a fraud, forgotten and all but lost, makes fascinating reading. Hjalmar R. Holland, whose book *America 1355-1364* is devoted to the Knutson expedition, rediscovered the stone and after forty years of effort saw it enshrined in our National Museum. Equally thrilling is the search for mooring rocks and similar exploration being done today by Mr. Pohl, a work in which the author has had the privilege of participating in a very small way.

The men who marked the Kensington stone had presumably come from Vineland via the Atlantic Coast north to Hudson Strait and into Hudson Bay. Their boat with her ten guards was left on the Bay's shore near the mouth of the Nelson River. The natural water route led them southward up the river, through Lake Winnipeg and up the Red River into the heart of Minnesota. Their fate is surrounded by vast darkness. Mooring stones, located where they would naturally have been bored, lend strong evidence to the authenticity of this bold voyage. A wide variety of other pieces of evidence has been found and the search is continuing.

The bulk of the expedition had established a semi-permanent camp at what is now Newport, R. I. There is even some reason to think that the old Round Tower still standing there may have been built by this colony. The Newport colonists eventually gave up for lost the explorers who had been sent North to find their way around Vineland. Led by Knutson the survivors headed for home, reaching there in 1364.

The Norse exploits between 1000 and 1364 proved that long voyaging on a substantial scale and with colonists was not impossible. Although their discoveries were not publicized to any degree it is to the Vikings that the major credit must go for opening the great era of exploration which led to the colonizing of the entire globe by Europeans. A second result of this Norse era was the ending of the age-old dependence upon oars. Long rows of oars as shown in the sketch going with this chapter were common still on ships of war. It is thought most likely, however, that Leif's ships used oars only at bow and stern. Leif's cousins, who settled in Normandy at about the time he was landing in North America, had just about given up the use of oars. The ships they used two generations later in the invasion of England under William had no oars.

A discovery was made near Sandefjord in Norway in 1880 that has been of much help in restoring the Viking ship. Known as the Gogstad ship, the relic uncovered was a coaster. It was buried under a large mound of blue clay, a burial mound. A replica was built and crossed the Atlantic in 1892 to visit the Chicago World's Fair. She made ten knots. The boat uncovered was seventy-eight feet long, sixteen feet wide and six feet deep. Built of oak, she had a sharp bow and stern topped with curved dragon heads.

The rudder of the Viking ship was placed on the right side aft. It took the form of a giant steering oar. It was on the right because most people are right-handed and because of the ancient belief that the right arm, eye, leg and the whole right side were stronger than the left. It was natural that this side was known as the steerboard side. It has since been simplified to starboard side. No vessel would dock with her right or steerboard to the land, because the board might be damaged. So the left side came to be known as the loading or lading board side or, as it came down to modern times, the larboard side. This was always the side facing port, and when the term larboard was abandoned the word "port" was a natural substitute.

The MAYFLOWER

JUST as much of the lore connected with the Vikings cannot be scientifically proved, so many of the details surrounding the *Mayflower,* of Pilgrim fame, are lost and gone forever. There is no doubt of the vessel's existence, of her name, of her captain and of the fact that she brought William Bradford and his heroic band of 103 settlers to America. There should be no doubt that she is one of America's most famous ships, a "wave-rocked cradle of our liberties," as Henry B. Culver so aptly described her. But there our facts stop. A web of legend has developed around the tiny craft.

Among the many yarns that shine in the shadowy, cob-webbed attic of our knowledge of the *Mayflower,* two stand out. One is that she was one of the two ships by that name which served England and democracy in the British fleet which defeated the Spanish Armada in 1588. The second, even more astonishing, is that she still exists today in the timbers of an ancient barn in England.

The *Mayflower* was a typical British trading vessel. She went on charter on voyages to a wide variety of destinations. She knew the hazards of Cape Horn. British records describe her goings and comings in the years 1609 to 1624. Nowhere, however, are her dimensions recorded. No picture of her survives to this day. We know only two positive things about her size: that she was not as big as the Pilgrims would have liked her to be and that she measured about 180 tons. We know the name of her master. He was Christopher Jones. A comparison of ships of that day whose dimensions are known, with the *Mayflower,* whose tonnage is known, suggests she may have measured along her keel between fifty-two and seventy-three feet, with a beam of from twenty-four to twenty-seven feet and a depth of ten to thirteen feet.

A series of articles on the *Mayflower* have been written by William A. Baker, naval architect, for the magazine *The American Neptune.* Mr. Baker describes as a "shaky claim" the contention that the *Mayflower* may have participated in the defeat of the Armada. He discounts with a single sentence the theory

This is what the Mayflower may have looked like. There is a story that her timbers still exist in a British barn

that a barn in Buckinghamshire is built of her timbers.

The highly-respected *Christian Science Monitor*, however, has lent its name to an article upholding the barn legend.

Twenty miles outside of London, this claim maintains, rests all that remains of the *Mayflower*. The aged craft was bought in 1624 for $500 by a Buckingham farmer named William Russel, knocked down and transported to his farm where it was carefully reassembled as a livestock shelter. Wood was very scarce in England. The barn is owned by the Society of Friends, who bought it directly from Russel in the seventeenth century. William Penn was among those who were arrested on this farm and dragged off to a prison in 1670. The barn is not advertised as a tourist attraction, although many travelers visit it.

There have been bitter quarrels over the authenticity of the barn timbers, despite the peaceful traditions of the Friends Society. A fifteen-foot-long crack in one of the arched beams is said by some to tally exactly with the crack described in Bradford's diary as having developed on the *Mayflower's* voyage to America in 1620. The bricks used in the barn's foundation are held by those who are on "the barn's side" to be clearly of 1618 vintage.

No one can deny that suggestions of an iron keel may be found on certain of the uprights, and that there are many treenails in the barn, suggestive of ship construction. What is thought to be an iron keel plate is there too, and the timbers are curved. Best of all, however, it is said that the entire barn is undeniably impregnated with salt.

A replica of the *Mayflower*, built in England in 1955, is due to sail to America in 1956. It is one of the projects of the Plimoth Plantation, Inc., of Plymouth, Mass. In the fall of 1955, Comdr. Alan John Villiers, author-skipper, was named to command the modern *Mayflower* on her 1956 voyage to the United States. The 183-ton replica was designed to be given to the people of America as a goodwill gift. Her voyage was scheduled to begin July 4, 1956.

The GRIFFIN

BETWEEN 900 and 1500 A.D. vast new areas of the globe were opened up through a series of discoveries. The Viking Age came first and was followed by one historic voyage after another by Spaniard, Portuguese, English, French and Italian. North and South America lay waiting for exploration. The seething cauldron of Northern Europe was nearly ready to boil over, pouring settlers into the New World. The vast open plains, the great rivers of the Americas were the province of the few bold navigator-explorers. They were spurred forward by stories of gold, furs, and a route to the fabulous Orient, and by the zeal to convert the hostile Indians to Christianity. Ships of all sorts and types were their indispensable allies.

The discovery of the Bahamas, Cuba and Haiti by Columbus was followed by a rapid series of voyages to the Americas. In 1497 John Cabot and his son Sebastian rediscovered the mainland of North America. Central America was located the same year by Pinzon and Vespucci. Vasco da Gama rounded the Cape of Good Hope the following year finding a sea route to India. In 1498 Columbus discovered South America proper. Labrador and Newfoundland were reached by Gaspar Cortereal, a Portuguese navigator, in 1500. Thirteen years later Balboa discovered the Pacific. In 1519 Magellan began his voyage around the world.

Meanwhile others were penetrating the vast green wilderness of the North American continent. Francisco de Garay found the mouth of the Mississippi. Cortes captured Mexico City, Verrazano reached the most magnificent harbor he had ever seen, little realizing that it would one day be the world's greatest port—New York. Jacques Cartier began the exploration of Canada and Cortes found California, establishing Spain's claim to the state of the Golden Bear. The sixteenth century had only begun.

De Soto, later to give his name to an American cargo ship as well as a popular make of automobile, landed in Florida. The first permanent settlement in North America was made by Huguenots in 1564 and was named St. Augustine. Less successful was Raleigh's colony twenty-two years later at Roanoke. Acadia, now Nova Scotia, was founded in the opening years of the seventeenth century. In the same year, Bartholomew Gosnold attempted a settlement on Martha's Vineyard, part of the area known by the Vikings 250 years earlier as Vineland. Whether he saw the great Round Tower built of stone and believed by many to be headquarters of the Knutson expedition to Vineland has never been ascertained. The age of exploration was not yet over, but a new age of settlement was dawning.

Another unsuccessful colony, this time in Maine, is known today as the launching site of the first ship ever built in America. It was on the banks of the Kennebec that discouraged colonists of the Popham settlement completed in 1607 the "faire pinnace" *Virginia* of thirty tons to take them home. No picture of this craft has come down to us, but she was a sturdy vessel and lived to make several crossings of the boisterous North Atlantic. Adrian Block, of New Amsterdam, built the first decked-over vessel seven years later. All along the Atlantic Coast new settlements appeared, spreading, overlapping and all loosely hung together by ships. The sea was their basic source of food, it was their road home and their safe refuge against attack by Indians.

Sixty-four years after the Great Lakes had been discovered by Champlain, and over 300 years after the Vikings of Paul Knutson's expedition had been lost in Minnesota, the French explorer René Robert Cavalier built the *Griffin*. She is known today as the first ship ever to make a voyage on the great Inland Seas, that 1,200-mile chain of deep-water lakes linking New York with Minnesota. Cavalier, better known as LaSalle, had built a small boat on the shores of Lake Ontario some days earlier, but this craft had been lost.

With a flying griffin as a figurehead and a carved eagle aft the Griffin *doubtless frightened many an Indian*

The year was 1679. Only six years before Joliet and Marquette had discovered the Mississippi. LaSalle and his trusty priest-associate Father Hennepin set to work to build the *Griffin* to explore the vast reaches of the Great Lakes. They hoped to find a through route by water to the Orient. The new craft's name did honor to the armorial bearings of LaSalle's patron Frontenac. It was a name well chosen. In mythology the *Griffin* was an imaginary rapacious animal of the eagle species whose duty it was to watch over gold mines and hidden treasure. The *Griffin,* or *Le Griffon* as she is sometimes referred to, was laid down in a clearing on the east bank of the Niagara River near where Cayuga creek drains into the rushing waters and above the great falls. Hostile Senecas looked on with forebodings and would have destroyed the new vessel had they been able. The town of LaSalle claims to be the site of this historic shipyard.

The size of the *Griffin* is uncertain. No contemporary prints of her exist. We know, however, that she mounted a figurehead on her jib boom. It was a huge flying griffin, no less. As if to carry out the precepts of mythology, a giant eagle was carved aft. The griffin motif was frequently used in ancient days as a vertical support for a table. Several examples in Pompeii show the head of a lion at one end and an eagle at the other end of the support. To some degree this ornamentation may have been designed in LaSalle's ship to frighten away the Indians. The curious red men, watching each step of the *Griffin's* construction, dubbed her "Great White Bird" at first sight of her billowing canvas sails.

By standards of her own day the *Griffin's* forty-five to sixty tons made her no small craft. Hume, writing at the end of the sixteenth century, records that only 217 of Great Britain's entire fleet of 1,232 merchant vessels were of over eighty tons. However, LaSalle's vessel was by no means the largest ship to be built in America up to that time. History records that a Puritan minister, the Rev. Hugh Peters, built a ship of 300 tons in Salem in 1641. The Rev. Mr. Peters, incidentally, should have remained in the Colonies. He returned to join Cromwell during the British Civil War, only to be hung when the Stuarts returned to power.

The *Griffin* had two masts and a jib. With all sails set she could have fitted into one of the smokestacks of the superliner *United States*. Armed with five cannon and a supply of muskets and with a crew of thirty-four, including several Jesuit missionaries, she set sail Aug. 7 on what was to be her first and only voyage. Just a century and a half later the same Niagara River was to give birth to another equally illustrious ship—the *Walk-in-the-Water*, first steamboat on the Upper Lakes. Who can tell but that the great-great-grandsons of the Indians who gazed in surprise at the approach of the "Great White Bird" were among the natives who saw the first chugging paddle motions of the *Walk-in-the-Water* as she entered Lake Erie.

At the outset of the *Griffin's* voyage the entire ship's complement fell on their knees and called upon God for protection. They entered Lake Erie singing *Te Deum Laudamus*. Father Hennepin, who was to become a noted historian, jotted down in his record that they were heading into those "vast and unknown seas of which even their savage inhabitants knew not the end." A thousand doubts assailed the weaker members of the crew. They had no charts, their captain and leader was navigating on faith and gumption.

Three days sailing and Lake Erie was behind them. Fresh provisions were secured at the mouth of the Detroit River and the voyage continued. The beauty of this river filled Father Hennepin with wonder. "It was thirty leagues long, bordered by low and level banks, and navigable throughout its entire length," the good Jesuit wrote. "On either side were vast prairies, extending back to hills covered with vines, fruit trees, thickets, and tall forest trees so distributed as to seem rather the work of art than nature."

The site of present-day Detroit was passed. Frequent stops were made, and on the day of the Festival of St. Claire they entered a new and wondrous lake. LaSalle promptly named it Lake St. Claire. He gave the same name to the river which linked it with Lake Huron, into which the *Griffin* moved with calm serenity that belied the fears of many aboard. Hardly had the passage on Lake Huron begun than a furious storm enveloped the "Great White Bird." Her crew's worst fears appeared to be realized. Their hearts were filled with terror. Even bold LaSalle was prompted at the storm's height to vow that if they were delivered he would build a chapel in memory of the patron saint of the sailor—St. Anthony of Padua. And then, just as suddenly as it had arisen, the wind died down, the storm vanished and the *Griffin* rode quietly. Such was not to be the case in her next encounter with a storm on Lake Huron.

The little craft came to anchor at a Jesuit mission recently established among the Ottawas in Michilimackinac Bay, the Straits of Mackinac. On then to Lake Illinois, now Lake Michigan. The voyage ended at a trading post on the spot of the present city of Green Bay. A treasure of furs was waiting there and LaSalle ordered them loaded aboard. He needed money, and the furs would bring $12,000 in gold. History reports that LaSalle was warned not to risk a stormy voyage back to Lake Erie. It is fortunate that he himself did not feel called upon to accompany the little vessel. She sailed on Sept. 18 with a master and a small crew. The *Griffin* was never to be seen again.

It is thought by many that the *Griffin* foundered in a gale similar to the one she had survived on Lake Huron. Rumors were current at first that she was captured by the Indians and destroyed. Then it was thought her crew might have mutinied, sold the furs and made for the Atlantic as best they could. Father Hennepin, who fortunately was too valuable to LaSalle to be allowed to leave his side, leaned toward the storm theory.

Many Great Lakes communities of today point with pride to battered skeletons of ancient ships, claiming the bones are those of the *Griffin*. Manitoulin Island, which separates Lake Huron from Georgian Bay, has an old shipwreck on its westerly shore which has been scientifically examined. It is said that an analysis of the metal found in the wreck suggests that it may date back far enough to be the *Griffin*. No one will ever know, but neither can anyone deny that from her winged lion's head to her crested eagle transom the "Great White Bird" was every inch a famous American ship.

The *REBECCA*

THE EARLIEST American shipping gave promise that new thinking was going to produce new vessel types. Little is known of the first ship built in Massachusetts. She was named *Blessing of the Bay,* and was launched in 1631. But Yankee builders were not the ones to duplicate the high superstructures and

The Rebecca *was a big improvement on Old World ships. From her developed the famed Grand Bank schooners*

many-storied forecastles common to the ships which had brought them to the New World. The famed fishing banks, whose rich harvests meant everything to New England, required different designs.

It was the sacred cod that did much to shape our first new craft. Stripped of the upperwork of old, with sharper bows and narrower hull, the schooner as we know her today was evolved through a century of trial and error. She was a fast ship, could carry more sail. She had no need for a tall poop. Fewer and lower deck structures followed. She would sacrifice all for the sake of a good hull full of salt cod, so popular in the Old World.

There is a yarn about the invention of the schooner. It may have some basis insofar as the application of the name is concerned. In olden days boys who lived by the seaside used to throw flat stones into the water, just as they do today. But then they called the skipping antics of the stones "scooning." And so it was that an onlooker shouted out "see how she scoons," as he watched a new, particularly narrow-hulled boat slide into the water in 1713. This chance remark produced the name "schooner." The schooner was America's greatest early gift to marine architecture. The builder of this first schooner was Captain Andrew Robinson, of Gloucester. It is thought she was named *Mayflower,* and there would have been reason for Capt. Robinson to pick this name. He was a direct descendant of the John Robinson who preached at Leyden to the Pilgrim Fathers before their historic voyage on the *Mayflower* of 1620.

The fishing schooner *Rebecca,* shown in the accompanying drawing, must have been of much the same design as Robinson's craft. She was built in 1798 at Marblehead. Relatively sharp, clean hull lines mark her as a far cry from the blunt styling of ships of the Old World. Her two masts each carried a fore and aft sail set from a boom and gaff, just as with Capt. Robinson's vessel. Up until the schooner, ships with more than one mast had depended on square sails. The square sail hangs at right angles to the fore-and-aft axis of the ship's hull. The fore and aft sail hangs parallel to the length of the craft. The square rig was more complex, more costly, harder to handle. It required twice as many ropes. It is no wonder that it gradually disappeared up and down the Atlantic Coast.

The schooner rig had other advantages. It was far better suited to short tacks, necessary when beating a course up river. It was ideal for the thousand and one inlets and rivers of our coastline. Schooners were quickly adopted in Europe, and schooner types are still common from the Baltic to the Mediterranean. Nowhere, however, were they so universally accepted as in America. No other nation continued to use them on into the age of steam as did Americans.

A picture of the French harbor of Brest in World War I, for example, shows the port filled with American schooners. Four-, five- and six-masted schooners were relatively common a generation ago. Even at this writing a 500-foot steel schooner is under study as a possibility. The extraordinary seven-masted schooner *Thomas W. Lawson* gained short-lived fame as the only one ever to have so many masts. Unfortunately she was ungainly and was lost with all hands off the United Kingdom in 1907, only five years after her completion.

The BETHEL

BETWEEN the earliest voyages of discovery and the period of permanent settlement in North America, there is somewhat of a vacuum insofar as most histories go. Such is not the case for years between the era of colonization and the Revolution. Traits we now proudly call American became evident early in

The Bethel, *a Yankee privateer, captured a huge Spanish galleon loaded with
100,000 pounds sterling*

this period. In shipping these American characteristics were apparent early in
our annals. As evidence, the tales of our first maritime development show rich
profits in both legitimate and not so legitimate enterprises. Strictly legitimate
were the letter-of-marque ships, or privateers as they became better known. On
the less legitimate side were the fortunes made from slave trading and smuggling,
fortunes that were the foundation of many of our best families.

A well-known letter-of-marque ship was the *Bethel*. Ships of this type were
authorized by the authorities to seize vessels of an enemy nation. No phase of
American shipping right down through the War of 1812 provided a more
profitable, and, shall we say, exciting career than privateering. On occasion privateers were hung as pirates.

The *Bethel* sailed out of Quincy. She was of the larger class of Massachusetts-built ships. A painting shows her with traditional lines, extended bowsprit raising forward at a substantial angle. She had the standard ship rig of that day, with square sails on fore, mizzen and mainmasts. A lateen sail, common on ships of that period, hung at a forty-five-degree slant half way up the main. The painting of the *Bethel,* incidentally, is one of the few pictures of ships of this era to survive. Ship portraits were rare at that time. Her gun ports were all on one deck. Her niche in fame rests largely on one encounter. In 1748 she sighted a large Spanish galleon returning home with gold aboard. By what is described as sheer Yankee bluff she captured the huge enemy ship despite the Spaniard's twenty-four guns and crew of 110 men. Her own crew numbered thirty-eight, and her guns only fourteen. The captured gold was valued at nearly 100,000 pounds sterling.

Despite frequent wars with the Indians, and later with the French and their Indian allies, trade and shipping in New England prospered in the more than century and a half following the earliest colonization. Shipping was not a big business in the southern colonies, but ships were equally vital to their economy. The rich plantation owners of Virginia needed ships to export their rice and tobacco and to bring home in return silks and scholarly books from France, expensive clothing and rich paintings from England. Ships were the trucks, automobiles, railroads, canal barges and airplanes of our day all rolled into one. They were more; they even provided the basic means of communication, for through roads were slow in developing, particularly in the South.

New England, on the other hand, and particularly Massachusetts, were predominantly maritime communities. This was not at all what the Founding Fathers had intended, but it was all for the good. Nature made seamen out of would-be farmers, sea captains out of school teachers, rich traders out of shop-keepers, shipbuilders out of carpenters. The vital need for a domestic merchant marine was evident early in Colonial development. The great Civil War of 1641 in England made it obvious that local trade must have local ships as insurance against the time when shipping from across the sea might be withdrawn. The crisis of 1641 was a real one. New England corn was worthless unless it could be shipped abroad and sold in trade. The market in England was suddenly cut off, a new one must be found, and that market proved to be the West Indies. Trade with the West Indies came naturally for New England. Lumber, dried fish and provisions were exchanged for sugar, rum and other West Indian products. Basically the trade was vital in that it pumped new blood into the mercantile life of the colonies, and gave them a taste of independence from England. It was important too in that it served as a splendid incubator period for our maritime enterprise. The sons of captains in the West Indies trade were to seek wider areas of conquest in the Mediterranean and even the Far Orient.

The Grand Turk, *whose picture now adorns a brand of shaving cream, helped open our fabulous China trade*

PART TWO

Some Famous Firsts

There follow eight chapters covering the first half century of America's national development. Maritime enterprise blossomed, the War of 1812 notwithstanding. It developed new trade routes and earned capital that helped New England's industrial revolution. Our Grand Banks schooners caught the cod, which, salted, appeared on the world's dinner table. By-products of our pioneering in steam were the foundation of our patent law and the establishment of Federal control over interstate commerce. Ships sewed our eastern seaboard to the vast new area around the Great Lakes and beyond the Mississippi.

The GRAND TURK

THE *Grand Turk* was the first New England ship to reach the Orient. Two other ships must share her glory. They are the *Experiment*, a tiny 80-ton sloop, not much larger than a lifeboat on a modern liner, and the *Empress of China*. The *Experiment* and the *Empress of China* both beat the *Grand Turk* to China, but pictures of them have not come down to us and we therefore chose the *Grand Turk* as our featured ship for this story. The sketch of this famous vessel is copied from what appears to be a reasonably conscientious rendition on a fancy bowl of Oriental Lowestoft china. She is shown with every piece of canvas spread. In actual practice it is doubtful if her twenty-eight sails would ever have been pulling at the same time.

The *Experiment* was built in Albany. She was commanded by Stewart Dean, who had earned his sea legs as a privateersman in the Revolution. She sailed in 1784, crossing the Pacific, returning in only four months and twelve days. It was daring such as this, laid on a foundation of skill and adorned with enthusiasm, that warned British maritime interests to look to their laurels. She made a grand arrival at Canton, we are told by an eyewitness. She is said to have swung into her assigned wharf frigate fashion, with strains of martial music intermingling with the piping of the boatswain's whistle with all the pomp and style of a war vessel. With a crew of only fifteen, counting boys, we wonder who

17

could have been spared to play music. The *Experiment* was armed, it might be added, with six guns, muskets, boarding pikes and cutlasses, since the Malay pirates were feared as much as or more than the typhoons of Japan.

The voyages of the *Experiment, Empress of China* and *Grand Turk* were of real importance to America. The Revolution was over. We had won, but we had also lost. Our losses could have been calamitous. We were no longer a member of the British family of colonies. Our West Indies commerce was largely lost, our triangle trade denied to us by the British. Our greatest market was gone. Our native produce was a drug on the market. We ourselves could use only so much cod or corn. We needed above all a new market and a new type of specie to trade. The early voyages to the Orient provided the market. Our next famous ship after the *Grand Turk*, the *Columbia*, provided the commodity to trade.

The days were dark for American shipping after the Revolution, and, as a result, for America as a whole. Not content with barring us from the West Indies, the British banned American-built ships to their own shipowners. This was a serious matter, for at the start of the Revolution, one out of three British flag ships had come from Yankee shipwrights. The cost to build a ship in America was from $24 to $38 a ton, while British yards could charge no less than $50 a ton. This had been a particularly sore point to the motherland. British animosity to our shipping reached a peak after the Revolution when a certain Lord Sheffield wrote a pamphlet advocating coldly that the Barbary pirates were a blessing because they preyed on American ships. But a much greater blessing, even, from the British point of view, was Jefferson's Embargo Act which laid up American shipping and left ocean-borne commerce in British hands.

Three months after the evacuation of New York by the Redcoats, the *Empress of China* sailed for China. She sailed on Washington's birthday. It was an event of major importance to New York. While she was away a London newspaper wrote that the Americans had given up all thought of the China trade because it could not be carried on to advantage without colonies in the East Indies. The return of the *Empress of China* gave the lie to this report. Her voyage, which lasted nearly fifteen months, was a big success. Several more like it and the ship would be paid for with plenty to spare.

Elias Hasket Derby, of Salem, was no one to be far behind if a new trade route showed promise. His *Grand Turk*, a celebrated privateer in the Revolution, had been en route to the Cape of Good Hope when the *Empress of China* sailed for the Orient. The *Grand Turk*, in fact, was the first American ship to reach the Cape. Immediately upon her return to Salem, she was sent off to Canton in the wake of the *Empress*.

Salem's Derby was one of the great names in early American shipping. Sightseers today in the now quiet waters of this New England harbor can still see Derby wharf and Derby Street, once the hub of maritime enterprise in America.

An anecdote about Mr. Derby may help explain his success.

The master of a British schooner was brought into Mr. Derby's prosperous counting house near Derby wharf one day in 1784. He had been picked up in a small boat at sea by one of Derby's great fleet of trading ships, the *Atlantic*. His crew had mutinied and set him adrift alone. Several days later the British captain saw his own ship standing in to Salem harbor. The mutinous crew had brought their "prize" into the well-known port to sell her, never dreaming their former master would be there to spot them with a spyglass from Derby's office. One of Mr. Derby's brigs was hastily armed. Commanded by none other than merchant-shipowner Derby himself, the brig took the British crew by surprise, overcame them and turned the ship back to her delighted and grateful British master.

The *Grand Turk's* return from China brought great wealth to Derby. Her bales upon bales of silks and nankeens and her boxes of exotic teas were vied for eagerly by Boston storekeepers. Keeping up with the Cabots now meant having a China silk gown, a chest of Hyson tea or fancy painted chinaware.

A later *Grand Turk* made history as a most profitable privateer in the War of 1812. Privateers were almost entirely former merchant ships of this type. Their officers and seamen were ordinary civilians. Their successes in the Revolution, in our unofficial war with France and in the War of 1812 did much to establish America's reputation as a foe not to be taken lightly. For their own part, the profits in privateering were often so great to the privateersmen that the temptation to continue on as pirates after peace came was too much for many.

As a postscript to the story of the *Grand Turk* it may be of interest to note that a direct descendant of Salem's famous Derby is Dr. Richard Derby, of Oyster Bay, whose wife is the former Ethel Roosevelt, daughter of the late President Theodore Roosevelt. Dr. Derby saved the author's life in 1926 with an emergency operation for ruptured appendix.

Thousands of men today see a picture of the *Grand Turk* every day but may be none the wiser. Her outline is featured on a line of men's toilet articles under the "Old Spice" trade name.

The COLUMBIA

IF ONE ship can be said to have saved America's economy in its earliest and most trying days it was the *Columbia*. It was this same eighty-three-foot vessel which gave America its earliest and one of its best claims to the entire Oregon territory. Finally the *Columbia* was the first American ship to circle the earth. Few ships have more right to a place in our maritime hall of fame.

The Colonies survived the Revolution impoverished, cut off from the vital West Indies route and lacking a trade which would provide gold or silver. The

Grand Turk and *Empress of China* found the much needed new trade route when they opened the way to the Orient, but the Chinese didn't want codfish or corn. Boston merchants had heard that sea-otter skins, which could be bought for a few pennies' worth of trinkets, would sell in China for up to $100 a skin. Such skins might be available in the vast, unknown Pacific Northwest. On this hope of profit rested much we hold dear today.

Chosen for the venture was the ship *Columbia,* built in 1773 but still sturdy. She had been launched on the North River, Scituate, a tiny Massachusetts stream now sand-choked, which in its busiest days had seen more than 1,000 sea-going vessels built on its shores. A two-decker of 213 tons, she was small for her time. A ninety-ton sloop, *Lady Washington,* accompanied the *Columbia.* Two able men commanded these vessels, Capt. John Kendrick, the *Columbia,* and Capt. Robert Gray, the *Lady Washington.* Charles Bulfinch, who later became a famous architect, was one of the men who put up the sum of $50,000 to finance the expedition. Special medals were designed for the voyage to be distributed among the Indians. Many of these along with State of Massachusetts coins given out by the *Columbia's* men turned up years later among the Spaniards of South America, the Oregon Indians and the Kanakas of Hawaii. The expedition was of such importance that the crew was picked with great care. In addition to excellent officers and seamen, the *Columbia* carried a trained furrier, a surgeon, a clerk and an astronomer or schoolteacher.

The voyage around the Horn was nearly disastrous. Both craft took a frightful beating from wild and mountainous waves. On one occasion the *Columbia* was thrown on her beam ends and nearly lost her three masts. The vessels were separated and proceeded alone to the point of rendezvous at Nootka Sound, on Vancouver Island, fur trade headquarters of the West Coast. The little *Lady Washington* arrived first, after having lost Captain Gray's cabin boy in a brush with the Indians en route. When the *Columbia* hove into sight a week later she was a sorry spectacle. Her crew was so weakened by scurvy and yellow fever that they were using only the sails that were easiest to set. Two of her men had died. It was before the day of lime juice as an antidote to scurvy, and fresh vegetables were out of the question. The voyage had taken a year.

The expedition was glad to move out of the cramped quarters on their vessels, and quickly built log huts ashore where they spent the winter of 1788-89. Although they were under the strictest orders to treat the Indians fairly, they took no chances with the red men and maintained constant guard against attack. In their idle hours they set up crude forges and hammered their supply of iron into rude chisels and other tools in which the Indians had shown a keen interest. When trading began in the Spring each chisel brought an otter skin. As the Indians learned the ways of the white men, the value of chisels declined, until it was necessary to trade eight for one skin.

Russian hunters in ages past had introduced sea-otter skins to China. Prime

Battered and blown in a furious gale rounding Cape Horn, the Columbia *took one year to reach the West Coast*

pelts were two feet wide by five feet long. They were described by one fur merchant as, next to a beautiful woman or a lovely baby, the finest natural objects in the world. To get them the *Lady Washington* scoured every inlet and bay along the coast, visiting the Indian villages one by one. To everyone's surprise the Jews'-harps, snuff bottles and rat traps they had brought to trade were not wanted. Pocket mirrors were popular. Beads, buttons and tools went rapidly.

"They do not seem to covet useful things," the clerk aboard the *Lady Washington* noted, "but anything that looks pleasing to the eye, or what they call riches."

Captain Kendrick exchanged commands with Captain Gray and took the little forty-foot *Lady Washington* into the Hawaiian trade. Gray, who had extraordinary qualities of leadership, sailed with the *Columbia* for Canton with nearly a full cargo of furs and an eagerness to return.

Chosen for his talents in spotting new objects of trade, Capt. Kendrick spent the rest of his life trading between the West Coast, the Hawaiian Islands and China. On one occasion his son Solomon was killed and scalped by an Indian. A man of great control and charity, he quietly turned the murderer over to the latter's own chief for whatever punishment Indian law demanded. The little *Lady Washington*, several years later, attempted to open trade with Japan. Although she was ordered to leave without landing, she gained the distinction of being the first American ship to reach the waters of Nippon. She was sixty years ahead of Perry's squadron which finally opened Japan to commercial relations with the rest of the world.

The story of the *Columbia* was far from over. She sold her furs in Canton, loaded a cargo of tea and returned to Boston. She had been gone nearly three years, had logged 41,899 miles, had been the first American ship to girdle the globe, but what's most important, she showed how Yankee grit could find a trading commodity the Chinese wanted. Now the luxuries of the Orient were at the command of the merchants of the New World. It was not necessary for American buyers to pay heavy duties to British or Dutch East India Company ships for the teas and silks of the East. A new, two-way outlet for our shipping and mercantile interests had been found.

Even more important, perhaps, to the average citizen of Boston, were the rumors that the *Columbia* had on board a Sandwich Islander, a King from "Owyhee." With the twice-fired, thirteen-gun salute of the *Columbia* still ringing in their ears, Bostonians could hardly believe their eyes as Attoo strode ashore. He marched behind Captain Gray, for he was none other than the Yankee skipper's new cabin boy, a young Hawaiian prince. With a feathered cloak of golden suns on scarlet, he must have made a proud appearance as he strode along to pay his respects to Governor Hancock. He had saved his Greek-like feather helmet especially for this occasion. Governor Hancock was pleased. He honored the officers and owners of the *Columbia* at a state dinner.

Captain Gray was given little time for festivities. He was quickly assigned to refit the *Columbia*, to see that new masts were stepped, new yards, new equipment provided. Once again his instructions were to beware of the Indians, to have nothing to do with the Spaniards and to carry himself as would any other "free, independent American." Many of his former crew sailed with him, including Robert Haswell, a skilled pen and pencil artist who had been his third mate on the first trip. Haswell was first mate now. Gray's ship's carpenter was Samuel Yendell, who with Gray was a veteran of the Revolutionary Navy. Yendell was later to help build *Old Ironsides*. He is known chiefly, however, for having been the last survivor of the *Columbia's* crew. He lived until 1861.

Attoo went along, too, and Captain Gray lived to be grateful to the tall, brown Hawaiian lad. Attoo's time to serve came not long after the vessel had resumed fur trading in the Northwest area. A conspiracy to destroy the *Columbia* and her crew was hatched by tricky Indians near Clayoquot, where Captain Gray had set up camp to build a new sloop as consort. The plot was discovered by Attoo. The Indians urged him to throw in with them and offered to make him a chief if he would soak down the vessel's supply of gunpowder. He refused and exposed the plotters. The sloop, the first vessel to be built on the West Coast, was finished and the expedition continued on its way.

It is odd how the whole course of history at times seems to be determined by what appears to have been an accidental combination of circumstances. Captain Gray was to discover the mouth of the Columbia River because of a British sea captain's belief in the infallibility of his own judgment, and thereby help establish our claim to the entire Oregon territory, a fact of tremendous consequence. Had we been there to watch, the odds in his favor would have seemed slim. For in the neighborhood was the famed British navigator George Vancouver, veteran of voyages with the even more illustrious discoverer, Captain James Cook. Vancouver had at his disposal a squadron of three ships. He was exploring the Northwest coast in line with a recent British treaty with Spain. He met and talked with Gray but pooh-poohed Captain Gray's assertion that a great river must be in the neighborhood. Vancouver continued on northward. Gray remained and a few days later discovered the river which he named after his ship.

Many years later those American statesmen who were to hold that it was our natural right to expand clear to the Pacific Coast were to base much of their thinking on this voyage and this ship. The discovery of the Columbia River by Gray came twelve years before the Lewis and Clark expedition, nineteen years before John Jacob Astor founded Astoria, the first settlement in the area by men from the United States.

The *Columbia* returned to fur trading, sold her rich cargo of pelts at Macao instead of Canton, because she had developed a leak, and set out for home via St. Helena. She completed her second circumnavigation of the world July 29, 1793.

In the words of historian Samuel Eliot Morison:

> On her first voyage, the *Columbia* had solved the riddle of the China trade. On her second, empire followed in the wake.

JOHN FITCH'S STEAMBOAT

WHILE SAIL was supreme, long before it reached its zenith in the American clipper, there were stirrings in the minds of half a dozen inventors which would lead to the steamboat. There are many who may share in the glory of inventing the steam-propelled vessel. In England there were Hull and Symington, in France the Comte d'Auxiron and Jouffroy. America produced no fewer than six rivals to John Fitch and Robert Fulton: Henry, Morey, Rumsey, Roosevelt,

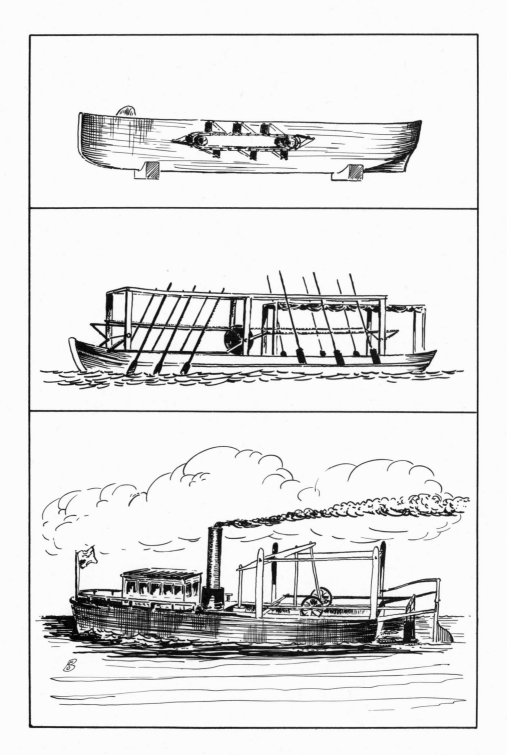

Three steamboat designs by John Fitch: (a) a skiff, (b) his Indian war-canoe-dream boat, (c) his successful 1790 craft

Livingston and Stevens. No tale is more extraordinary than that of John Fitch whose third and final steamboat actually traveled from two to three thousand miles during the summer of 1790 on the Delaware River at a speed of up to eight miles an hour.

Few Americans in the days following our Revolution were much interested in the steamboat. To them it seemed merely a clever toy. Subsequent developments have of course proved how wrong they were. As a sort of by-product, the invention of the steamboat and the wranglings and problems arising out of the original invention greatly influenced the writing of our patent law. John Fitch was the most important pioneer in this picture, and he was followed by Robert Fulton, perhaps less inventor than promoter. We are told by James T. Flexner, in his book *Steamboats Come True:*

> If Fitch had not been a misfit—marvelously skillful yet impractical as a mad man; brilliant, visionary, quarrelsome, wild and strange—the result of his labors would have been very different.
>
> Thus his perpetual rebellion against his environment; his tragic, frustrated childhood; his disastrous marriage which made him a homeless wanderer for life; his ludicrous adventures in the American Revolution; his arduous years as a wilderness surveyor and his terrible months as an Indian captive; his great manual skill that made him successively brass founder, clockmaker, silversmith, map maker, and engine builder; the strange compulsion that forced him to set himself up as the Messiah of a new religion, rival of Christ and Mohammed: all these are part of his strange story.

Fitch's first model of a steamboat, shown in the accompanying illustration, was that of a skiff. An endless belt of flat paddles was fixed on one side of the twenty-three-inch model. We do not know how Fitch planned to connect the paddles with his little two-boiler, two-cylinder atmosphere engine. Plans of the model were submitted to Congress and quickly pigeonholed. Fitch's reaction was quick and revealing; he wrote:

> Determining to revenge myself on the committee of Congress and prove them to be but ignorant boys, I determined to pursue my scheme as long as I could strain a single nerve to forward it. I at that time did not look so much for the benefit, as to prove to the world by actual experiment that they were blockheads.

Fitch actually did win interviews and some measure of support from Franklin, James Madison and Patrick Henry. He even talked with Washington, who had earlier promised James Rumsey a steamboat monopoly on the Potomac. His days were filled with interviews, presentations before this Philosophical Society or that state legislature. One prospect he talked with was John Stevens. Little did Fitch dream that by calling the attention of Stevens to steamboats and their possibilities he would give incentive to a man who was to become a steamboat inventor himself. Not only that, Stevens was to interest Robert R. Livingston, his brother-in-law, in the subject, and Livingston was to turn for help to none other than Robert Fulton.

Fitch next designed and built a craft the like of which had never been seen before. Its inspiration came from a dream about Indians paddling their war canoes.

The boat had four sets of three long oars. They were attached to arms which moved by the turning of a crank. The two forward sets would dip into the water together, move aft and lift up, alternating with the two latter sets of oars. Six oars would always be in the water, while six were in the air. The oars were mounted on a wooden frame rising out of a low, narrow hull. A small canopied section aft was presumably designed for the comfort of the boat's navigators.

The boat worked. The little engine amidship steamed merrily, the perpendicular oars lifted and fell with a crawling motion and the craft moved. But try as they might, Fitch could not win more than three miles per hour from his primitive engine and awkward oars. A rowboat could outrace his pride and joy. Stagecoaches along the Delaware would leave him far in the rear.

Fitch did make some advantage out of what otherwise was a failure. It was 1787 and the Constitutional Convention was meeting in Philadelphia. There were many visitors. The little craft was busily engaged on trial runs with distinguished guests aboard. His successes gave momentum to a law Fitch had been eagerly pushing which gave him a monopoly on the waters of Virginia. Virginia, at that time, stretched far West across the Mississippi Valley to the Pacific. The monopoly was for fourteen years. But it had one condition. Fitch must in three years have two vessels of twenty tons in operation on the waters of the state.

Meanwhile others were active. Rumsey built a jet boat. He wrote pamphlets contesting Fitch's right to a monopoly and gained wealthy friends. John Stevens became actively interested in steamboat inventing. Abroad Watt continued to perfect his steam engine. In both England and France steamboat inventors were rampant, each thinking his was the first. Rumsey went abroad and nearly reached an agreement with Watt which might have assured him of real success. Symington built *his* first craft. It worked briefly. People began attaching names to their steamboat inventions. Rumsey called his *The Columbian Maid*. Symington built a *Charlotte Dundas*. Poor Fitch, on the other hand, temporarily lost his tried and true partner, the capable engineer Henry Voight. Their disagreement was over a lady friend.

And then the sun seemed to shine again for Fitch. His engineer friend returned, new ideas poured into both their brains and a new boat began to emerge. This time they abandoned the tall pole-like oar and used the duck paddle style. This consisted of large, snow-shoveled paddles, three or four of them, extending aft over the transom and moved one by one against the water by a crank. Progress was temporarily set back by a fire which forced Fitch to scuttle his own craft in the early hours of a winter day near the end of 1789. But Fitch persevered, wrangling with financiers, reinventing shortcuts discovered a decade earlier by Watt and surviving derision and dispute. And then the trial run for his third and final steamboat. It was April 16. He wrote:

> Although the wind blew very fresh at the northeast, we reigned Lord High Admirals of the Delaware, and no boat on the river could hold way with us, but all fell astern. Several sailboats, which were very light, and had heavy sails—that brought their gunwales well down to the water, came out to try us. We also passed many boats with oars, which were strongly manned. We also ran round a vessel that was beating to windward in about two miles, which had about 1½ miles start of us, and came in without any of our works failing.

There followed formal tests, with flags and measured distances. The remarkable speed of eight miles an hour was thoroughly accredited. Fitch objected strenuously to the high, fancy cabin that his backers, flushed with success, built on the vessel so she could carry passengers in comfort. He was overruled. Repeated trips were made from Philadelphia to Burlington, New Jersey. Funds for a second boat were gathered to live up to the terms of the Virginia monopoly franchise. Newspaper advertisements lured the curious to *The Steamboat,* as Fitch's craft seems to have been called. Flags for the craft were bought by Governor Mifflin and the State Council of Pennsylvania, but Fitch became moody over the Governor's refusal to officiate at formal presentation ceremonies. Voight's boiler blew out on three occasions. There were other accidents, but apparently no fatalities. A minimum of six miles an hour was regularly achieved. And yet passengers continued to prefer the stage. Efforts to build up a trade to Gray's Gardens on the Schuylkill failed, despite the elegant cabin and the availability of sausages and beer, rum or porter.

A second boat was built and named *Perseverance.* She was torn loose from her moorings and badly damaged by a storm. Meanwhile the Virginia monopoly franchise time limit passed. Fitch was hopelessly in debt. The year 1790 had seen him operating a mechanically successful steamboat all summer, but financially he was a failure. His backers deserted him. His competitors belabored him. Patent troubles plagued him. He was evicted from his rooms. His first successful boat had been junked to get money and parts to complete the *Perseverance.* A second and more serious dispute with Voight brought their partnership to a close.

Fitch's closing years were spent in wanderings abroad and in the West. His dream of establishing steam on the Ohio and Mississippi lasted until the end. It ran counter, however, to important political developments. Congress was

The Clermont, *or actually* The North River Steamboat *as she was officially listed, also known as "Fulton's Folly"*

afraid of a growing Mississippi Valley. Spain controlled New Orleans and was trying to break up the new United States and establish a new Spanish-dominated state in the West. The time was not ripe from the American standpoint for a development which would have stimulated settlement of the great untouched area west of the Alleghenies.

Fitch became a silversmith again. He began drinking too much. In 1796 he moved to Kentucky where in his earlier years he had staked formal claim to a great plantation for himself. Squatters had taken over his property and his last chapter is devoted to a series of never-ending lawsuits to regain these 1,300 acres. Alcohol and so-called opium pills finally brought relief for the tired inventor. His grave was unmarked until 1910 when the John Fitch Chapter of the Daughters of the American Revolution raised a small stone in his honor.

The CLERMONT

ROBERT FULTON would have had few if any passengers on his first brave trip from New York to Albany with the *Clermont* in 1807 had it not been for his partner Robert Livingston. Better known as Chancellor Livingston, Fulton's partner was a patrician, an inventor as well as a feudal lord. It was largely his money that was used to build *The North River Steamboat*, or the *North River*, as the *Clermont* was actually known by people of her day. And it was his relatives and friends who gingerly stepped aboard the long, narrow craft on that warm August 17.

Some historians say a huge crowd gathered to watch the strange craft begin her maiden run. Others hint that the adventure began almost unnoticed. There were many more exciting things taking place. The news of Aaron Burr's trial as a traitor was uppermost in most people's minds. Another burning issue was the *Chesapeake* affair, in which the British warship *Leopard* wantonly attacked our naval vessel and seized four alleged deserters from her decks. Fulton's dreams were interlaced with both these events. His dream of a successful steamboat envisaged a craft able to move up and down our great Western rivers and tie together the newly won Louisiana Purchase area with the thirteen original colonies. With such a development another Burr conspiracy would be impossible. A successful *Clermont* would also lead the way to the use of steam in ships of war. With such craft flying the Stars and Stripes there would be no more *Chesapeake* affairs.

The one newspaper that deigned to record the departure of the *Clermont* on her first voyage was the *American Citizen*. It said:

> Mr. Fulton's ingenious steamboat, invented with a view to the navigation of the Mississippi from New Orleans upward, sails today from North River, near State's prison, to Albany. The velocity of the steamboat is

calculated at 4 miles an hour. It is said it will make a progress of 2 against the current of the Mississippi, and if so it will certainly be a very valuable acquisition to the commerce of the western states.

The *Clermont* was a completely new-looking type of boat to those who saw her on that morning. A roughly pointed bow, a deck without sheer, a low-lying hull and small cabin aft suggested virtually no trace of kinship to vessels common on the waters of the world at that time. This is not to mention the weird-looking smokestack amidship and the bulky and formidable steam engine, much of which was visible above deck. Fulton had been forced to hire strong-arm protection for his craft while she was being built. Her appearance had struck fear into the minds of river boatmen and navigators.

As if to bear out the worst apprehensions of her timorous passengers, the *Clermont* came to an unceremonious clanking stop after having moved barely a few moments from her wharf. Fulton wrote later to describe this tense moment:

> I could distinctly hear repeated, "I told you it was so. . . . It is a foolish scheme. . . . I wish we were well out of it. . . ."
>
> I elevated myself upon a platform and addressed the assembly. I stated that I knew not what was the matter, but if they would be quiet and indulge me for half an hour, I would either go on or abandon the voyage for that time.

It is easy to imagine the quiet that must have followed. Perhaps Harriet Livingston, to whom Fulton had become engaged only three weeks earlier, was on the shore watching with tense sympathy. She was the cousin of the Patriarch himself. She and Robert knew instinctively that the *Clermont* must be a success or their wedding might never take place. Fulton reminisced:

> I went below, and examined the machinery, and discovered that the cause was a slight maladjustment of some of the work. In a short time it was obviated. The boat was again put in motion. She continued to move on. All were still incredulous. None seemed willing to trust the evidence of their senses. We left the fair city of New York; we passed through the romantic and ever varying scenery of the highlands.

The chugging, splashing sound of the engine and paddle wheels must have soon brought a feeling of confidence to the select group of passengers. The impossible was happening and they were right in the midst of probably one of the most extraordinary events of American history. We are told that the gaily dressed guests soon moved to the *Clermont's* stern deck. Some raised their voices in song. They waved at spectators along the Hudson, many of whom were aghast while others cheered. One country bumpkin raced headlong home, slammed his door, closed his shutters and confided in whispered gasps to his wife that a devil was sailing up river in a sawmill.

As evening came we can imagine hampers being unpacked with a general passing around of delicacies, wines and good cheer. Sandwiches always taste better on a picnic and no one minded an occasional salting of wood smoke from the *Clermont's* tall single smokestack. As night fell the ladies repaired to one cabin, the men to another, for this was no mere afternoon's sail.

It would have been an ideal time for Fulton to muse quietly alone at the bow. He was past forty, his life had been busy but not until then startlingly successful. Twenty of his years had been spent abroad where he had met most of the great men of England and France. He had failed as a painter, gained reputation as a canal designer, built and operated a successful steamboat on the Seine, built and submerged for six hours in a submarine, dabbled in international intrigue and come home with a glamorous reputation and light purse.

Many have tried to explain why Fulton succeeded where others failed. For one thing, Fulton went at things in the modern scientific manner. If something didn't work, he found out why it failed. Others had simply tried something different. Adequate financing was another important factor, although Fulton knew well what it meant to be without enough money to pay for his next meal. Fulton consciously combined the best of earlier inventions. He knew how and why each component part worked. He cared less for originality and more for the result. And finally Fulton seemed to have all or most of the best features his illustrious line of steamboat precursors had shared. He was brave in the face of unending obstacles, he breathed a fire of enthusiasm, he loved hard work, he always insisted on doing the most difficult, even dangerous chores himself.

The *Clermont* chugged and groaned along through the night at a steady five miles an hour, three knots slower than Fitch's last and most successful boat of seventeen years earlier. When morning came she was well up the great river. News of her feat had gone on ahead. More and more people waved at her from the shoreline. Flags flew and small boats cut in and around the 100-ton *Clermont*. There was a festive air ashore and aboard. The Chancellor himself joined in the elation of the moment and as the *Clermont* approached his country home at Clermont the great man called out for silence. Addressing the guests who rose to hear his words, he gracefully announced Harriet and Robert's engagement. He went farther. Steamboats would make the name Fulton famous the world over. They would even some day cross the Atlantic.

The *Clermont* anchored at Livingston's estate twenty-four hours after she had left New York City, 120 miles down river. That night her passengers had a good rest in the Chancellor's commodious home, something they probably welcomed heartily. But back they trooped the next morning for the last leg of the voyage, an eight-hour, forty-mile churn to Albany. The voyage had taken thirty-two hours sailing time, in contrast to the best passage by sailing sloop of sixteen hours. It was far from a record, but much more impressive than this comparison suggests. The average time by sailing craft was four days between New York and Albany.

The *Clermont's* first commercial voyage to Albany made Sept. 4 was much more widely celebrated. The boat had been rebuilt, strengthened and fitted with twenty-four bunks. Fourteen of the berths were filled on this trip. One wonders how Fulton was able to crowd as many as ninety aboard the *Clermont* only a month later. A complete rebuilding, from keel to cabin, was called for during the winter months. No effort was spared to make the passenger quarters luxurious. Polished wood, oil paintings, gilt decorations suggested the sumptuous accommodations of later-day river craft. The *Clermont* now had fifty-four berths. She had a galley, bar, pantry and steward's cabin. But best of all, she was to have a sister ship, several sister ships, for she was a paying proposition.

The *Clermont* and her successors faced no mechanical problems that proved as grave a handicap to steamboat development as did one human barrier. The ghosts of Fitch and Rumsey seemed to have descended over the scene. While bigger, more powerful boats were designed and built, the clammy hand of litigation obstructed free use of our waterways. Fulton and Livingston, later joined by Stevens, tried their best to stop all others from operating steamboats. Profits made by the *Clermont* went into lawsuits. Opposition steamboats were seized and scrapped whenever possible. A web of legal snares was woven around Fulton's great invention. It took two of America's greatest men to clear away the barrier. In doing so they paved the way in the establishment of basic principles which were later applied to all forms of economic enterprise and took their place in the foundation of our way of life.

Daniel Webster, as a counsel aiding the Attorney General of the United States, successfully convinced the Supreme Court that the whole structure of steamboat monopoly rulings by state legislatures was contrary to the best interests of the nation as a whole. It is doubtful whether the early states would have been able to stay together had not the freedom of interstate commerce been established once and for all in the Ogden vs. Gibbons case of 1824. Expansion westward would certainly have been vastly hindered had state lines continued as barriers. The steamboat monopoly decision that opened the navigable waters of the Union to all remains to this day one of the outstanding decisions handed down by Chief Justice John Marshall.

The NEW ORLEANS

JOHN FITCH, inventor of steamboats, had failed in his great dream. It had been his chief purpose to put steam propulsion on the Ohio and Mississippi. But Spain owned New Orleans and it was not American policy in Fitch's day to encourage commerce on these rivers. There was fear that the regions through which they passed might grow rich and become independent. The Spanish government and later the French government contributed to these fears, as did some American conspirators, notably Aaron Burr. But when Fulton was ready with his *Clermont* things had changed. One of the prime movers in the Louisiana Purchase which gave New Orleans and the vast Mississippi Valley to the United States was none other than Chancellor Livingston, Fulton's partner and cousin by marriage.

Romance and the heroic qualities of pioneer womanhood have a part in the story of the *New Orleans,* first steamboat on the Ohio or Mississippi. Nicholas J. Roosevelt is the hero, his wife the heroine. Before the story ends we are to see them facing every type of obstacle from wild Indian, sneering unbelievers, hostile river bargemen, and engine failure, to mention only a few. Even nature seemed to conspire to make things difficult for the *New Orleans* and her first voyage to the Gulf. The Roosevelts rose to the occasion against flood, earthquake and the arrival of their first child in the middle of the trip. No wonder that such stock was to produce two of our greatest Presidents.

It was 1809 and the hated Embargo, which had halted all our shipping and trade for fifteen months, had just been repealed. New Orleans was again humming with activity, although it would not be until 1835 that our foreign trade would again reach the $246,000,000 level of the pre-Embargo year of 1807. Canal boats using vast new canal networks would soon be funneling immigrants into the areas bordering on the Ohio. Cities were growing and the bands of communication with the East were stretched to the breaking point. An all-water route down the Mississippi and up along the coast was the missing element. It was a noble challenge that lured young Roosevelt.

Roosevelt was a prominent New York engineer. He had been employed by Livingston in some of the Chancellor's earliest and least successful steamboat adventures. Not one to be backward, Roosevelt had the gall to apply for a patent on the invention of the paddle wheel, a device used for a thousand years in sawmills. He got the patent and was to exact payments from many early steamboat operators.

The success of the *Clermont* led Fulton and Livingston to seek new empires on the Mississippi and the Great Lakes. They chose Roosevelt to be their emissary on the Father of Waters. Young Roosevelt took especial care in building the flatboat at Pittsburgh which was to take him to New Orleans on an exploratory voyage. It was to be his honeymoon as well. It was a flatboat the like of which was probably not to be found anywhere. A bedroom, dining room and pantry were constructed for the Roosevelts aft. The forward cabin housed bunks for the crew and a brick fireplace in the galley.

The honeymoon began in midsummer, 1809. The news of Roosevelt's purpose traveled before him. Many frontiersmen warned that steamboats could never survive the treacherous currents of the Ohio, or of the Mississippi, for that matter. Roosevelt took notes. When he found coal deposits, he arranged for their mining and set up coal-loading sites along the river. His craft was invaded

Two different views of what the New Orleans *first Mississippi steamboat looked like*

one night by Indians. Fortunately they were made happy with a gift of whiskey and left in a jovial mood. From Natchez to New Orleans, the last leg of their voyage, the young couple went by rowboat, spending several nights ashore. And then home to New York by coastal sailing ship and stagecoach; then he penned his report.

Mrs. Roosevelt's wanderings were only briefly interrupted. Despite the fact that she was to become a mother, she left New York in the fall of 1810 for Pittsburgh. Nicholas was sent there to watch the *New Orleans* take shape. The new boat was to be 116 feet long and twenty wide. Like the *Clermont* she was to have two masts and sails. There is some dispute as to whether she had a recessed stern wheel or paddle wheels. Two old prints, published some time ago by the Cincinnati *Post,* have been copied to show both versions of how she may have looked. Roosevelt's close association with the paddle wheel is probably sufficient reason to believe that this was her mode of propulsion. As if eager to get on with her historic task, the *New Orleans* almost went down the ways in a partly built state when flood waters inundated the shipways.

The new vessel was launched on Saint Patrick's Day, 1811. She made nine knots, with the current, a remarkable speed for that day. Three officers and six men made up the $40,000 craft's complement. Mrs. Roosevelt insisted on joining her husband on the first, perilous voyage down river. No one could make her stay at home despite her condition. She was determined to be with him in his triumph or defeat.

Everywhere the new boat was greeted with great interest and great skepticism. Her smoke drove off threatening Indians; escaping steam when she anchored at Louisville caused some to think it was the end of the world. Three interesting things happened at Louisville, the Kentucky city on the Ohio. First the Roosevelts were honored at a public dinner. Next, the Roosevelts returned the favor with a dinner in the main cabin of the *New Orleans.* The guests were comfortably enjoying the ship's hospitality when suddenly the craft began to vibrate. The clanking of machinery suggested that something out of the ordinary had happened. To a man, the diners rose and hurried to the deck. They were under way! Ever the showman, Roosevelt was taking them up river, mindful of the skeptics who had chuckled that it was easy to sail with the current, but "what about going against it, what then?" With the thunder of the Ohio River falls just below the town in their ears, Roosevelt's passengers were suddenly keenly interested in the little steamer's ability to overcome the current. She did, and a new confidence was born in the hearts of the guests that night.

The third development at Louisville was the arrival of the Roosevelt baby. The brief period of enforced idleness resulting was spent to full advantage by Roosevelt in taking the *New Orleans* on a round trip cruise to Cincinnati.

Negotiating the Ohio River Rapids was the next crucial moment of the voyage. Mrs. Roosevelt and her tiny infant were aboard when the dauntless little steamer set out with a special pilot in the wheelhouse. He ordered full speed. People lined the river banks, prepared for the worst. Fortunately it was high water. The rapids, now bypassed by a two-mile canal, were held in great awe. Despite her bulky engine, tall stack and substantial cabin superstructure, the *New Orleans* made it. The rest of the trip would be easy, the Roosevelts confidently hoped. They were unprepared for what was to come.

Tiger, a big Newfoundland the Roosevelts had brought with them, suddenly leapt up and braced his paws on the *New Orleans'* wooden deck. If a dog's face can show surprise and fear, his probably did. They were quietly riding at anchor below the rapids, but the vessel suddenly began to shake and tremble. Swishing spurts of water rose in what had been calm. Trees toppled over the bank. It was the great New Madrid earthquake, felt throughout the entire Mississippi Valley and as far east as Massachusetts. In a few brief moments the boat's down river course was to be virtually wiped clean of landmarks. Flooded banks, uprooted trees, lost channels, disappearing islands, floating barns were to make the voyage to Natchez a nightmare. As if to add to the difficulties Mrs. Roosevelt must have experienced caring for her new baby, fire broke out. The cook had piled freshly cut wood too near to the stove. The fire was put out. We hope that young Roosevelt kept some of his other problems from his wife. Perhaps she never knew that at this point their supply of coal gave out. From then on they had to chop their fuel from the forests on the river bank.

At New Madrid, Mo., center of the tremendous quake, all was havoc. Great openings in the earth, giant holes along the river bank, gaping chasms and floods were everywhere. Terror-stricken settlers begged for passage down river on the *New Orleans*. Repeated earth tremors made the trip one of continuing danger. Popping gas geysers along the shore sprayed them with mud. One night a mooring rope was tied securely to a tree growing on a river island. When dawn came the island was gone. The rope was still taut, but it led down into the water. The tree and its island had disappeared. As they drew nearer to Natchez, however, the shocks became less frequent. From Natchez to New Orleans, the sailing was easy. Moreover, there was paying cargo aboard now, for, against the earnest counseling of his associates, a Natchez plantation owner had entrusted his cotton to the hold of the *New Orleans*.

The famous boat reached New Orleans Jan. 12, 1812. She immediately went into passenger and freight service to Natchez, making weekly trips. The fare was $25 to Natchez, and $18 to New Orleans. Her passenger lists often numbered as many as eighty souls. The profits from her barroom paid for her provisions and she showed a net gain of $24,000 for her first year of service, not bad for a craft costing not much over $36,000.

The Roosevelts lived to reap rich profit from the voyage, in fame and wealth. Although the *New Orleans* was to be supplanted soon by a new type ship especially designed for river service, her fame was assured.

The *New Orleans* was lost in 1814. She suffered an odd fate, being impaled upon a sunken tree trunk. Moored to the bank at high water, her hull was pierced by the hidden stump as the water sank. Efforts to free her only made things worse and she went to the bottom.

The WALK-IN-THE-WATER

AN INDIAN who saw Robert Fulton's *Clermont* went home and described the craft to his people as the "Walk-in-the-Water." His apt name came to be widely known. It was used to christen a new craft building at Black Rock, near Buffalo, in 1818, which was to be the first steamboat to sail on Lake Erie or the upper lakes.

For long years the *Walk-in-the-Water* was called the first steamer on the Great Lakes. It has since been demonstrated that the steamers *Frontenac* and *Ontario* operated on Lake Ontario in 1816 and 1817. As early as 1809 the *Accommodation*, a steamer of sorts, sailed between Montreal and Quebec. Nevertheless a goodly share of fame remains for the *Walk-in-the-Water*, in part, perhaps, due to her quaint name.

Great things were going on up and down the Hudson and the reactions were felt well into the Lakes. Indiana had been admitted into the Union in 1816, Mississippi the next year. There was already talk of the great Erie Canal, which was to be completed in 1825. Far-sighted merchants and shipping men in New York could easily see their port becoming the through way for the trade that would spring up with the new West. New York itself was humming. In the 175 years before the Revolution New York had slowly acquired a citizenry of 20,000. In the next twenty-five years the city quadrupled its population and became the leading seaport of the country. New York's population was to leap ahead to 152,000 in 1820, 242,000 in 1830, 696,000 in 1850 and past a million by the Civil War. And in this gain New York owed more to ships and shipping than to any other factor.

"We are children," murmured a group of incredulous Indians as they watched the *Walk-in-the-Water* chug and puff her historic way up the Detroit River on the conclusion of her maiden voyage in August, 1818. Here was proof, they must have thought, of an ancient legend that some day they would see a vessel pulled through the water by sturgeons. How, thought the Indian braves, could they fight such a race, people who could command the very fish of the sea?

A puff of white smoke followed by an echoing boom may well have punctuated this train of thought, for the *Walk-in-the-Water* was arriving at her destination. There were no such things as steam whistles in those days and a small cannon on her forward deck served the purpose of announcing her arrival at Detroit. A special wharf had been built to accommodate the great vessel, for the

This tiny craft, the Walk-in-the-Water, *could carry 150. Built in 1818, part of her engine was in use until 1902*

338-ton ship was all that to Judge Augustus B. Woodward and the other Detroit dignitaries who awoke early to greet her. Her time from Buffalo: 44 hours and 10 minutes.

The *Walk-in-the-Water's* engine was built by Robert McQueen, in New York City. It had come up the Hudson aboard a sloop. It took several six- and eight-horse wagons from fifteen to twenty days to haul the engine from Albany to Buffalo. Apparently this effort was by no means in vain, for the engine out-lived the *Walk-in-the-Water* by a quarter of a century, and was used in two later steamboats. Nevertheless it was not strong enough to take the little craft unaided from her Niagara River shipyard to Buffalo where she was to begin service. Eight yoke of oxen pulling from the shore were needed to help her pass the Niagara rapids. In still water she could make eight miles an hour.

The accompanying drawing was made from a sketch designed at the time for use on bills-of-lading printed for the boat's freight. In reality the *Walk-in-the-Water* had much more graceful, finer lines. Not shown in the sketch is the carved figurehead of Commodore Oliver Hazard Perry, hero of the Great Lakes in the War of 1812. The spread eagle emblazoned on her paddle box shows that this spot was already recognized as well suited for decorative purposes. Paddle-box artistry was to be expanded into a rich field of decorative art culminating in the four-deck-high many-colored gilt creations of the lush Mississippi era.

Sails remained important to the *Walk-in-the-Water's* design. She was brig-rigged. with two masts and topmasts. Her passenger accommodations consisted of a women's cabin forward, a men's cabin, small dining saloon and still smaller smoking room aft. She would carry 150 passengers. The fare was $8 to Erie; $15 to Cleveland and $24 to Detroit. She had twenty-nine aboard on her first trip. Rates were high, but the vessel had cost the enormous sum of $50,000. Her owners also had paid the Livingston-Fulton monopoly a substantial fee for the operating privilege on the Great Lakes.

Comparatively little is known about the three seasons that the *Walk-in-the-Water* operated on the Lakes. Passenger and freight traffic was still in its earliest stage. Only one dividend was paid the vessel's owners from earnings. She ran regularly between Buffalo and Detroit, with stops at Cleveland, and Sandusky. James Calhoun, her Hudson River-bred engineer, usually made the voyage to Detroit in three days. Capt. Job Fish and the three masters who succeeded him were all Hudson River-trained boatmen. The choppy, short-wave patterns of the Lakes were quite different from the swells and milder motion of the Hudson.

In 1820 and 1821 the *Walk-in-the-Water* made several cruises to Mackinac Island and one eight-day voyage into Green Bay, of Lake Michigan. It was late in the latter year that accident put an end to the doughty little craft's short career. Lake historian Dana Thomas Bowen believes that her owners were stretching the season a bit in allowing her to sail Oct. 31 for Cleveland and Detroit. It was a dangerous time of year for shipping on the Lakes.

She let go her lines at four in the afternoon at Black Rock landing with a few passengers and some cargo. The sun was already low in the horizon and the sky was threatening. She had bravely pushed out into a gray and rough Lake Erie when a strong gale blew up, whipping the water into white-capped fury. Capt. Jedediah Rogers pushed on, but by eight that evening leaks were reported in the hull. The ship was brought about and a course set for Buffalo. More leaks developed and the ship's pumps were soon fighting a losing game. They were making no progress toward Buffalo, and so Capt. Rogers dropped his three anchors. The ship's complement prepared for a rough night.

With all hands struggling to stem the leaks and with the winds increasing instead of slackening, it was indeed a terrible night. At ten, one anchor rope snapped. Another went at midnight, leaving only the third clawing vainly at the Lake bottom. The ship slowly dragged toward shore. She hit at about 4:30 the morning of Nov. 1. The storm slowly passed as dawn came, but the ship was firmly aground. The passengers and crew were all saved, making their way ashore in the ship's lifeboat with the aid of a stout line between ship and shore. The closeness of the wreck to shore made it possible to save most of the fittings. The engine was removed and installed in a new steamer, the *Superior*. When she in turn was wrecked the engine was again salvaged, this time going into the steamboat *Charles Townsend*. A report has it that the engine's main cylinder lasted as late as 1902 in use in an engine works in Buffalo.

The SAVANNAH

THE *Savannah*, of 1819, was a failure by almost every standard. Begun as a sailing ship, she was completed as a steamer. Sent to Europe in the hope she could be sold for a fancy price, she found no buyer. Restored to a sailing craft rig, she blew ashore off Long Island when only three years old and was lost. Yet today, over 130 years later, the *Savannah* is reckoned one of the world's most illustrious ships. She made the first crossing of the Atlantic under steam.

This judgment of history is no chance development. The *Savannah* has a right to her niche in immortality. She was an historic vessel of the first import, despite the countless historians who belittle her voyage. The *Savannah* and her twenty-nine-day crossing to Liverpool were high points in a great American maritime epoch.

These were important years in our national development. New states were being admitted to the Union in a regular pattern. The "era of good feeling" gave a political tranquillity to our nation such as it had not known before, and was not to know again. Our war with England had come to a satisfactory, though perhaps not altogether glorious, conclusion. No longer were our seamen to be impressed or our ships searched by the British. Well over seventy-five percent of our foreign trade was born in American ships. Great things, too, were expected of the *Savannah*.

It is true that she was building in 1818 as a sailing craft. But she was hand picked for conversion from countless others of her type also on the ways along the coast. She was selected by Capt. Moses Rogers, a man who would have been famous in his own right had he never commanded the *Savannah*. Moses Rogers had been master of the steamer *Phoenix* on her historic voyage from New York to the Delaware in 1809. This was the first ocean trip by steamship. He later commanded Robert Fulton's *Fulton* on the Hudson. He was the guiding spirit behind a group of Savannah shipping men who formed the Savannah Steamship Company. He commanded that company's one ship—the *Savannah*.

Moses Rogers bought the *Savannah's* engine from Stephen Vail, later associated with Morse in the invention of the telegraph. The engine was an inclined direct-acting proposition, with one cylinder having a forty-inch bore and a sixty-inch stroke. It was designed to be of ten pounds steam pressure, developing ninety horsepower which would drive the ship at six knots, without sails.

The *Savannah* was launched August 22, 1818, at the Crockett and Fickett's shipyard at Corlear's Hook, New York. A descendant of Francis Fickett is now on the staff of the Columbia Broadcasting Company, New York. Local citizens of the day referred to the *Savannah* as a "steam coffin." It was necessary to recruit a crew from New London, home town of Moses Rogers and his brother-in-law, Steven Rogers, who was sailing master on the vessel.

The completed *Savannah* made her trials in New York Bay in March, 1819. Only one contemporary picture of the vessel has come down to us. It was by a Frenchman named Marestier, sent to America to study American steamboats. This drawing shows several of the experiments in design credited to Captain Rogers. One is the swivel smokestack, designed to direct sparks away from the sails. Another is the collapsible paddle wheels. The sketch does not show the iron frame and canvas cover which took the place of the even then conventional paddle box.

There can be no doubt of the speculative nature of the *Savannah* enterprise. It is seen in the novel ideas which went into her construction. It is evident in the way Captain Rogers grasped at every opportunity that came along to publicize his vessel.

For example, when she reached Savannah on her first voyage it was discovered that President James Monroe was up the coast at Charleston, making a tour of the South. Up anchor and away went the *Savannah* to Charleston. Captain Rogers hurried ashore at the South Carolina port, met the President, and urged him to continue his southward journey as far as Savannah on the new ship. The President declined. It is reported that he feared his popularity in South Carolina would suffer if he left the state in a vessel whose home port was in Georgia.

But Captain Rogers was not to be done out of his publicity stunt. When President Monroe's party reached the Georgian seaport, there was the *Savannah* ready and waiting. We can imagine she had all her flags flying May 11 when she took the President and his suite for an all-day excursion to Tybee Light and return.

The *Savannah's* logbook, bound in heavy canvas probably from the ship's own sail locker, is in the Smithsonian Institution, Washington. It shows that the 320-ton craft left her pier under steam at 9 A.M. on May 22, now celebrated throughout America as Maritime Day. She anchored at noon at Tybee Light, remaining there until 6 A.M. the 24th. Two hours later she dropped her pilot and her cross-Atlantic voyage was really under way. For fuel she had seventy-

Referred to as a steam coffin, the Savannah was the first steam-propelled vessel to cross any ocean

five tons of coal and twenty-five cords of wood. It permitted only between eighty and ninety hours of steaming time on the whole voyage.

The vessel's approach to the Old World was marked by two episodes worthy of note. In one she was chased by a British revenue cutter whose master thought she was on fire. In the other she neatly confounded efforts of a British sloop of war to force her to lower the United States flag.

The revenue cutter *Kite* had been sent to the relief of the *Savannah* by the admiral of a fleet lying in the cove of Cork. The station at Cape Clear had sighted her with smoke belching from her bent stack and concluded she was on fire. The surprise of the Britishers can be imagined when the *Savannah*, without a sail set, out-distanced them completely. It was not until after the exasperated cutter's crew had fired shots at the American vessel that she stopped and gratified their curiosity.

Proud of his new ship and with memories of the War of 1812 still in his mind, Captain Moses Rogers refused to follow the custom at British ports of flying the Union Jack above the Stars and Stripes while lying off the bar at Liverpool. The captain of a British sloop took this as a personal insult and a boat was sent out to order the American colors down. Threatened with force, sailing master Steven Rogers, who was on deck at the time, turned to his engineer and said, "Get the hot-water engine ready." Although there was no such engine, the idea of a bath of scalding water was enough to cool off the Britisher, who dropped the whole matter.

The *Savannah* did not have many pleasant experiences in England, although her trip up the Mersey was watched by thousands. She was generally viewed with suspicion. Newspapers of the day surmised that "this steam operation may, in some manner, be connected with the ambitious views of the United States."

Ten days of her thirty-three-day run to St. Petersburg, Russia, were under steam, with the engines running for spells of fifty-two hours on two occasions. Eighteen hours was the *Savannah's* longest period under steam while on her Atlantic crossing. She did not use steam on her return voyage to Savannah because of rough October and November seas.

To deny that a ship which uses steam for ten out of thirty-three days is a steamship is like arguing how many angels can stand on the point of a needle. But such denials are common. For the last word, however, we could not do better than to depend upon a first-hand, on-the-spot account published in *The Times* of London. It is in connection with the *Kite* episode. *The Times* reported: "The *Savannah*, a steam vessel, recently arrived at Liverpool from America, the first vessel of the kind which ever crossed the Atlantic."

As an epilogue, we quote a poem believed to be contemporary with the *Savannah's* famous voyage:

THE *SAVANNAH*

Sail on, Oh Sea Bird of the deep
  That plows the Ocean wave;
We gave a hearty joyous cheer
  When you were launched upon the wave.

When on the "Stocks" near river front
  We watched and prayed you would succeed;
Thou hast redeemed a nation's pledge,
  Thou hast a nation's honor saved.

A Yankee boat has won renown,
  From foreign lands come laurels now,
And word is sent from shore to shore
  That steam is conqueror evermore.

The name *Savannah* now resounds
  In every household in the land;
The greatest wonder ever seen,
  The *Savannah* was the Ocean Queen.

The *ALBION*

IN THE first half of the last century the Stars and Stripes completely dominated passenger ship service and fast freight traffic on the Atlantic. There was no French Line, Italian Line, North German Lloyd, Hamburg American Line, and the great Cunard Line was a fledgling.

American sailing-ship packets were the luxury liners of the era. Regularity and speed were their guiding principles. They were notorious for their so-called bucko mates and packet rats. Their fame is kept alive today by the rollicking rhymes of old sea chanties. It was in such craft that the first great surge of immigrants came to America. A crossing on such a ship in steerage was rough indeed.

From five to eight hundred immigrants, generally Germans or Irish, would be crowded aboard. Although the few first-class passengers were fed in elegance, immigrants brought their own food. Water and a stove were all the ship provided. In rough weather little cooking could be done and the suffering passengers lived on cold gruel. When high seas made the decks dangerous, the steerage passengers were herded below to uncomfortable and cramped quarters. The hatches were lashed down often for what must have seemed an eternity. Eastbound voyages were as fast as seventeen days. Westbound runs often lasted forty days and more.

The Albion *was a packet. Some packets were known as "blood boats" because of frequent knifings among the crew*

Aboard the *Pacific,* one of the earliest packets, first or cabin class was in sharp contrast. Every comfort of the best hotels was provided. Mahogany and bird's-eye maple cabins, rosewood card tables, shiny coffee urns, black haircloth seats, satinwood panels, white Italian marble pillars and individual staterooms were regular features. A Christmas dinner menu of a typical packet shows that good food was not lacking. First came soup, then boiled codfish and boiled potatoes. Next roast turkey, followed by stewed chicken and macaroni pie. Roast or more boiled potatoes with mashed turnips followed. Freshly baked bread, sea biscuits, pickles and odd fixings were always available. The meal was topped off with plum pudding and champagne.

Bucko mates ruled supreme aboard these fabulous American packets which flew such famous company house-flags as that of the Black Ball Line, the Swallow Tail Line, the Dramatic Line, the Red Cross Line, the Black X Line and the Black Star Line. The rage for speed made such men vital to the shipowners of that day, for the crews knew only one law: force. The packets satisfied this craze for speed though it meant driving the seamen almost to and beyond human endurance.

The ordinary seamen on these flyers reveled in the title of "packet rats." Basil Lubbock, well-known sailing ship historian, says that "they were, with little doubt, the roughest and toughest customers that ever sailed the seas." They prided themselves above all on being able to face the iron fists and devil's heart of the most fiercesome mate. Some packets were known as "blood boats" because of the constant knifings and blood-letting between crew members.

The *Albion,* shown in the accompanying sketch, was one of the first Black Ballers. The Black Ball Line began packet service between New York and Liverpool in 1818. The idea of sailing on a fixed schedule, cargo or not, was new. It meant a revolution in Atlantic trade and a host of rivals sprang up. The *Albion* and others of her company ships were known by their large black ball painted or sewn on their fore topsail. The famous packet *Dreadnought,* about which more will be heard later, had a red Crusader cross on her sail. The packets were built of live oak and often lasted fifty or more years, being used in their later life as whalers.

Not only did the packets cement American leadership on the Atlantic. They helped New York on its way to being the nation's greatest port. They provided many a generation with lusty chanties, most notable of which was "Blow the Man Down." It went in part as follows:

> Come, all you young fellows that follow the sea,
>   To me way—aye, blow the man down!
> Now pray pay attention and listen to me.
>   Give me some time to blow the man down!

The second and fourth lines were repeated with each new two-line verse. It should be noted that "blow the man down" meant knock the man down in the vernacular of the time. Other verses follow:

> On a trim Black Ball liner I first served my time,
> And in that Black Baller I wasted my prime.

> It's when a Black Baller's preparing for sea,
> You'd split your sides laughing the sights you would see,

> At the tinkers and tailors and sojers and all,
> For you'll seldom find sailors aboard a Black Ball.

'Tis when the Black Baller is clear of the land
The crew musters aft at the word of command.

Lay aft, is the cry, to the break of the poop,
Or I'll help you along with the toe of my boot.

Pay attention to orders, now you one and all,
For see, right above you there flies the Black Ball.

'Tis larboard and starboard on deck you will sprawl,
For kicking Don Thompson commands that Black Ball.*

As a ship, the *Albion* was strangely unlucky. She was built with iron knees, or reinforcements to the hull. As a result her compass was affected and would not point correctly until it was placed high above the deck on a platform. Her builder was Sidney Wright, great-grandfather of Ralph E. Cropley, modern-day marine historian attached to the famous model museum of the Seamen's Church Institute of New York. Wright went on to build Perry's fleet on Lake Erie. A Liberty ship named after him in World War II was President Franklin D. Roosevelt's pet ship.

Built in 1819 the *Albion* was lost off the Irish coast in 1822 with all but eight of her fifty-four passengers and crew. Capt. John Williams went down with his ship.

The difference between packets, whalers and clippers has often provoked questions. Hard and fast definitions are impossible, but with this broad limitation in mind the following rough explanations will probably stand scrutiny.

A packet was a heavily built, deep hulled sailing craft whose chief purpose was the transportation of mail and passengers. Packets generally were not among the largest sailing vessels, although in later days some reached proportions rivaling the large clippers. The *Dreadnought* was a packet because of her full hull and heavy construction.

Whalers were often old packets. Even through the end of the nineteenth century they did not develop into large ships. Today's steam whalers are of course completely different, being large and thoroughly mechanized ships with all modern facilities.

Clippers were the greyhounds of the sea. Sharp, curved hulls, designed to reduce resistance to a minimum, supported unbelievably tall masts on which were hung many small square sails. Clippers were not intended for bulk cargoes, but instead were most successful when carrying high-priced goods. Extremely long and tapering bow and overhanging stern were the clipper's trademark.

* The words of the sea chanty are taken from *Roll and Go,* by Joanna Colcord, published 1924 by The Bobbs-Merrill Co.

Specialized shallow-draft steamboats like the George Washington *made possible the slogan "Go West Young Man"*

PART THREE

Steam Advances on All Sides

From shiny spittoon to red-plush ladies' lounge, nothing better displayed the new America than the steamboat—or steamship if you speak of an ocean craft. During the forty years before the Civil War, it was the new world in its Sunday best. It was America in capsule form. . . . From Maine to New Orleans, from the Great Lakes to San Francisco time was measured between sailing days of the steamer. Steam advanced on all sides . . . particularly within our vast new land, binding our frontiers together, supplying our outposts.

The GEORGE WASHINGTON

I TELL you, young man—you deserve well of your country, but we shall be compelled to beat you in the courts."

This hard-boiled remark was made to an inventive young barge captain by a New York blue blood. It neatly summarized the stand of the Fulton-Livingston monopoly faced with a strong rival with a new boat on the Mississippi. The captain was Henry M. Shreve. The Easterner was Edward Livingston, none other than brother and business representative of the Chancellor. It was he who had backed the first steamboat, the *New Orleans,* to navigate the Ohio and Mississippi.

First with his *Enterprise* and then with his ill-fated *Washington,* Capt. Shreve challenged the Fulton-Livingston group. A series of trials, vessel seizures and court decisions eventually resulted in abandonment of the claim by the Easterners. Meanwhile the *Washington* in 1817 had made her famous 25-day voyage from New Orleans to Louisville, a voyage hailed as proving to the world that steamboat navigation on the Father of Waters was practical. Daniel French and the *Enterprise,* with Shreve as captain, had done the same thing earlier by

49

two years but with less public acclaim. Capt. Shreve's *Washington,* which had had a serious boiler explosion on her very first voyage, was eventually sunk by a second such accident, forerunner of a long line of explosions which were to plague river boats.

The development of steam on the western rivers was one of the most significant chapters in American history. In a sense it divided the East from the West, but in a greater way it united the new country. It broke the domination of eastern wagon-train operators and canal-boat men over commercial expansion in the West. At the same time it opened new incentives to colonization, drew the states closer together and insured that they would remain one nation. Not since the great burst of canal building had a movement so transformed an area.

Before Mississippi steamboating could become the stampeding, pulsating, revolutionary economic and political force it was to be, one more development was necessary. The conventional, ocean-type boat was not suitable. A new design was called for, modeled along the lines of the flat-bottomed canal boats, whose part in American history should not be underrated. For generations Capt. Shreve and his *Washington* have been credited with pioneering this new Mississippi style. River historian Louis C. Hunter has shown, however, that the flat-bottomed, two- and three-deck river boat came gradually over perhaps as many as three decades.

Shreve's *George Washington,* 1825, featured in this chapter, was one of the first boats to show progress in this trend. Although of about the same length and tonnage, her depth of slightly over eight feet is in contrast to the 12-foot depth of both the *New Orleans* and the *Washington.* She was a side-wheeler, as shown in the accompanying sketch. Within fifteen years after the *George Washington* there were over 500 steamboats on the Western rivers. In 1842 Pittsburgh was home port to more steamboats than Boston, Philadelphia and Charleston lumped together. In the 1850's western river steamboats were within an iota of passing in tonnage the aggregate of steam vessels in the British Empire.

Capt. Shreve is credited with still one more innovation. Nothing earthshaking, it was the development of the term "stateroom." Up to his time steamboats did not have individual cabins for passengers. There would be only a large men's and a separate women's cabin, both lined with bunks. Shreve partitioned these areas into private cubicles, naming them after the different states of the Union, hence the designation "stateroom."

The NORTH AMERICA

SLAVERY was abolished in the State of New York in 1827. Abraham Lincoln, at 19, was best known as a champion wrestler. Nearly a third of our 12,000,000 citizens were now west of the Allegheny Mountains and the popular revolution that was to put Andrew Jackson in the White House was in the making. The

The North America, *from an old print. Note how her two walking beams are incorrectly placed far aft from where they must have been atop the paddles*

Clermont was just twenty years past, but her beautiful Hudson was now swarming with commerce. The opening of the Erie Canal in 1825 was one reason. Another was the extraordinary progress made in new steamers on the Hudson. Outstanding among these was the *North America*.

The *North America* was a beautiful vessel in every respect except for her spittoons. This was the comment of a Scotchman named James Stuart who was traveling up and down our Eastern seaboard in 1828, and making copious notes. A good traveler, he brushed aside the "spit-boxes," as he knew them, as a "necessary evil, I suspect, whilst cigars and tobacco in other shapes are fastidious." Mr. Stuart went so far as to note that spit-boxes "have only disappeared in Scotland within these thirty years."

Mrs. James Stuart recorded for posterity an example of racial discrimination that was surprising to her, since there were virtually no Negroes in Great Britain at that time. Walking on deck outside the well-stocked dining saloon aboard the *North America,* she met a comely colored woman. She asked her why she was not going in with the others to dine.

"She replied very modestly that the people of this country did not eat with people of colour. . . . The manners and appearance of this lady were interesting and could have distinguished her anywhere," Mrs. Stuart noted.

The *North America* was built by Robert L. Stevens, whose father, Col. John Stevens, had known Fitch and Fulton. The Stevens family were not only of an inventive bent, they were wealthy and highly educated. This combination produced a series of significant contributions to our progress, notably the first double-ended ferryboat, the first twin-screw-propelled craft, the first ocean-going steamboat, the first ironclad warship, and the first locomotive to run on a track. Robert L. devoted his brilliant mind largely to steamboats. The *North America* was one of his most successful efforts.

A far cry from the humble *Clermont* of only two decades before, the *North America* was fast and elegant. Her 218-foot length and 30-foot width could accommodate 320 passengers, with a berth for each. Captain Shreve's stateroom idea had not penetrated to the Hudson, however, and the *North America's* guests slept in two long cabins. The men's cabin also served as the dining saloon.

Her 145-mile voyage to Albany was made at a rate of from ten to sixteen miles an hour. Her best northbound voyage was made Sept. 22, 1832. Her time was an extraordinary nine hours and eighteen minutes, one quarter the time of the *Clermont.* Built light for speed, the *North America* was the first American steamboat to have a hog frame or truss to strengthen her hull. She used twenty-five to thirty cords of wood on her overnight run from New York.

The *North America* was built near the end of one of the Hudson's strangest eras, the period of the safety barge. A series of boiler explosions, often accompanied by large loss of life, led to the invention by William C. Redfield of the so-called safety barge. It was a craft without power, fitted with every luxury and towed behind a conventional steamboat. An earlier step to prevent casualties when boilers exploded had been the placing of the boilers outside the shell of the vessel's cabin. This practice, an invention of Robert Stevens, continued for many years. The safety barge, however, went even farther, and for a few years in the early 1820's was all the rage. An advertisement of the period read as follows:

> Passengers on board the safety barges will not be in the least exposed to any accident by reason of the fire or steam on board the steamboats. The noise of the machinery, the trembling of the boat, the heat from the furnace, boilers and kitchen, and everything which may be considered unpleasant on board a steamboat are entirely avoided.

Nothing in the long and successful life of the *North America* recommended the use of safety barges, and they faded from the picture after a few years. Accidents were quickly forgotten amid the luxuries of this splendid craft. Most of the passengers were light-hearted pleasure seekers, many headed for Saratoga Springs, which, even then, was a leading spa.

The *North America* was sold in 1839 to Isaac Newton. Late that year she ran into a field of ice just below Albany and sank. The progress which she represented beyond the *Clermont,* only twenty years her senior, was extraordinary. The refinements and new features brought into vogue during her twelve-year life were to make the Hudson River steamboat the most popular means of travel to the West.

Two BANGORS

HUSNI PACHA, Chief Naval Constructor of the Imperial Ottoman Admiralty, remembered well the old side-wheeler *Sudaver.* He used to make trips on her as a boy between his home in Constantinople and the Ottoman Naval College at Halki, one of the Princes' Islands. The old craft was thought to be one of the most commodious and comfortable passenger boats in the Mediterranean service, Husni Pacha told the American Vice-General Consul William Smith Lyte. No, she had definitely never been the yacht of a Sultan. Yes, she had been scrapped about 1888, after many repairs and quite a period of idleness.

This information was secured around 1903 by Vice-Consul Lyte in response to a query from steamboat historian John H. Morrison, of Brooklyn. The query was prompted by frequent claims that the famous old Maine coast steamer *Bangor,* built in 1834, was still in service in 1902 under the Turkish flag. There is no doubt, however, that the *Sudaver* was the *Bangor.* She had been sent to Turkey in 1842 for sale to local interests who first used her to carry pilgrims to Mecca. The fact that this frail little vessel, only 160 feet long and measuring 385 tons, could make the run to Gibraltar, is a credit to the craft of her East River builders, Brown & Bell, of New York. Her primitive cross-head engine was nicknamed *rokana* by the Turks who were reminded by its motion of the carpenter's plane, "rokana" in Turkish.

Although the *Bangor* served the Turks for over 40 years, her original appearance at Constantinople was not one which would have suggested a long career. She was greeted by a great lack of enthusiasm on the part of the pilgrims who were expected to throng aboard for their trip to Mecca. Not a Mussulman would buy passage. A hasty conference by her owners led to the discovery of what was wrong. The vessel was quickly given a coat of black paint, and the passengers crowded aboard. Someone had forgotten that white was the native mourning color. The *Bangor,* like all other American coastwise boats then and now, was white from bow to stern.

Two early coastal steamers were named Bangor. *The first (upper) outlived the second, spending her last years as a Turkish pilgrim ship. The second was one of the earliest ships using a propeller*

The tiny side-wheeler *Tom Thumb* was the first steamboat to serve along Maine's 2,000 mile in-and-out coastline. She was an open boat only thirty feet long and was towed from Boston to the Kennebec River in 1818. The rugged coastline made roads and overland travel difficult but proved ideal for steamboating, which prospered accordingly. The *Bangor* was probably the first new steamer put on the regular Maine service, earlier vessels being mostly old ships taken from other routes. She opened the first line between Maine and Boston in 1834. Her owners were the Boston & Bangor Steamship Company, later to become the Eastern Steamship Lines, whose last American flag ship was sold in 1955.

The *Bangor* had a remarkably modern appearance. Her two tall smokestacks were amidships, rising above her paddle wheels, which were enclosed in decorated paddle boxes. Her name was painted on the center portion of the paddle box on either side. A hog frame showed that Robert L. Stevens' innovation on the *North America,* eight years earlier, was now quite common practice. A long passenger cabin stretched from beneath the pilot house and foremast to the stern. The *Bangor* burned wood. The sale of the *Bangor* to the Turks was due in part to the opening of a railroad to Portland. A rate war between steamers and trains saw the fare from Boston to Bangor cut from $7 to as low as $1.

In 1844 a new *Bangor* was built, a ship that except for her very short life would rate an important spot in the maritime chronoscope. She is listed by *The Lytle Lyst,* an authoritative publication of the Steamship Historical Society of America, as being the first iron seagoing vessel built in the United States. She was also one of the earliest propeller-driven craft. Her 131-foot hull was made of lapped iron plates hung on iron ribs and secured by wrought-iron clamps.

A bad luck ship from the start, she tilted far over on her side during her launch but righted herself and slid into the water without serious damage. On her second trip she caught fire and was beached near Castine. Declared a constructive loss, she was later refloated, towed to Bath and rebuilt. Converted into a Mexican war transport the next year, she was renamed *Scourge.* Two years of war service so wore out the 450-ton craft that, at the war's end, she was sold for the meager sum of $2,300, and dropped completely out of sight.

Here is a postscript to the story of the first *Bangor,* first of the Boston boats. The *Belfast,* last boat of the Boston-Bangor line, sailed on her final voyage from Rockland to Boston in 1935, 101 years after the *Bangor* began the service. The railroads, fast automobiles and great trucks combined to ring down the curtain on this famous run. The *Belfast* lived on to see service in the Pacific as an American troopship. She was lost on the shore of the Columbia River. The *Camden,* her sister, was sold for service in Chinese waters after World War II trooping in the Pacific. She may still live to parallel the *Bangor's* forty-year service under a foreign flag far from her home waters off the rocky coast of Maine.

The JOHN S. McKIM

JOHN ERICSSON, Swedish-American inventor, is best known for his historic cheese-box-on-a-raft named *Monitor*. With this one "invention" he popularized the iron warship in the minds of the world's leaders. Her successes against the *Virginia*, known as the *Merrimac*, the Confederate iron-clad ram, made the *Monitor* and her inventor world famous. A much more practical invention popularized by this bewhiskered genius, but one almost completely ignored by historians, was the screw propeller. Ericsson designed the *John S. McKim*, one of the first commercial steamships in America to be driven by a propeller.

Our maritime picture in 1839, the year Ericsson arrived in America, was a strangely complex one. On the western rivers a completely new type boat was in use. It had a flat bottom, shallow draft, high superstructure and side-wheel somewhat aft of center. It was made of wood. On the Great Lakes, on our eastern rivers and bays less drastic changes in form had taken place. But equally amazing increases in size, speed and luxury were evident. Along our coasts shipowners were experimenting with iron hulls and propeller-driven steamboats, with sails still a strong competitor. On the oceans wooden sailing craft remained supreme, despite the *Savannah* of 1819. Our sailing packets and heavy-hulled whalers were unequaled, and the peak of our achievement under canvas was still a decade off. And yet regular British trans-Atlantic steam service had begun a year before with two lines of steamers. Of course these and all other steamers of this era still used sails, too. They had clipper bows, three masts and heavy spars and rigging.

Soon after his arrival in the United States, Ericsson made an important convert to his revolutionary ideas in the person of Thomas Clyde, founder of the Clyde Line. Mr. Clyde's interest was immediately engaged by the Swedish engineer, who had just won a one-fifth share of $100,000 awarded by the British government for the invention of the propeller. The two men immediately put their heads together, and in 1844 they brought forth the *McKim*, a 242-ton wooden steamer with three masts and clipper bow. The 177-foot craft had her single tall smokestack and engines aft, a feature widely claimed in 1955 by a big British company as revolutionary for passenger ships.

The *John S. McKim* had a flush deck, running from scrolled prow to square stern. A single lifeboat hung over her transom aft. Her hull was decorated with a white stripe punctured by square gun-portlike decorations. A long bowsprit spread two large jibs forward. She flaunted square sails on her foremast and fore and aft sails on the main and mizzen.

Thomas Clyde and his descendants were far-sighted men. Their many coastwise lines pioneered in the introduction of first iron and then steel in ship construction. Their *George W. Clyde* boasted the first compound engine built for a ship in the United States. They were among the first to order a triple

Another early propeller-driven craft was the John S. McKim. *She became a Mexican War transport, then a river boat*

expansion engine for one of their vessels. A company folder put out in 1913 goes so far as to hold that "to the Clyde family may be credited about all the advances made in steamship construction and improvements in this country during the past seventy-six years, with the exception of the turbine."

Unfortunately the *John S. McKim* stayed with the Clyde Line for only three years. The outbreak of the war with Mexico brought an urgent need for transports. The *McKim* was taken off the New York, Charleston and Savannah run and sold to the United States War Department. On one of her voyages to Vera Cruz, Mexico, she carried 500 Mississippi volunteers captained by a dashing young colonel whose name was later to become famous in half of the United States and despised by the other half. He was Col. Jefferson Davis, who became President of the Confederate States of America in the War Between the States.

After the end of the war, the *John S. McKim* was sold to a New Orleans shipowner who bought her at just the right time. Gold had been discovered in California and ships were at a premium. Even smelly old whalers were dumping their oil barrels overboard and picking up huge loads of passengers for the Golden West. Rough use as a transport made a thorough overhaul necessary, during which her length was reduced by nearly fifty feet. A hectic four-month voyage around Cape Horn brought her to San Francisco in October of 1849. Sacramento was the starting point for the gold trek into the hills. Her passage up the Sacramento River was hailed by thousands along the river banks and by booming cannon. She was the first large steamer to reach the gold port and it was a great day for the local citizens. For three years the *John S. McKim* had a new lease on life, serving between San Francisco and Sacramento, but time was taking its toll.

In 1851 she made a voyage to Panama. Returning via the Mexican port of Acapulco, now famous as a summer resort for the Hollywood set, she was detained at that spot by the Mexican authorities as unseaworthy. Her passengers were unceremoniously dumped and told to return home as best they could. Still a relatively young boat by modern standards, her trooping service and gold-rush traffic had apparently shortened her life considerably. It was necessary to remove her Ericsson engines, and rebuild her from keel up in order to regain permission to operate. A second deck was added. In the process her famed propeller was removed and replaced with conventional side-wheels, somewhat better for quick maneuverability as a river steamer. For some reason her name was abbreviated to the *McKim*. These alterations enabled her to continue in river service out of San Francisco for another seven years. The *McKim* was broken up in 1858, three thousand miles away from the home of John Ericsson, who by then was trudging from office to office with plans for his *Monitor*.

An even more revolutionary Ericsson invention developed during the lifetime of the *John S. McKim* was the caloric or hot-air steamer. Considerably larger than the *McKim,* this strange craft was intended to be propeled by the jet principle. Her engines, which were definitely very economical to operate, could generate only about half the speed they had been designed to make. They were eventually removed.

Upon his death in 1889, Ericsson's body was taken back to his native Sweden in state by ships of America's famous White Squadron.

The WASHINGTON

THE FOLLOWING notes were written in 1840 about a famous ship by a more famous man:

"Before descending into the bowels of the ship, we had passed from the deck into a long and narrow apartment, not unlike a gigantic hearse with windows in the sides; having at the upper end a melancholy stove, at which three or four chilly stewards were warming their hands; while on either side, extending down its whole dreary length, was a long, long table; over which a rack, fixed to the low roof, and stuck full of drinking-glasses and cruet-stands, hinted dismally at rolling seas and heavy weather."

The ship was the *Britannia,* first vessel of the famous British Cunard Line. The grumpy passenger—can't you guess?—was Charles Dickens. Perhaps it was the voyage across that was in part responsible for the bad mood which is so acidly reflected in his famous *American Notes.* At any rate Dickens chose not to return on the Cunarder. Instead he picked an American packet, the *George Washington,* of the Swallow Tail Line. The packet, it should be added, beat the Cunard steamship by twenty-nine hours. However, the British "smoke pot," as she was derisively called by Dickens, was to have her day, and that leads us to the featured ship of this section.

Despite the *Savannah,* first steamship to cross any ocean, America lagged in ocean steamship development. Britain's leadership became more and more evident, although our coastal shipping prospered and followed Britain's lead in both iron hulls and screw propulsion. In the early 1840's, however, Congress was forced to act to stimulate our deep-sea steam-shipping enterprise. It was not deeply concerned with shipping as such but was worried about the danger of an aggressive Britain.

A series of disputes with England brought about this state of mind. First there were our border tangles over Oregon and Maine. Our annexation of Texas provoked further bitterness. Feeling along the Canadian border ran high and Britain's subsidization of services to Canada and the West Indies brought further tension. Our security was threatened. Finally Congress acted, slowly, to be sure, but it acted. Our first ocean subsidy was authorized in 1845. A principal argument in favor of ocean subsidies was that merchant liners could become warships.

The sailing packet *George Washington,* Dickens' choice, was one of many ships named after our first President. There were thirty-five steamers honoring Washington in the first sixty years of steam navigation. The largest was one of America's first subsidized liners, the *Washington,* 1,700 tons. She was launched on a cold winter day in 1847 from the East River yard of Messrs. Westervelt and Mackay. When the cheering and cannon-shot echoes had died away, a representative of the Navy was heard to remark that the new 260-foot craft would "prove herself an excellent sea boat." He went so far as to add that she would be fast enough to beat "any steamer yet put afloat." The *New York Herald* hailed her as "the most complete and beautiful" vessel ever built.

By a coincidence the Cunarder *Britannia* sailed from Boston on the same

America's first regular ocean liner was the Washington. *A "Washington polka" was written in Bremen in her honor*

day the *Washington* left New York on her maiden voyage. The American press confidently expected the nation's first trans-Atlantic liner to easily outpace her older rival. Such was not to be the case. The British veteran beat the *Washington* by more than two days.

It was said that she was under-boilered. This was a serious matter to her owners, since the subsidy contract specified that she must be able to beat the Cunard vessels. The *Washington* was said by most to be a very comfortable vessel despite the London *Times* remark that she seemed "rather to roll along than steam through the water." Perhaps it was the figurehead of our first president which caused such dispeptic comments. The same journal called the new arrival from America "about as ugly a specimen of steamship building as ever went through this anchorage." Whatever the motives, the traditional new ship welcome dinner was proffered by the Southampton Dock Company and the *Washington* was on her way to a decade of successful service.

The welcome at Bremerhaven was far more sincere. German merchants had invested heavily in the stock of the Ocean Steam Navigation Company. It was to their interest that the vast river of immigrants from Northern Europe should flow at least in part through Bremen. A bevy of bedecked excursion boats escorted the new American steamer to her dock. On board was the son of Bremen's Burgomaster Smidt, returning home from Louisville, Ky., for the grand occasion. A gala dinner, dancing, shooting and fireworks marked the celebration. A six-foot model of the *Washington* was presented by the ship's officers to Bremen officials and the announcement was made that the liner's sister would be named *Hermann* after the German hero of ancient days. So great was the enthusiasm that a musician in the orchestra is said to have composed a *Washington* polka on the spot.

British coldness was turned into deliberate discrimination when the British Post Office ordered that double the normal postage be collected on all mail coming on the American ship. A lengthy squabble between Washington and London ensued, and finally the British were forced to backtrack. Other and more important factors were working to eliminate the American competition. The Civil War was approaching and Southern Congressmen, who had been so eager to help found the Bremen Line in 1847, became the enemies of Northern shipping interests. On the other side of the Atlantic, local shipping interests in Bremen became restive. Why support an American steamship line? Why not have our own?

The *Washington* brought an interesting innovation into Atlantic trade. She was the first ship to have second-class accommodations in addition to her luxurious first-class cabins for 112 passengers. Up to then the several British steamer lines in service had left this traffic to sailing packets. The *Washington* also forced a substantial reduction in first-class passenger fares and in cargo rates. A third effect was the decision by Cunard to operate out of New York instead of Boston.

In the Spring of 1854, the *Washington* chanced upon the Boston sailing ship *Winchester*, dismasted and in desperate straits. Aboard the sinking craft were 477 souls to whom the black hull of the *Washington* with its white strip of imitation gun ports must have looked like heaven itself. A volunteer lifeboat crew was soon lowered and battled the high waves toward the near-foundering *Winchester*. Records say that "the most expert and strenuous seamanship" saved every person.

In 1857 the *Washington* left the Atlantic. The withdrawal of her American subsidy and the decision of the Germans to start their own line were the deciding factors. The Bremen merchants' enterprise and experience gained with the *Washington* were to bear rich fruit in the establishment of one of the world's great steamship lines—the North German Lloyd.

Little is left to tell of the *Washington*. Built originally at a cost of $390,000, she was sold at a foreclosure sale for $40,000 for service to the Isthmus of Panama. Two voyages on this route and she was laid up. Two years later she journeyed to San Francisco under the house flag of the great Pacific Mail Line, just beginning its nearly century of Pacific service. Again, only two voyages on the western leg of the intercoastal run proved the old vessel was more than past her prime. She was laid up and scrapped in 1864.

The CALIFORNIA

ON FRIDAY, Oct. 6, 1848, the 1,058-ton steamship *California* sailed from New York to open what was to become America's most famous ocean steamship line— the Pacific Mail. She carried only a few passengers, although she was fitted out to accommodate some 200. Her cargo consisted largely of coal, a knocked-down engine and stores for the voyage around South America. It was to be a long voyage and a momentous one. Britain had just conceded our right to the Oregon border, a right whose earliest claim was based on the voyage of the sailing ship *Columbia* a half century before. Mexico had ceded to us the great area of California in a war won with the substantial aid of ex-merchant ships pressed into service. Our manifest destiny to rule the Continent from Atlantic to Pacific had become a reality. An alert Congress realized the need of water communications and offered a mail subsidy to stimulate the organization of a ship line to link the East Coast with Panama and Panama with the West Coast.

The *California*, little aware of the excitement that was stirring at Sutter's sawmill in the land she was named for, continued down the coast of South America. Engine trouble caused a protracted stay of three weeks at Rio de Janeiro. Rough going contributed to delay the voyage. The sturdy craft, built of live oak, maneuvered the difficult Straits of Magellan and headed north again.

In outline she was somewhat different from the *Washington*. A white band around her hull gave her a modern appearance. A much abbreviated clipper bow with an almost horizontal bowsprit set her apart from the sleek clippers just reaching their prime at this period. A tall single smokestack was placed forward of the paddle boxes. Square sails were rigged on fore and main with a large fore and aft sail on the mizzen. As was customary, a gigantic United States flag hung from the mizzen yard. A burgee with the name "California" in large letters on white flew from the top of the mizzenmast. A long, low cabin extended from the foremast nearly to the stern, almost hidden by the high wooden bulwarks. Two lifeboats, one on either side, were hung forward of the stack, and there were two more forward of the mizzenmast.

The California, *first steamer through Golden Gate. Dropping anchor her crew promptly deserted to mine for gold*

When the *California* sighted Panama her officers were surprised to note great activity on the dock. As she approached and it became clear that she was a large ocean vessel, great crowds massed along her course. Even before she tied up, her officers were besieged with calls asking for passage to San Francisco. The discovery of gold, vast gold deposits, in California had been confirmed. Stories of gold in the area had been common on the East Coast for years. The rumors became more persistent in the fall of 1848 and by December the news was out, given added credence by an enthusiastic endorsement by President Polk.

An irony of history was this discovery of gold in California. Some 300 years earlier Spanish gold hunters and explorers had opened the area to white men.

For three centuries their descendants had lived atop one of the world's richest gold layers. It was there for the scraping. And then, barely a year after American conquest, the discovery. A Mexican named Baptiste saw it ordered by Providence that the finding of gold be delayed until California became a part of the United States.

Crowded to the gunwales with 365 passengers, the *California* puffed up the coast for the new Mecca. The gold fever must have hummed and buzzed through every cubic inch of her 225 by 31 by 18-foot hull. Fabulous prices had been paid for her cabins, and many gladly accepted passage with no sleeping facilities. The *California's* arrival must have been a thrilling experience for all on board. She was the first ocean-going steamship to enter the Golden Gate. She was the symbol of the new sovereignty. On board was Major General Persifor Smith, the new Military Governor of the Territory. Her arrival date was Feb. 28, 1849. It was a day to be long observed by a group of her passengers banded together as the First Steamship Pioneers. It was a date that marked a new era of American history.

As the *California* rounded Clark's Point below Telegraph Hill the several hundred shanties and tents that were San Francisco came into view. We can imagine that most of the settlement's thousand citizens were on hand with bells on. In the harbor, riding high and impressive midst a motley assortment of deserted sailing craft were five ships of the United States Navy's Pacific Squadron, under Commodore Jones. They were probably the only vessels in the port whose seamen did not desert en masse for the gold fields. Sporting all officers in full dress the flagship *Ohio* and sisters were a fine sight. As the *California* approached, the squadron's entire complement, 1,500 men, manned the yards in salute. Roaring broadsides from each vessel gave noisy welcome. The *California's* anchor chain rattled and splashed into the blue harbor depths. With bated breath her passengers swarmed ashore. Her crew did too, for to a man they deserted, with the exception of Captain Cleveland Forbes and Third Assistant Engineer Fred Foggin.

The local newspaper (one had already been set up) went into raptures at the approach of the *California*. Interest was at a high pitch as the banner headline ran "Look Out For the Steamer!" A rhapsodic article followed:

> The knowing ones say that we may daily look for the first steamer. If this be so, ought not our citizens to take some steps to manifest their joy at an occasion so full of interest to this port? We most strenuously recommend the holding of a public meeting, the appointment of a committee of arrangements, and the raising of a fund for burning of powder and spermaceti on the occasion. It is an event so fraught with future hopes of advantage, that our memories will almost deserve execration if we do not celebrate . . . with proper style and spirit. It is an epoch. . . . Come, come, you that have amassed so much gold since the opening of the

mines . . . and let us show the newcomers that this is a land o'cakes, jollity, generosity, and kind-feelings, as well as a land of enterprise and gold.

When the Pacific Mail liner actually did arrive, the newspaper's enthusiasm mounted to new heights. The passage reporting the event is quoted in Kemble's *The Panama Route, 1848-1869* as follows:

> The *California* is a truly magnificent vessel, and her fine appearance as she came in sight off the Town, called forth cheer upon cheer from our enraptured citizens, who were assembled in masses upon the heights commanding a view of the Bay, and in dense crowds at the principle [that's how the editor spelled it] wharves and landing places.

Within a decade the trade between New York and San Francisco was supporting 29 steamships. They brought 175,000 passengers to the Golden Bear state, returning some $200,000,000 in gold. The railroad was still years away.

Among these early passengers were the famous "Mercer girls." Brought from the East by Asa B. Mercer, they were destined for Seattle, to meet the dearth of eligible young ladies as brides of the bachelor settlers. The first lot of eleven reached Seattle safely, but money problems stranded the second contingent of forty-six in San Francisco. There, according to Henry G. Alsberg's *American Guide,* local swains snatched away a goodly number. With the survivors Asa proceeded to his destination. Eventually he became President, and for a time the entire faculty of the Territorial University in Seattle (today's University of Washington). One of the "Mercer girls," we might add, became Mrs. Asa S. Mercer.

New gold discoveries in Australia and Alaska retained for the area a certain primitive flavor long lost in the East. Ships, both offshore and river, remained the handmaidens of progress and prosperity. The first steamship to cross the Pacific, it might be noted, was the *Monumental City.* The lure of gold had brought her. Built at Baltimore in 1852 she was wrecked on her first voyage in Australian waters a year later.

The *California* was to live on and on to the remarkable age of forty-six years. Hers was not an uneventful career. On one occasion she ran out of coal and had to burn her own spars. On another occasion an engine breakdown forced her to continue under sails alone. Another time she rescued the women and children and part of the mail from the newer and larger steamer *Winfield Scott* which had gone ashore. As new ships came out she was assigned to less important services and finally laid up as a spare boat. The trans-continental railroad was completed in 1869. Passing into different hands, the *California* was finally converted into a sailing craft in 1875. As a lumber bark she was long familiar up and down the coast under a foreign flag. She ran aground and was lost in January, 1895, off Peru.

The *BALTIC*

FROM sea-green, shell-shaped spittoons to fancy honeymoon staterooms, the *Baltic* was indeed a beauty. Built in 1850, a decade before the Civil War, she was unrivaled on the Atlantic not only in speed, but in size, luxury and popularity. It was not until a century later that the United States was to have a steamer which could break the Atlantic speed record and win the mythical Blue Ribbon.

Tiny in comparison to the superliner *United States* of today, the *Baltic* and her sisters established many "firsts." They were the first ships to be steam-heated, the first to offer a complete barbershop. Their bell systems by which passengers could call stewards were the first of their kind. Their straight stem, or bow, set the style for steamers for one hundred years. The *Baltic* carried and used sails but was essentially a steamship. Her twin half-moon paddle-wheel boxes were the outstanding feature of her high wooden hull. A shield of the United States was the central emblem on each paddle box. A gilded eagle graced the rounded stern. The *Baltic's* single smokestack reached higher than the beginning of the topmasts on fore and main. The ship's hull was black, except for a red band. An old-style anchor was slung over the side forward. Its chain looped down to a large hawsehole halfway up from the water line.

There was one deck of superstructure. The forward house contained officers' quarters, a pantry, kitchen and the barbershop. The barbershop attracted wide interest. A writer of the day described it as follows:

> It is fitted up with all necessary apparatus—with glass cases containing perfumery, etc.; and in the center is the barber's chair. This is a comfortable, well-stuffed seat, with an inclined back. In front is a stuffed trestle on which to rest feet and legs; and behind is a little stuffed apparatus, like a crutch, on which to rest the head. These are movable, so as to suit people of all sizes; and in this comfortable horizontal position the passenger lies, and his beard is taken off in a twinkling, let the Atlantic waves roll as they may.

The afterhouse contained a smoking room and a sheltered area for the helmsman, who steered according to bell signals from the bow. The smoking room communicated with the main lounge or great saloon just below it and adjacent to the dining saloon. Both rooms were about sixty feet in length, twenty in width. They were divided from each other by a steward's pantry lined with glass cases containing burnished plate and crockery of every description.

Of special note at the time were the suspended racks above the long tables in the dining saloon. They were to hold decanters and glasses so that they could be put on the table without risk of being carried from place to place during rough weather. Rose, satin and olive woods were used in both saloons.

The Baltic, *blue ribbon winner of 1852, was the last American ship to win the speed crown in 100 years*

Some of the tables had "beautifully variegated marble" tops with metal legs. Rich carpets and seat covers were used.

The cabin windows were of painted glass. Large circular glass ventilators were in the center of the saloons to let in light. There were many mirrors. A ladies' drawing room "full of every luxury" was near the chief saloon. There were 150 staterooms for passengers. Each berth had a bell rope which could be pulled to call a steward. Called an "Annunciator" the patented machine consisted of a framed panel with numbers corresponding to the staterooms. When the bell-rope was pulled the number of the passenger's cabin would be uncovered for the attending steward to note.

The many spittoons scattered about the *Baltic's* public rooms were proof that she was designed for Americans by Americans. It was the day of much tobacco chewing. The spittoons were large. Their upper section was shaped like a shell. They were painted a sea green or sky blue, according to an English observer who added that "they give ample facility for indulging in that practice of spitting of which Americans are so fond."

The *Baltic's* four boilers burned about eighty-three tons of coal in a typical 24-hour period, "and that is walking pretty fast into a coal mine," said an engineer of the day. But her engines were considered highly efficient in that era. They certainly performed! The *Baltic's* best time was nine days and thirteen hours. This was a voyage from Liverpool to New York in August, 1852. Her average speed was 13.34 knots, and she won the Atlantic speed crown. It would be exactly 100 years, minus a month, before another ship flying the American flag would win this coveted honor. The *United States* in July, 1952, broke the record held by the British *Queen Mary* with an average speed of thirty-five knots.

In addition to her powerful engines, her annunciator for stewards and the helmsman's bell, another mechanical contrivance on the *Baltic,* astounded visitors. This was a crude type engine-room telegraph. In the engine room was a box with five compartments. Each compartment was attached by wire to a bell pull at the side of the paddle wheel. The bell pull had five handles marked, respectively, "Ahead," "Slow," "Fast," "Back," "Hook on." When one of these handles was pulled a printed card with the corresponding signal appeared in the box in the engine room.

It is no surprise that the *Baltic* and her three Collins Line sister ships gained immediate popularity and quickly took the cream of the Atlantic trade away from their smaller, older and slower rivals. But they were expensive to operate. A British ship-line executive remarked dryly to the effect that "Mr. Collins is breaking our windows, but he is doing it with sovereigns, something he can't keep up very long."

The superior speed of the *Baltic* aroused that most venerable of all British humor magazines, *Punch,* to comment in the following "poetic" fashion:

> A steamer of the Collins Line
> A Yankee Doodle Notion
> Has also quickest cut the brine
> Across the Atlantic Ocean
> And British agents, no way slow
> Her merits to discover
> Have been and bought her—just to tow
> The Cunard packets over!

A certain Captain McKinnon, of the British Royal Navy, was high in his praise of the *Baltic* after returning to England aboard her. He had made his westward voyage in a Cunarder. Captain McKinnon said:

"I am only doing justice to these magnificent vessels in stating that they are beyond any competition the finest, fastest, and best sea boats in the world. I am sorry to be obliged to say this, but as a naval officer I feel bound in candor to admit their great superiority. Their extraordinary easiness in the sea cannot fail to excite the admiration of the sailor. I never beheld anything like it. No sea ever came on board, there was no violent plunging; the steering of the *Baltic* was the absolute poetry of motion. The reason why we allow Brother Jonathan to beat us on our own element is patent to the world, the British model is far inferior to the American."

For mouth-watering delicacies, fancy names for various dishes and variety, a dinner menu of the *Baltic* would rival that on a modern American passenger liner. Can you imagine yourself aboard the *Baltic* on the evening of Nov. 9, 1852, sitting down in her elegant dining saloon to this meal?

Soups	Green Turtle Soup; Potage aux choux.
Boiled	Hams; Tongues; ·Cold Corned Beef; Turkeys, Oyster Sauce; Fowls, Parsley Sauce; Leg of Mutton, Caper Sauce.
Fish	Cod-fish, stuffed and baked; Boiled Bass; Hollander Sauce.
Roast	Beef; Veal; Mutton; Lamb; Goose, Champagne Sauce; Ducks; Pigs; Turkeys; Fowls.
Entrees	Macaroni au gratin; Filet de Pigeon au Cronstaugh; Croquette de Poisson a la Richelieu; Salmi de Canard Sauvage; Poulets, pique, Sauce Tomato; Cotelette de Veau a la St. Gara; Fricandeau de Tortue au petit Pois; D'oyeis on cassi; Epigram d'Agneau, Sauce truppe.
Vegetables	Green Corn; Green Peas.
Salads	Potato and plain.
Pastry	Baked Vermicelli Pudding; Apple Fritters, Hard Sauce; Almond Cup Custards; Red Currant Tartlets; Apple Tarts; Open Puffs; Cranberry Tarts; Coventry Puffs; etc.

High operating costs, however, were not the only problem faced by Collins. In 1854 the *Baltic's* sister ship *Arctic* was rammed by an iron-hulled French steamer. The magnificent *Arctic* sank. Two years later, another sister, the *Pacific*, sailed out of Liverpool never to be seen again. She is thought to have struck an iceberg. In a day when disasters of these types were almost commonplace, the loss of two out of four ships was the beginning of the end for the great Collins Line.

The company was largely dependent on government funds, and with the Civil War approaching there were grave problems in Congress. Hostile members of Congress from the South were in no mood to continue Federal subsidies to a Northern ship line whose ships would be used against them in a war. The South had always been cold to an American Merchant Marine because it was largely a Northern industry. Southern planters were outraged at having to ship their cotton to Europe via New York or Boston. It hurt their pride. When the Collins subsidy came up for a vote, it was cut off and the line collapsed. Ship-owner Collins, after whom the line was named, died a pauper. He is buried in the Bronx, New York City, and his grave does not have a headstone; his family at his death was too poor to provide one.

The *Baltic*, which had made the last voyage of a Collins Line ship, was laid up for over a year. Eventually she was bought and put on the gold-rush run between New York and California. She operated on the Atlantic side, sailing between New York and Panama. She made several record passages, but in 1860 was laid up. At the outbreak of the Civil War, she was loaded with troops for Washington and supplies for the relief of Fort Sumter. The capital city was in danger of being captured and a fast transport of her type was eagerly acquired by the Government. Confederate guns prevented the *Baltic* from landing her supplies at Fort Sumter. She was forced to stand by until the fort's surrender. Major Anderson and his garrison are said by some to have been brought home aboard the *Baltic*. She was frequently chartered by the Government as a transport at from $1,000 to $2,000 a day.

For five years after the war ended the *Baltic* was again a transatlantic liner. She sailed under ownership of various companies, all more or less unsuccessful because of higher American operating costs. In 1870 the *Baltic* was sold to California shipowners. Her engines were removed and she was converted into a full-rigged sailing ship. She retained her name. Her new owners put her into the Australian and European grain trade. German interests bought her in 1875. Badly strained on a voyage between Bremen and Boston, she was again laid up. For five years the once proud record holder of the Atlantic rotted slowly in a state of complete neglect. She finally caught the eye of a ship breaker. He bought her and scrapped her in 1880 at Apple Island, Boston.

The MEMPHIS

CAPT. SHREVE'S *George Washington* set the style for all future steamboats on the Mississippi. A far cry from the slim, thoroughbred clippers or the sturdy Pacific Mail type steamships, the Mississippi River steamer was nevertheless one hundred per cent American. She was the prototype of river steamers now on the Volga, on the Amazon or the Nile. But Capt. Shreve did more than develop the Mississippi type. He was instrumental in making river navigation safe so his *George Washington* could be succeeded in years to come by speedsters like the great *J. M. White*, the *Rob't E. Lee*, or the *Memphis*.

His snag boat *Heliopolis*, developed in 1829, is said by some to have been his greatest single contribution. A twin-hulled vessel, she had an ingenious, wedge-like snagbeam forward which loosened and ripped up the deadly snags, cause of

For luxury, color and romance the Mississippi packet of the 1850's was unsurpassed. This is the Memphis

more river disasters than any other hazard. His title, Federal Superintendent of Western River Improvement, was well earned. Thirty years after his death a grateful government recognized at long last his claims to having invented the snagboat and awarded $50,000 to his heirs. Shreveport, La., is named for him.

The *Memphis* of 1852 represents the Mississippi steamboat in her heyday. A towering structure with main, boiler and hurricane decks, her pilot house was some fifty feet above the water. She measured 319 tons. Her giant paddle wheels were far aft and rose well above the saloon deck. Cords of wood were stacked forward beneath the ornate promenade deck with its gilt gingerbread railings and ornate joiner work. A tall flag mast at the bow rose sixty feet, with its round ball decoration at just about the pilot house level. Two great booms suspended from tall, thin king posts on either side of the saloon deck forward raised or lowered two long, narrow gangplanks, permanently carried aboard the craft on her voyaging between St. Louis and Memphis. Atop of it all were two giant smokestacks, abreast and supported by ornate iron struts from óne to the other. Taut guy wires strengthened the stacks in their commanding position. Many-pointed and bulbous were the cowls from which the rolls of wood smoke and sparks shot skyward. Speed was the watchword. The *Memphis* could make eighteen miles an hour in still water. She could reach twenty-four miles an hour with light draft and high pressure. The *Memphis* was abandoned in 1860.

As Mark Twain wrote, the steamboats of this day:

> —were finer than anything on shore. Compared with superior dwelling houses and first-class hotels in the Valley, they were indubitably magnificent, they were palaces.
>
> When a citizen stepped on board a big fine steamboat he entered a new and marvelous world; chimney tops cut to counterfeit a spraying crown of plumes—and maybe painted red; pilot house, hurricane deck, boiler deck guards, all garnished with white wooden filigree work of fanciful patterns; gilt acorns topping the derricks; gilt deer horns over the big bell; gaudy symbolical pictures on the paddle box, possibly; big, roomy boiler deck, painted blue; and furnished with Windsor arm chairs; inside, a far receding snow white cabin; porcelain knob and oil picture on every stateroom door; curving patterns of filigree work touched up with gilding, stretching overhead all down the converging vista; big chandeliers every little way, each an April shower of glittering glass drops; lovely rainbow light falling everywhere from the colored glazing of the skylights; the whole a long-drawn, resplendent tunnel, a bewildering and soul-satisfying spectacle; in the ladies' cabin a pink and white Wilton carpet, soft as mush, and glorified with a ravishing pattern of gigantic flowers.

We won't print what Charles Dickens said. His choleric attitude toward everything American made him dislike these extraordinary vessels just as much as Mark Twain liked them.

A word, in passing, on two subjects most people think of when they think of Mississippi steamboats: explosions and races.

The greatest maritime disaster of all time, in point of lives lost, took place in 1865 on the Mississippi. Licensed to carry 386, including crew, the big, new *Sultana* loaded 100 ordinary passengers, 2,400 war-weary soldiers and a crew of eighty. It was April, the same month as the *Titanic* disaster many years later. A boiler explosion turned the ship into a torch. Officially there were 1,547 dead, but more are thought to have been lost. The *Titanic* took down with her 1,503.

What is probably America's best known steamboat race is also part of Mississippi folklore. It pitted the *Rob't E. Lee* against the *Natchez* and it took place in 1870. Although captains of both boats publicly denied there was to be a race some 10,000 people watched the two racers leave Canal Street, New Orleans, for St. Louis. The *Lee* won, making the trip in 3 days, 18 hours and 13 minutes, as the roustabouts on her freight deck sang:

> Shoo fly, don't bodder me!
> You can't catch up wit' de *Rob't E. Lee.*

The WESTERN WORLD

AS IF to match the sea-green spittoons of the *Baltic* and not to be outdone by the many-colored skylights of the *Memphis,* the Great Lakes shipbuilders of 1854 proudly offered the *Western World.* A $250,000 sensation, this 348-foot-long mistress of the Inland Seas boasted paddle wheels that were four stories high. The elegant joiner work adorning her saloons, cabins and other public rooms was of rosewood. Stained glass domes, a weird combination of Greek, Ionic and Doric architectural forms and a dining saloon which could seat 200 put her on a par with the gaudiest and grandest vessels on any sea. She had a tonnage of over 2,000, not much less than the Atlantic blue ribbon holder *Baltic.* She could speed between Buffalo, her home port, and Detroit in 14 hours, a great improvement on the five weeks of the *Griffin* or the five days of the brave little *Walk-in-the-Water.*

The 1850's were years of significance for Great Lakes shipping and for America as a whole. The opening of locks at Sault Ste. Marie gave Chicago, Detroit, Cleveland and Buffalo a direct approach to the vast ore and wheat areas of Lake Superior. The first year's traffic in 1855 was 106,296 tons. This rose by twelve times in less than twenty years. Forty years after the Soo Canal was opened 8,000,000 tons passed through its locks. At this writing, as the Soo celebrated its century of service, twice as much tonnage passes through its gates during the ice-free months of each year as goes through the Panama and Suez Canals combined in a full year. The new St. Lawrence Seaway will probably continue the phenomenal rise of marine activity on the Great Lakes, our new and fourth coastline.

The *Western World* was built by the New York Central and the Michigan Central railroads to serve as a link between New York and the West. With the *Plymouth Rock,* her sister, she was designed by Isaac Newton, steamboat titan of the Hudson River. These steamboats were similar to the great Fall River liner *Metropolis,* whose story will follow.

Before the *Western World* was four years old she was laid up, never to operate again. Railroads rimming the Lakes were soon completed. They were not icebound during the winter. What they lacked in tinted domes and Doric joiner work, they made up in speed, and speed was the watchword of the day.

The *Western World's* hull was used for a while as a floating drydock at

A mammoth wooden paddle wheel steamboat, the Western World *was the pride of the Great Lakes in 1854*

Cleveland. Her machinery was removed and shipped to New York. Fifteen-hundred-horsepower plants were not lightly to be scrapped. Her engines had been built in New York in the first place, by the Allaire Works, one of the best known engine concerns in the business. The engines eventually found a new career. They were installed in the hull of a craft with a frightening name, a name that would never have been chosen for an American vessel, particularly at a time when boiler explosions were not at all uncommon. The name was the *Fire Queen*. Her owners were Yangtze River operators and she was a grand success in China, serving between 1864 and 1878. The engines of her sister ship the *Plymouth Rock* also went into a new craft built in New York for Chinese service. Many American excursion boats were built for sale to China. The story of their daring voyages for delivery in the Orient around the Horn and across the Pacific mark one of the boldest chapters in American maritime enterprise.

The METROPOLIS

THE SPEED queen of Long Island Sound and one of the earliest and most famous Fall River liners was the *Metropolis*. She made one voyage at an average of over twenty knots when new in 1855, a speed about twice that of *Liberty* ships of World War II. When going at her best speed she seemed to be pushing a great mass of water ahead of her. Hers was the largest and most powerful single marine engine ever built up to that day. Its cylinder was the largest that had ever been cast up to that time. Her four great boilers burned from forty to sixty tons of coal each night on the 180-mile course linking Boston, via Fall River, with New York. A tall smokestack rose on either side, each stack serving two boilers. Her two iron paddle wheels were forty-one feet in diameter, larger even than the *Western World's*. Each had thirty-two thirteen-foot iron buckets which propelled her up and down the Sound for nineteen years.

The *Metropolis* measured 342 feet overall, longer by far than the *Washington, California* or *Baltic*, the three ocean liners described above. The *Himalaya*, giant British Peninsular & Oriental liner generally thought to be the world's largest ship of that time, was shorter by two feet than the Fall River queen. The longest vessel of her day was the *New World*, of Hudson River fame, which boasted a length of 371 feet. In tonnage the *Metropolis* measured 2,108 tons, a good 1,300 tons smaller than the *Himalaya*. Nevertheless she was occasionally referred to in contemporary descriptions as the world's largest ship.

The *Metropolis* was in many ways an ocean-type vessel. Her hull construction marked a startling departure from earlier Long Island Sound and river boats. Her center keelson was of white oak, four feet deep. Her frames, of live oak and locust, were strapped diagonally with iron bars. So rigid was her great length that the hog frame was not necessary. For the first time on a steamer of her type the main deck was extended forward to the stem and closed in. A gaily decorated paddle-wheel box below the giant walking beam just abaft the two tall funnels touched off the glistening white hull of the *Metropolis*. Her overall design was far more modern than the oddly impressive four stacker *Newport* which came after her.

The fastest voyage of the *Metropolis* set a record which was to stand unchallenged for fifty-two years, according to author Roger McAdam. It began at 5:09 p.m. at Pier 3, North River, New York. She passed through Hell Gate at flood tide and began the long almost straight course up the Sound. Her best time was made from Saybrook Light, Conn., to Watch Hill Light, R. I., during which stretch she raced on through the night at 21.93 miles per hour. This was substantially above the best speed of contemporary Atlantic liners. It was still

FRANK O. BRAYNARD

She was speed queen of the Fall River Line, and some claimed the Metropolis *was the world's largest ship*

dark when the *Metropolis* docked at Fall River, only 8 hours and 51 minutes running time from New York.

The story of the *Metropolis* and her picture were the featured subjects on a "steamboat Christmas card" sent out some years ago by William King Covell, Fall River Line historian. Each year Mr. Covell's Christmas greetings to fellow members of the Steamship Historical Society were sent in the form of a little printed folder describing one of the famous Fall River steamers.

The last years of the *Metropolis* were not eventful. She was dismantled at Newport about 1873 for use as a car ferry. Some think she was intended for the Staten Island run in New York harbor. At any rate she never was used as a ferry since her wheel shafts were so high that cars could not run from one end of the boat to another. Laid up at Newport she was sold in 1879 and taken to Boston where she was stripped and burned for scrap.

The Fall River Line was a pioneer in marine construction and ship safety. The line operated the year round, occasionally having as many as four ships with up to 4,000 passengers aboard at one time. Only one passenger died through an accident in its 90-year history, 1847-1937. The line led in the use of the double-bottom hull, electric lights on shipboard, automatic fire alarms and the fire-sprinkler system. Many of the fire-safety devices made law in 1934 and 1935 after the *Morro Castle* disaster had been in use for decades on the great floating palaces of the old Fall River Line.

It fell to the originator of the phrase "Tin Pan Alley" to immortalize the Line in song. Harry Von Tilzer's "On the Old Fall River Line," written in 1913, has comfortably taken its place with his other hits as a classic. Inspired by frequent voyages his heart was in his work as he penned these lines:

> On the Old Fall River Line,
> I fell for Susie's line of talk
> And Susie fell for mine
> Then we fell in with a parson
> And he tied us tight as twine.

The VANDERBILT

CORNELIUS VANDERBILT was a genius. He was a genius at deals, a genius at making money and a genius at shipping. Most wealthy men in the days before the Civil War had a hand in ships and shipping if they lived above the Mason-Dixon line. Vanderbilt had both hands and both feet in the game, and loved it. His steamer *Vanderbilt* lived a life which compares well with her namesake in accomplishments, thrills, quick changes and interest.

Built in 1857, she was in use up to 1930. Laid down as a steamship, she spent many years as a full-rigged sailing vessel. Intended for transatlantic passenger service, she ended her career as a coal hulk at Gibraltar. Her naval record in the Civil War is worth a book in itself. She nearly caught the raider *Alabama,* which was destroying the Union merchant marine. With fifty feet of ironplating on her bow, she could have sunk the *Merrimac* had the *Monitor* not got there first.

The *Vanderbilt* began as a 331-foot beauty with two giant smokestacks and two raked masts. The funnels and masts did not have the same rake, although many contemporary prints suggest they did. Though shorter than the *Metropolis* she was of greater tonnage. She cost $800,000. Although of wooden construction, she had four watertight compartments. America, it should be noted, continued to use wood long after Britain had turned to iron, just as we stuck to sail longer than England. In each case we suffered as a consequence.

The *Vanderbilt* was designed to compete with the highly subsidized British Cunard Line on the Atlantic. With her ran the *North Star,* originally Vanderbilt's sumptuous private yacht in which he toured Europe with a party of twenty-five ladies and gentlemen, to the consternation and wonderment of the monarchs and upper crust of the lands he visited. His steamship line began its service as the Collins Line was folding. It continued with some success until the Civil War, with the *Vanderbilt* sailing only in the summers. The Commodore's immense wealth made such a venture possible.

When the Civil War broke out the big craft was chartered for three months as a transport for $2,000 a day. The government was considering buying her when the Union side was thrown into turmoil by the success of the ironclad *Merrimac.* Vanderbilt, longing for some part in the war, hurried to Washington and offered the *Vanderbilt* as a ram to destroy the Confederate menace. He talked with Lincoln and so impressed the President that he was allowed to carry out all arrangements himself and to personally take command of the vessel on her mission. The liner was placed under the ægis of the War Department, for Vanderbilt was having a feud with the Navy at the time.

Eager with a sense of importance, the Commodore rushed home from the White House and supervised the installation of ironplating on both sides of the *Vanderbilt*'s bow some fifty feet aft. A ram was built at the stem. Her twin walking beams were protected with 500 bales of cotton and her vulnerable paddle-wheel boxes were strengthened. Twelve 9-inch and two 100-pound guns were swung aboard. All this took a week. Then came his commission as her Commander and his orders to stalk the *Merrimac* off Norfolk. Although the *Monitor* stole the show, much credit remains for the *Vanderbilt.* Her next assignment was to seek out and destroy the Confederate cruiser *Alabama.* The Commodore's ship reached the Cape of Good Hope, rendezvous point of the British-built *Alabama,* hours before the latter got there. But the *Vanderbilt* missed the Confederate raider. Her guns, however, did succeed in capturing several Confederate blockade runners. It might be noted here that the *Alabama* and her sisters were responsible for the decimation of the Union merchant marine. High insurance rates due to the raiders' depredations and the transfer to foreign flags of half our fleet meant the beginning of the end for the deep-sea American cargo and passenger fleet. A law prohibiting the return to the American flag of former United States ships, after the war, capped this disaster to our shipping. Our eyes were to the West.

Apparently Vanderbilt believed he had only loaned the *Vanderbilt* to Washington. He was somewhat taken aback to receive in 1864 a resolution of thanks and gold medal from Congress for his "fervid and large-souled patriotism."

"The damn, dirty thieves. What'n hell do I want with their twenty-five-dollar gold medal? What's a medal, anyway? I want my steamer! I never said I'd give 'em the *Vanderbilt.* They took her. They stole her."

From luxury liner, to Civil War armed auxiliary, to fast sailing ship went the fabulous Vanderbilt's *career*

These are his reported words.

However, he soon settled down to bask in the medal's favorable publicity and to turn his attention to railroading.

The *Vanderbilt* then went to the Pacific as a cruiser, the fastest in the Navy. In 1868 she was laid up in San Francisco Bay. After five years of idleness she was sold for a mere $42,000 and rebuilt as a sailing ship, with clipper bow and three masts. She was renamed *Three Brothers*. Her lack of sheer gave away the fact that she was originally a steamship, but she made many fast voyages up and down the California coast, to New York and to Liverpool. In 1885 she became a coal hulk at Gibraltar and in 1928 was sold to a Spaniard for firewood for the piddling sum of $2,500. She was scrapped two years later.

A popular Currier & Ives print hailed her in her last years as the "world's largest sailing ship." This print is widely used today as a calendar picture, and was hanging in the author's kitchen as this chapter was prepared.

No reference to ships in the Civil War period would be complete without mention of two extraordinary ship types developed by the Confederate States of America: the blockade runner and the raider.

Probably the best known blockade runner was the celebrated schooner yacht *America*, best known for bringing home the "America's Cup" from the international yacht races off England in 1851. Her high speed and light draft made her ideal for the trade, and she smuggled countless cargoes of quinine, morphine, surgical instruments and even ammunition through President Lincoln's blockade.

The best known Confederate raider was the powerful steamship *Alabama*, which the *Vanderbilt* unsuccessfully chased. Built in England, her sale to the South nearly brought on war between Great Britain and the United States. England was finally required to pay American shipowners for the vast damage done by this commerce destroyer. Perhaps less known but with an equally interesting story was the *Shenandoah*, commissioned in 1864 and also built in England. Her most famous raid took place two months after war ended. Four days after General Lee surrendered she headed for Alaska in search of northern whalers. In one week during June of 1865 she captured twenty-three of them. It was not until August that she met a British vessel with certain evidence that hostilities had ended.

PART FOUR

The Last Stand of Sail

In the quarter century before the Civil War American maritime enterprise under canvas reached new heights. Why use iron when we had the finest forests in the world? American whalers outnumbered all others 3 to 1. Our renowned clippers were the envy of every merchant marine. But our allegiance to wood and sail spelled shoals ahead. Equally dangerous to our maritime strength was to prove the concentration of maritime enterprise in northern states, for the Civil War was to virtually sweep American shipping off the high seas.

The ANN McKIM

THERE are those who say that the clipper ships actually contributed to the downfall of America's maritime might. Clippers were so fast, so illustrious and above all so profitable that shipbuilders were lulled into a prideful sense of security. Whether we rejected progress because of our clippers or not, the clipper-ship era remains a magnificent chapter in our history.

It was an era of glamor, success and achievement. Its deepest roots reached back as far as the first schooner of 1713. The ketch *Eliza,* built in 1794 in Salem, was another forebear, with her curved stem and hollow waterlines. Her navy-cutter stern and substantial deadrise were suggestive of the Baltimore clippers and the famous cup racer *America.*

"A thing of beauty was the *Ann McKim,*" writes William M. Williamson, son of a sea captain and a notable authority on sailing ships. She was launched in 1833 at Baltimore. We must glance back to some of the things that were said about her on that warm June 4th, for she is today regarded as the prototype of the clipper.

A selection from the next day's newspaper follows:

The launch of the elegant ship *Ann McKim* took place yesterday afternoon in the presence of thousands of spectators. Soon after five o'clock, and at the precise moment that the steamboat *Columbus* was passing the front of the shipyard, she was released from the last stay that prevented her motion, and glided into her destined element in the most beautiful and imposing style, amidst the shouts of the assembled multitude. She is a splendid vessel, and richly merits all the praise that has been so universally bestowed on her.

A small craft, the *Ann McKim* was 143 feet long. She was hailed as "the most masterly and beautiful specimen of naval architecture which has perhaps ever been produced at the shipyards of this or any other city in the United States." Seldom before or since has such high praise measured true in performance.

Isaac McKim, rich Baltimore merchant, built the *Ann McKim*, which he named in honor of his wife. Money was not spared to make the craft complete. Spanish mahogany hatch combings, rails and skylights were fitted on her handsome flush deck. She had twelve brass guns, brass capstan heads, brass bells and was her owner's pet. After five years in the China trade she was sold to a New York firm. This same company is said to have used her lines when they built the illustrious *Rainbow*, the first true clipper. The *Ann McKim* was sold in 1847 to a Valparaiso shipowner. Her fate under the Chilean flag is hidden in obscurity. She marked the beginning of the Baltimore clipper as the *Mary Whitridge*, of 1854, marked the climax. The *Mary Whitridge* on her maiden voyage ran from Cape Charles to the Rock Light, Liverpool, in 13 days, 7 hours.

Just when or how the term "clipper" was coined is uncertain. Some think it was because such craft used to go along at a good clip, for speed was their chief claim to fame. Then again they clipped days off speed records.

Clippers could be distinguished by the line of their stem reaching forward from keel to bowsprit in a graceful concave curve. Thin lines in the forward hull made for faster passage through the water. The greatest breadth of hull was farther aft than in previous vessels. Greater speed came from increased length in proportion to beam. Finally, and perhaps most distinctively, it was the mass of canvas, more and higher than ever seen before, that set clippers apart from other sailing ships.

We are indebted to Lawrenze Gardiner, of the Shipbuilders Council of America, for the following filip regarding the *Ann McKim:*

The direct descendant of the Ann McKim after whom the famous ship was named lived in Baltimore. Though high in the social circles of the city, she kept an antique shop in her little pink house with blue shutters at the end of a lane. A maiden lady, she always used to say she never needed a husband because she had a cat, a dog and a parrot. She would say:

The cat stayed out all night.
The dog growled and the parrot swore.

The best of everything from brass to polished woods went into the beautiful
Ann McKim, *first of the clippers*

The CHARLES W. MORGAN

AN AMERICAN whaler was the first ship to reach a British port after the close of the Revolution. The local Commissioners of Customs were dumbfounded at such effrontery. Never before had the red, white and blue flag with its thirteen rebellious stripes flown at peace in British waters. They did not know just what to do "on account of the many acts of Parliament yet in force against the rebels in America," according to a contemporary account in a London newspaper. But the ship eventually was cleared, sold her cargo of oil and returned to Nantucket with a handsome profit.

Such was the spunk of the American whalers. Their story adds up to one of the most astounding, heroic life-and-death epics in all our past. Whalers supplied fuel for our lights, bone for our clothing and perfume for our fashions. Whaling and whalers took the American flag to every port in the world. The cornerstone of our deep-sea shipbuilding industry was the whaleship. Whaling men made up the backbone of our Navy in the War of 1812 and the Civil War. Whaling was one of the greatest incentives to exploration and led to pioneer discoveries by Americans in both the Arctic and the Antarctic. Whaling may almost be said to have been an American monopoly. In 1842 there were 882 whalers, of which 652 were American.

The *Charles W. Morgan*, built in 1841, may be said without fear of contradiction to be America's most illustrious whaler. She is preserved today as queen of Mystic Seaport, maritime Williamsburg operated by the Marine Historical Association at Mystic, Conn. An active and successful whaler for 80 years, the *Morgan* made thirty-seven voyages. She sailed on every ocean, including the Arctic and Antarctic. Her log shows she took more whales, and sailed greater distances than any other American whaleship. She was named after a famous whaling merchant.

In 1954, 67,533 adults and 17,748 children saw the *Morgan* at her berth in Mystic River. She has been a museum ship at Mystic and before that, at New Bedford, since 1925. One would suppose that these last few years would have been quiet years of retirement for the sturdy *Morgan* with nothing more serious to contend with than dry rot or souvenir hunters, but not so. She has survived two major hurricanes. In 1938, while at Round Hills, Mass., she was lifted six feet out of her bed of sand by the Sept. 21 hurricane. Her copper sheathing was almost entirely washed away, a strip of planking was torn loose from her port quarter and her beautiful carved wooden eagle sternboard was lost. Otherwise she was undamaged. Hurricane Carol in 1954 saw her better ready for the worst nature could hurl.* As a whaler the *Morgan* survived hurricanes, mutinies

---

* The author's parents took refuge from this hurricane aboard the *Joseph Conrad,* near the *Morgan,* while their small sailing boat tossed wildly about tied up at the same pier.

The Charles W. Morgan, *built in 1841 and today enshrined at Mystic, Conn.,
is America's most famous whaler, a sight to see*

and groundings. She was struck by lightning not once, but three times. She was even set afire by her own crew on one occasion.

Henry Beetle Hough's fascinating book *Whaling Wives* describes what happened when another crew set fire to their whaler. The whaler's captain, Nathaniel M. Jernegan, would never go after a whale on a Sunday, but how he handled the crew on the occasion of the fire shows of what stern stuff whalemen were made.

His ship had caught fire and he was sure some crew members had started it deliberately. After failing to discover the culprit in a solemn hand-on-Bible ceremony, Captain Jernegan picked ten of the toughest seamen and put them in irons. Still no confession. Next he picked from the ten three of the meanest, strung them up to the rigging so they could barely touch the deck on tip toe. A personally-administered lashing with a new rope finally brought out the story, implicating two of the ten in irons, and a third. Each of the three was beaten with 400 lashes. It is not known whether Abigail, the captain's wife, watched this punishment. She was aboard.

The ship was still burning, and no one knew whether the fire could be extinguished; in fact, things looked pretty bad. The captain, however, was not through with the arsonists. While Mrs. Jernegan and the rest of the crew made ready to abandon ship and seek refuge on a nearby whaler, Captain Jernegan offered the guilty men their choice of two courses. He would have them hanged immediately, or he would tie them to the rigging of the sinking craft and let them go down with her. The men chose to be hanged. Night saved them, however, and on the next day the fire was put out. Their lives were not taken. It scarcely need be added that they deserted at the first opportunity.

The *Morgan* seemed to have a charmed life. On one occasion at her home port, New Bedford, a burning passenger steamer drifted toward her, sinking under her lee. Some blistered paint was the only memento of the affair.

Originally rigged as a single topsail full-rigged ship, the *Morgan* was altered in 1876 into a bark. In 1925 she was again given a ship rig, that is, her fore and aft sails on the mizzenmast were re-rigged as square sails. The accompanying drawing shows her with bark rig, as she was for fifty of her eighty years of active life.

Whereas the modern freighter's life expectancy is twenty years, it was not uncommon for whalers to live and work fifty to sixty years or more. Two whaling ships' lives span our national history: the *Morgan's* and that of the *Maria,* built in 1782 and not scrapped until 1863.

Whalers had to be good ships; their work was strenuous, to say the least. It was not unknown for a whaling ship to be attacked by a whale. There are several cases in which whales actually destroyed whaling vessels. The *Essex,* for example, was sunk by an immense sperm whale in only two charges. She was a substantial vessel for her year—1819. In tonnage she was the same size as the first *Bangor,* described above. Whales are the largest living things, larger than the greatest dinosaur of the past. Of tremendous power, they are known to have gone as fast as twenty-five miles an hour when harpooned. Some accounts hold that the sulphur-bottom or the finback could make fifty miles an hour at the start of a race for life.

Go see the *Morgan* at Mystic. You will enjoy this direct touch with America's great whaling era.

When kerosene supplanted whale oil as the chief fuel for the lamps of the world, whaling declined. This, plus the Civil War, killed our whaling industry. Whaling today is done largely by giant, thoroughly-mechanized Norse whaling ships. International regulations carefully limit the season in which whaling may be done and the number of whales which may be caught. Not a single whaler flies the American flag.

The *FLYING CLOUD*

SHE was truly a "Flying Cloud," an expanse of canvas, a white-winged mistress of the blue, a great, living, racing creature. She typifies the middle years of the nineteenth century, truly the halcyon days of sail. Before 1840 man's progress under sail had moved slowly ahead, so slowly at times as to seem at a snail's pace. And then there slid from the greased shipways of America a succession of such craft that were the wonder of the world. The *Flying Cloud* remains today perhaps the most perfect clipper, the most famous sailing ship of all time.

She came at a time when America was booming. Some $50,000,000 worth of California gold was flowing each year into the veins of our new country, new in its extent from coast to coast. Wheat fields stretching westward into Minnesota were producing gigantic surplus crops, much of which was exported. Our $100,000,000 cotton industry supplied nearly half our sales abroad. Over seventy percent of our foreign trade was still being carried overseas in American ships, sailing ships to a large extent. Almost half of our 23,000,000 people were now Westerners. Britain had repealed her hostile Navigation Acts. In England, vast sums went into new steamships, with the founding of the Union Line to South Africa, and the Royal Mail and the P. & O. Britain was spreading her steam lines in a great network round the world. In America, private maritime capital for ocean services largely went into wooden clippers.

Built in East Boston in 1851, the *Flying Cloud* was designed by Donald McKay. His flare for names was evident in the selection of hers. Other grand-sounding McKay names were *Stag Hound, Lightning, Glory of the Seas,* and his masterpiece, *Great Republic.* The *Flying Cloud's* figurehead, in keeping with her name, was that of an angel with trumpet extended. She was 235 feet overall, much smaller than the Fall River queen *Metropolis,* but larger than Baltimore's *Ann McKim.* While not an extreme clipper, she excited keen interest for the

The Flying Cloud, *the perfect name for the perfect ship. She was a queen among queens*

beauty of her lines. She was sold on the stocks for a price reported to be twice that of her entire cost. On her first voyage, New York to San Francisco, she set a record of eighty-nine days, a time never since beaten by sailing ship, although twice equaled. So proud were her owners that they published on silk with letters of gold her log of this historic voyage.

Gilded pilasters, elegant wainscoting of satinwood, mahogany and rosewood made her passenger accommodations well regarded, although she was basically a freight carrier. Her speed, in all sorts of weather, made her a choice link between New York and the gold rush communities of California. Her master, Captain Josiah P. Cressy, of Marblehead, Mass., was a demon with his canvas. His first voyage was an example. The log shows a succession of lost sails, sprung masts and trouble with officers and crew, due probably to overwork and extreme tension.

On one occasion Capt. Cressy notes releasing men from irons "in consequence of wanting their services, with the understanding that they would be taken care of on arriving at San Francisco."

Again Capt. Cressy reports that he has "suspended first officer from duty, in consequence of his arrogating to himself the privilege of cutting up rigging contrary to my orders, and long-continued neglect of duty." The mate sued Capt. Cressy for damages. By some odd chance the Captain was mistakenly reported as having died on a voyage to Canton from San Francisco. The Captain had the pleasure of reading his own obituary. He saw it in a paper passed over to him by an outward bound ship on the voyage back from the Orient. He made no note of it in the log, but whatever his reaction it saved him considerable harassment. The offending first mate had also read it, and dropped his suit.

On one voyage the *Flying Cloud* logged 374 miles in a day, an average of over fifteen knots. Records fell at every turn, and lavish praise was given Cressy. His wife came in for her share of honors, and justly so. She was in her cabin on a passage home in 1855 watching through a port the warm waters of Madagascar rushing by astern at twelve knots. Suddenly she was amazed to see the waterswept form of a man wildly clutching at the foam swirling past. He had been washed over, and none but she had seen him. Racing on deck, she gave the alarm and threw a life buoy to the fast disappearing figure. The Captain stopped the ship and lowered a boat which returned some time later empty-handed. Captain Cressy was not satisfied. Two boats were sent back to search, with orders not to return until darkness made any further looking hopeless. They found him! He was picked up four hours later and two miles behind the *Flying Cloud*. Mrs. Cressy nursed him back to health in her own cabin, reports Basil Lubbock. Only parallel to this tale is the modern miracle whereby the American freighter *Santa Clara*, Grace Line, retraced her course several hours after a man had fallen overboard. No one had seen him go, but he was missed. He too was found, a triumph of seamanship against winds and tides.

Mrs. Cressy's bravery, reminiscent of the bravery of the whaling wives, recalls the heroic tale of Mrs. Patten of the clipper *Neptune's Car*. While rounding the Horn her husband broke down with so-called "brain fever" and was incapacitated. The first mate was in irons, the second was no good. Bully Mrs. Patten took command; she had interested herself in the art of navigation on an earlier voyage. Fifty-two days later she brought the 1,800-ton clipper safely into San Francisco, with her husband on the mend, thanks to her care. She was only nineteen.

The depression of 1856 led to the laying up of the *Flying Cloud* for a spell. Built of soft wood, as were other American vessels, time was beginning to tell. Her record voyages were fewer. Her hull became heavier and waterlogged. New owners, new ports and more years of service followed. She became an emigrant ship to Australia under the house flag of James Baines, of Liverpool, a shipowner who was to give his own name to another of Donald McKay's finest creations. The *Flying Cloud's* sale to British owners was an example of how the best and finest of our merchant fleet left the flag, during the Civil War, never to return.

As late as 1870 her angel-trumpet figurehead still gave promise of speed, still proudly spurred the *Flying Cloud* to new achievement. Loaded with 387 emigrants, she raced from Liverpool to Hervey's Bay, Australia, in the excellent time of eighty-seven days. Again she averaged just under sixteen knots on a four-day coastal run "down under."

The last chapter of her life was spent on the North Atlantic as a lumber ship. She flew the Black Ball Line house flag. In 1874 she grounded off New Brunswick, was refloated and taken to St. John for repairs. A shipyard fire so badly wracked her that she was broken up for her iron.

Her life spanned the clipper ship era and more. America was a new land when she burned in St. John, a different country from the America of 1851. In two short decades a continent had been won, torn apart and cemented together again, and was ripe for internal expansion. Vast hoards of immigrants were flowing westward. Churning, muddy rivers were being cleared for commerce. Indians were being rounded up and driven back onto reservations at the same time that the buffalo were being exterminated. Money for railroads, packet boats and mines was flowing in from abroad to make us a debtor nation. Brother Jonathan was slowly being transformed as our national symbol to Uncle Sam. The fame of our clippers was an opiate which would lull us into a belief in our maritime supremacy for years. The churning wonders of our river steamers and the gilded palaces gliding up and down our coastline blinded us to the fate of our deep-sea shipping, blighted by the Civil War and ignored in the decades to follow while all eyes turned west.

The DREADNOUGHT

THE American Merchant Marine can well be proud of the packet ship *Dreadnought*. This ship, which to this day holds the transatlantic speed record for a sailing ship, was once as well known in the homes of America as the superliner *United States* is today. In addition to seventy-five fast passages across the Atlantic, the *Dreadnought* is perhaps best remembered as the ship which sailed at night into New York through Hell Gate from Long Island Sound. She is known, too, as the vessel which sailed stern first in a gale for 280 miles after her tiller and rudder had been blown away. Her master, the fabulous Captain Samuel Samuels, was a national idol.

The *Dreadnought* has become an American legend. She is honored in story and song. Here are the words of an old chanty:

> There's a saucy wild packet, a packet of fame
> She belongs to New York, and *Dreadnought's* her name,
> She is bound to the Westward, where the strong winds do blow.
> Bound away in the *Dreadnought* to the Westward we'll go.
> She's the Liverpool packet—O, Lord, let her go!

The *Dreadnought* was built in Newburyport, Mass., by Currier & Townsend. She had been jointly ordered by E. D. Morgan, Francis B. Cutting, David Ogden and other New York shipping men for their prize master, Capt. Samuels. Her keel was laid in June, 1853, when regular steamship service across the Atlantic for passengers and freight was already over a decade old. The ship was named after a famous vessel in Admiral Nelson's fleet. Her owners sent to England to get the proper spelling and found that it was "Dreadnought" and not "Dreadnaught."

Capt. Samuels, who had already made himself one of the Atlantic's best-known skippers, was given supervisory charge during the *Dreadnought's* construction. He had more than a little to say as to her rigging and sail plan and even her hull design and inboard arrangements. Although only thirty years old, Capt. Samuels had been a master for nine years when he was assigned to what was to become known as "The Wild Boat of the Atlantic."

The *Dreadnought* was not strictly a clipper like her famous contemporaries under the American flag—the *Flying Cloud, Sovereign of the Seas,* etc. Her hull was fuller and her lines less fine. She was designed to bear driving to the limit in the worst the North Atlantic could give. "She would stand up to her canvas until the breaking strain of rope, spar and sail was reached," writes Basil Lubbock. In light weather she was not outstanding.

The *Dreadnought* was first planned for the Racehorse Line, which ran between New York and California, for the gold rush was still on. But high rates for cargo and increased immigrant traffic made her owners change their minds and she was put under the house flag of the St. George's Cross Line. The red cross on her fore-topsail was soon to become unique, for all the other ships of the company were lost through accidents shortly after the *Dreadnought* slid into the water. She was a large ship, as sailing vessels went, measuring 1,400 tons. She was 200 feet long, and 39 feet wide. On Nov. 3, 1853, she set sail from New York on her first run to Liverpool.

Capt. Samuels and the *Dreadnought's* owners made $40,000 on her first round trip, but, even more important, the ship's reputation was firmly established. The two-way voyage was made in fifty-eight days. On the return passage she beat the Cunard steamer *Canada*. She had left Liverpool a day later than the flush-decked paddle wheeler of 400 horsepower. On the day the *Canada* reached Boston, the *Dreadnought* passed the Highlands of New Jersey, inward bound. Capt. Samuels was so sure of his craft after this that he henceforth guaranteed to make cargo deliveries within a certain time or forfeit freight charges. This bold bid induced shippers to pay him rates halfway between those of other sailing packets and what the steamers were getting.

It was also on her maiden voyage that the *Dreadnought* sailed through Long Island Sound and past treacherous Hell Gate—at night! She was the first full-rigged ship to do this.

As time passed the *Dreadnought* cut her own record almost with every voyage. Her best runs were made in winter, when her rather full hull could take full advantage of heavy winds. On Dec. 4, 1854, she made 320 miles on an eastbound run. Fifteen- and fourteen-day passages became almost common with the new ship. Her best through passage was made early in 1859. She made the 3,018-mile run from New York to Liverpool in 13 days and 8 hours.

If we can depend on a statement made by Capt. Samuels in his old age— he lived until 1908—an even better voyage was in the making on another occasion. The Atlantic leg of the trip from Sandy Hook to Queenstown, now Cobh, Ireland, had been made in the phenomenal time of 9 days, 17 hours. Light and variable airs killed what might have been the most extraordinary passage under sail of all time, and the final leg to Liverpool took six days. Since his logbooks have long since been lost, and his own records washed overboard in a storm, there is no way to prove or disprove this claim by the *Dreadnought's* doughty skipper. Authorities today accept his account as quite possible.

The *Dreadnought's* feat of sailing backwards for 280 miles took place in 1862. A huge sea put Capt. Samuels out of action. The wheel was ignored and the ship became helpless. A jury rudder failed and it was found impossible to turn her about. Her headsails and those on her foremast were taken in. With her main and mizzen yards braced until every sail was flat aback, she slowly gathered sternway in the direction of the nearest land. A second jury rudder was finally fitted and the *Dreadnought* reached port. It was eleven months, however, before

She would stop for none, the Dreadnought *sailed best in bad weather. Her
Atlantic speed mark still stands*

Capt. Samuels was back in service, so serious had been the compound fracture of his leg.

In 1864 the *Dreadnought* was put in the Cape Horn trade. While en route from New York to San Francisco in 1869, the famous craft, now old for her type, hit a calm while close in under the rock coast of Tierra del Fuego. There was a heavy swell rolling with a current in toward the rocks. After all other efforts to stop her failed, as a last desperate old-school try her crew took to the boats and actually attempted to tow the brave old ship clear of the slowly approaching shoreline. To pull a fully-loaded ship of 1,400 tons in a Cape Horn swell was simply out of the question. Quickly she was caught by the breakers, hove inshore and all was over. But all was not forgotten. For many years the chanty hailing the *Dreadnought's* fame was popular on shipboard and in tavern. It concludes:

> Then a health to the *Dreadnought* and to her brave crew,
> To bold Captain Samuels and his officers too;
> Talk about your flash packets, Swallow Tail and Black-Ball,
> The *Dreadnought's* the flyer that can lick them all.

The JAMES BAINES

CLIPPERS had class. They were noted for their smooth seams, polished dull black hulls, holystoned pine decks that gleamed a cream-white.

"Many had sumptuous staterooms, cabins and bathrooms for passengers that put the old-time stuffy Cunarders to shame," says Samuel Eliot Morison in his *The Maritime History of Massachusetts*. One had a library costing some $1,200.

But if the British were chagrined by the superior accommodations on American clippers, they were positively blue in the face when it came to their inability to compete as to speed. Morison notes that British firms in Hong Kong paid 75 cents a cubic foot freight on speedy American clippers bound for London while British craft could claim only 28 cents. He adds:

> Crack British East Indianmen humbly awaited a cargo in the treaty ports for weeks on end, while one American clipper after another sailed proudly in, and secured a return freight almost before her topsails were furled. When the Yankee beauties arrived in the Thames, their decks were thronged with sight-seers, their records were written up in the leading papers, and naval draughtsmen took off their lines while in dry-dock.

All was not well, however, for despite our naval architects, often likened to cathedral builders of the thirteenth century, and despite our pounding, strong-willed masters, one important element came to be lacking.

From 1850 on it became more and more apparent that the American deep-sea seaman of old was a disappearing breed. The gold rush, high-paying coastal and river-boat jobs and unlimited opportunities in the booming West were

The graceful clipper James Baines *was named by her British owner after himself. He also modeled for her figurehead*

responsible. As a result, many American clippers were manned largely with foreigners. As another way around the problem, many American clippers were built for British merchants and run with British seamen. Such was the case with four of Donald McKay's finest vessels, the *Lightning, Champion of the Seas, James Baines* and *Donald McKay*. They were built for James Baines, of Liverpool, owner of the Liverpool Black Ball Line of Australian packets. Baines had appropriated not only the name but the red flag with its familiar black ball from the much older American line of the same name.

The *James Baines*, built 1854, was Donald McKay's finest, some say. She ran head and head with the *Lightning* for all-time speed honors, a bit faster in heavy weather, perhaps slightly slower in light breezes. She measured 2,515 tons, 500 more than the *Lightning*. Her figurehead was none other than Baines himself, drooping whiskers, peg-top trousers and chimney-pot hat, a fine contrast to the graceful lady with golden thunderbolt on the *Lightning* or the angel and trumpet of the *Flying Cloud*. When Baines insisted on naming his fourth ship after Donald McKay himself, the naval architect refused to permit his own effigy to be used as a figurehead, but ordered instead a Scot with the McKay tartan.

Queen Victoria inspected the *James Baines* at Portsmouth in 1857. High praise from her indeed was the comment that she didn't know her merchant marine possessed such a great vessel. On her maiden voyage, the *James Baines* set a new Atlantic speed record for clippers, 12 days, 6 hours from Boston to Liverpool. She made twenty knots in flashes while cutting along the Irish coast. On her first voyage as an Australian immigrant ship, she carried 700 passengers, 1,400 tons of cargo and 350 sacks of mail in a record passage of sixty-three days. The distance: 14,034 miles. The average speed: 9.2 miles an hour.

Later voyages, while not record passages, were outstanding. On one occasion she reached twenty-one knots "with main-skysail set." She became a troop-ship in 1857 taking British soldiers to India. Before sailing she was again visited by Queen Victoria, who offered her master one hundred pounds a day as a personal bonus for every day he saved on his contract time, so concerned was the Queen over the Indian mutiny. We don't know how much Capt. McDonald collected from the royal coffers, but he tried. This much is attested to by the report of a fellow shipmaster who sighted the great *James Baines* surging along India bound with the astonishing spread of thirty-four sails pulling. Included in this cloud of canvas were three skysails, sky-stunsails and a moonsail. Her rails were lined with cheering red jackets.

The *James Baines* burned upon docking after her return from India, a sudden and shocking end to a masterpiece. Her hull became the basis for the Liverpool landing stage from which in the decades to come thousands of emigrants were to step aboard Atlantic liners for the land of Donald McKay.

The GREAT REPUBLIC

Lo! The unbounded sea!
On its breast a Ship, spreading all her sails—an ample Ship,
    carrying even her moonsails;
The pennant is flying aloft, as she speeds, she speeds so stately—
    below, emulous waves press forward,
They surround the Ship, with shining curving motions and foam.

THESE were the words of Walt Whitman in his "Drum Taps." They may well

Her masts rose higher than the superliner United States. *The* Great Republic *was largest of all clippers*

have described the great *James Baines* or even her larger sister the *Great Republic,* whose story ends this section on sail's last stand.

In a sense the *Great Republic* will forever be something of a ghost ship, a ship that never really was. We may class her with the *Principessa Jolanda,* Italian luxury liner of pre-World War I days, which was launched mid pomp and luxury and with smoke coming from her two tall stacks only to turn over as she hit the water and sank, good only for scrapping. Or she may even be compared with the two giant four-funneled American Line ships *Boston* and *Baltimore* which, although completed on the artist's drawing board and widely heralded, never were built. Launched late in 1853, the *Great Republic* was the world's largest ship. She was Donald McKay's pride, and might well have set records for speed under canvas that even the *Flying Cloud* could never match.

Her sails covered more than 15,683 running yards, one and a half acres, if spread flat. Her main yard was twice the length of LaSalle's *Griffin* or 120 feet long. She was exactly 53 feet broad and 334 feet in length, slightly shorter than our friend the Fall River liner *Metropolis.* Her tonnage was 4,556 registered tons, far and away the greatest of any ship in the world in her day. But excepting her voyage at the end of a towrope from Boston to New York preparatory to her maiden trip, she never sailed as originally built.

It was the night after Christmas. The *Great Republic* was loading at her South Street dock. She was intended for the Australian trade and was preparing to sail for San Francisco en route. A warehouse nearby caught fire and sent sparks flying into the winter sky. The winds blew the sparks into the fresh white canvas and tarred rigging of the great sailing ship, to the horror of all concerned. Her four masts, towering more than 200 feet, higher even than the mast of the superliner *United States* of today, were soon a mass of smoke and flame. She burned for two days. To save her hull, she was finally scuttled and allowed to sink to the muddy bottom of the East River.

The *Great Republic* was finally raised, with the use of a giant cofferdam. She was rebuilt up to her third deck and rigged in a more conservative fashion. Even then, as a four-masted bark, she was a great and fast ship. Her reconstruction was done under the watchful eye of Nathaniel P. Palmer, the discoverer of the Antarctic Continent.

"What wonders of speed might this ship of ships have performed, as Donald McKay built and rigged her," wrote Morison. As it was she made many fast passages, including a ninety-two-day run between New York and San Francisco. Later, chartered to the French Government as a troopship in the Crimean War, she was said to be faster than the best of steamers in a leading wind and under full sail. Her best run was 413 miles in one day, a remarkable figure equaled only half a dozen times by other American clippers.

PART FIVE

Two Famous Marys

As the Civil War began, two ships were built whose stories were to be far from similar. Both were launched in the same year. Both had compound names beginning with "Mary." Their lives, a contrast in fortunes, make an interlude in this maritime chronology of America, a pause between the halcyon clipper-ship days and the shipping doldrums of the latter part of the nineteenth century. . . .

The MARY CELESTE

THE sea was cruel to Mrs. Nathan Briggs, of Rose Cottage, Marion, Massachusetts. Four of her five sons were shipmasters. Three of them never returned from voyaging on the sea. Her only daughter was lost in a shipwreck. Her daughter-in-law Sarah and her granddaughter Sophia were also drowned. Of these six victims, three died in what remains today perhaps America's strangest, best-known mystery of the deep.

The story of the *Mary Celeste* may begin for our purposes at the North River pier of the old Fall River Line in New York. It was a Sunday morning, October 27, when Sarah Elizabeth Briggs and Sophia Matilda, her two-year-old daughter, left the gold carpet and white pilasters of their overnight boat and met sturdy, square-jawed Captain Benjamin Spooner Briggs. Capt. Briggs, who had come on from Rose Cottage a week or so before, escorted his family by carriage to Pier 50, East River, where his new command lay. She was the *Mary Celeste*, a rebuilt brig 103 feet long of about 282 tons. Built in 1861 in Nova Scotia she was a sturdy craft well able to sail around the world. Originally named *Amazon*, she had been transferred to the American flag in 1868 and was

99

owned by J. H. Winchester & Co., who later were to manage the giant liner *Leviathan*. At this writing (1955) they remain an important New York shipping firm. The Atlantic Mutual Insurance Co., also still prominent today, held a part of the insurance on the trim little *Mary* in that year of 1872.

The family settled quickly in their tiny cabin aboard the *Mary Celeste*. Sarah had brought her sewing machine, music books and handsome two-pedal melodeon. It must have been a tight fit, for there was barely room in the cabin for one large bed. Two small ports opened out on deck. A skylight gave added illumination from above. It provided the only ventilation during the Atlantic passage when it was necessary to batten up the windows with canvas and boards. Two adjoining cabins housed two other officers.

"It seems real homelike since Sarah and Sophia have got here and we enjoy our little quarters," Capt. Briggs wrote his mother in his last letter to her. Sophia was a great joy to them.

"She behaved splendid and seemed to enjoy the ride as much as any of us," the Captain said of his baby daughter after they had taken his wife's brother and wife on a buggy ride through Central Park. A strange disease had stricken so many horses in the city that the horsecars were not running on the East Side. It was confining for his wife, but Captain Briggs promised her they would "make up for it" when they returned.

The family had left their seven-year-old son Arthur at home with his grandmother. Everyone missed him, particularly little Sophia who "calls for him occasionally and wants to see him in the Album which by the way is the favorite book of hers," the Captain wrote. "She knows your picture in both Albums and points and says 'Gamma Bis.' She seems real smart—has got over the bad cold she had when she came and has a first-rate appetite for hash and bread and butter. I think the voyage will do her lots of good.

"We enjoy our melodeon and have some good sings. . . . We finished loading last night and shall leave on Tuesday morning if we don't get off tomorrow night, the Lord willing."

There followed instructions as to how his mother was to address letters to follow the voyage through its various stops in the Mediterranean. On Nov. 5 they cast off and moved out into the Bay. For two days they were delayed off Staten Island because of unfavorable weather. The pilot boat, last vessel to see the little *Mary Celeste* before tragedy struck, brought back a final message from Sarah, the daughter-in-law. It was a homey letter. Sarah had sailed ten years before on a similar voyage to the Mediterranean. It had been her honeymoon.

"Sophy thinks the figure 3 and the letter G on her blocks is the same thing so I saw her whispering to herself yesterday with the 3 block in her hand— Gam-gam-gamma," the mother wrote. Little Sophia was a lucky child, in one way at least. Her parents apparently spared nothing to make her happy on the voyage. She brought a big doll, too, named Sarah Jane.

This is the trim little Mary Celeste, *still most tantalizing mystery ship in America's maritime legend*

"We had some baked apples (sour) the other night about the size of a new-born infant's head. They tasted extremely well."

With that the curtain drops on Capt. Briggs, his wife and child and their crew of seven.

One month less three days later the brigantine *Dei Gratia,* flying the British flag, sighted a sailing vessel ahead on the port bow. She was under short canvas and was behaving strangely. They were almost halfway between the Azores and Spain. Hailing the unknown and deserted-looking craft brought no response. A boarding party rowed over to her. She was the *Mary Celeste.* Not a living soul was aboard. Some slight weather damage was noted, and yet every sign indicated a most hasty departure by her crew. The logbook was found on the desk in the mate's cabin, although the Captain's chronometer, sextant, navigation book and the ship's papers were gone. The craft's one longboat was missing. The beds in the three cabins aft had all been mussed as if recently used. On the master's large bed it seemed as if the impression of a child's body could be made out. Toys and women's clothing indicated the presence of the master's family. The pantry was intact, well equipped with utensils and food. The melodeon was in fine shape. It was eventually sent home to Captain Briggs' brother's family.

What happened to the *Mary Celeste* has been the subject of countless newspaper yarns, magazine articles and books. Every variety of wild tale has been circulated. The late Lincoln Colcord, famed writer on maritime subjects, stated that this ship's story "has held more fascination for lovers of the sea than any similar tale of marine accident or disaster." The fact that she was found on a calm sea in relatively perfect condition has whetted the appetites of mystery lovers for nearly a century. Did the crew mutiny? Her officers and cook were high-type American lads. Her four seamen were Germans, all young, all respected in their home towns. Was it true that hot food was found on the stove, a half-eaten meal on the galley table, the captain's watch still ticking on the bulkhead, a child's dress in the sewing machine? These and a thousand other questions have risen over and over again. And many weird answers have emerged from the fog of time. There have been those who have said they were survivors. In one case a book was written based on the accounts of one Pemberton who, apparently without any proof whatsoever to support his claim, maintained that he had been the cook aboard. But back to the ship and her fate.

A lengthy legal battle ensued at Gibraltar when the *Mary Celeste* was brought there. Her salvage was not inconsiderable. Surveys, correspondence, hearings, testimony, made the matter drag on and on. Captain Briggs had found an old sword during his wanderings. This object was discovered under his bed and an excitable Irish Queen's Proctor tried to prove there was blood on the blade. He was certain it was the key to the case. Nothing was ever settled. Eventually the *Mary Celeste* was restored to her owners, who themselves had come under suspicion during the trial. She returned to happy obscurity and was lost from sight. A sum amounting to one-fifth the value of the ship and her cargo was awarded for salvage and to pay court claims. Nevertheless, the effects of the mysterious disappearance of Captain Briggs and his family and crew were to bring embarrassment, however undeserved, to his family and son for the rest of their lives.

What really happened will never be known. An excellent theory was advanced recently by Charles E. Fay in a publication of the Peabody Museum, Salem. The *Mary Celeste* had a cargo of 1,700 barrels of alcohol. Bad weather may have kept her hatch closed for several days. The well-kept log shows there had been bad weather. When calm came Captain Briggs may well have sought to ventilate his hold. Did he open the hatch only to be panicked by a rush of fumes? A rumbling roar accompanying the upsurge of alcohol fumes from leaky barrels may well have led the Captain to fear an imminent explosion. Rousing his family and crew the entire party hastily lowered their craft's longboat and dropped back the length of a handy towline. The rest is simple, starkly tragic. A sudden "blow" and the wallowing longboat, already low in the water, capsized. That was the end.

The MARY POWELL

FOR every sad twist to the story of the *Mary Celeste,* there are half a dozen happy yarns to tell about another Mary. The *Mary Powell* was indeed America's happy boat. She was a vessel of many legends, an extraordinarily beautiful, successful and long-lived boat.

Built in 1861, the same year as the *Mary Celeste,* she ran through September, 1917. In fact she lives on in the shape of the "Mary Powell House," a cottage built of wood from her housing. Prominently displayed on the cottage is the *Mary Powell's* name plate so long fastened on her pilot house. The cottage is near Rondout Creek, Kingston, where the *Mary Powell's* hull was left to rot away after she had been dismantled. Her two tall funnels were there up until 1938, lying beside the remains of her hull. Her walking beam was not taken away until 1947. Her first owner and famed original master is probably doing just what one of his passengers of long ago predicted he would be doing after having "crossed the bar." The passenger gazed up at his captain's commanding figure and proud handle-bar mustache and exclaimed: "Captain, I believe you'll run a steamboat in Heaven."

Capt. Absalom L. Anderson and two of his sons were devoted attendants of Queen *Mary Powell.* Their lives were completely wound up in the graceful craft. Being master of a steamboat—*the* steamboat—was the pinnacle of success to them. Unfortunately Capt. Anderson's eldest son died in early middle age and could not take over from his father. The younger son, Capt. A. Eltinge

Anderson, more than lived up to his father's dreams, becoming the *Mary Powell's* part-owner as well as her very popular master up until 1914.

His deep affection for the *Mary Powell* was shown the year before his death when a new and larger vessel was added to the Hudson River Day Line. Due to changes in the operation of the line, it was necessary for him to utilize for his command another landing near the Kingston terminal for lay-over purposes and as winter quarters. The landing was called, of all things, Rat Dock. Taking matters into his own hands, Capt. Anderson conspired with Albert Benson, the ship's carpenter, to have a quantity of sunflower seeds planted on the shoreside pier. When these bloomed in profusion, it was natural that the wharf's name be changed to Sunflower Dock, and that was done.

The *Mary Powell* was a fast boat, perhaps the fastest on the Hudson. In her youth she sped to new records, many of which stand to this day. As she aged, she gracefully submitted to being the standard for speed, with every new contender seeking first to measure his ship against the *Mary Powell*. It was the *Mary Powell* that was selected by famous yacht designer Herreshoff to test the new steam yacht *Stiletto*. Even when the *Mary Powell* was fifty years old she was "still the boat to beat," in the words of Donald C. Ringwald, the "Queen's" biographer. In terms of land speed, she could do a steady twenty-four to twenty-five miles an hour at her best, and she kept it up from the days of the Civil War to General Pershing's time.

She was a family boat, a favorite for school reunions, commuters, day excursions. She participated in many public functions. In 1877, for example, she brought the body of General Custer to West Point. Nine years later she joined in the ceremonies accompanying the unveiling of the Statue of Liberty. Incidentally, she had her own statue of the Goddess of Liberty. It was six feet high and stood atop her pilothouse. This Miss Liberty spent some thirty years "sightseeing on the river," Mr. Ringwald notes. The *Mary Powell* led the first of the ten squadrons of merchant vessels in the sea parade commemorating the centennial of Washington's first inauguration, 1889. She joined in the dedication of the tomb of General U. S. Grant, who, as President, walked aboard her one day, as any other passenger would, and sailed from Kingston, cigar in mouth and newspaper in hand, enjoying a seat up forward.

General Custer's funeral was not the most elaborate or touching in which the *Mary Powell* participated. In 1890 Daniel H. Bishop, her mate since she had come out twenty-nine years before, died at New Hamburg, one of her stops. She didn't let him down. A special excursion was arranged from Kingston down to his home. No charge was made for anyone wishing to join in the funeral. It was a Sunday, and the *Mary Powell* never made a regular voyage on the Sabbath. Her pilot house was draped in black. Her flags were at half-mast. She picked up more mourners at Poughkeepsie, and at New Hamburg all went ashore. Mr. Bishop had been dressed in his first mate's uniform when placed in the coffin.

The happy ship Mary Powell, *best known and best loved of all Hudson River excursion boats*

At the conclusion of the service his old ship's bell began to toll. Leading the procession back to the ship with the Mate's body were the *Mary Powell's* famous Negro waiters carrying flowers.

The waiters were famous in their own right. It was their custom in the 1870's to strum the guitar and sing in the dining saloon after passing Poughkeepsie homeward bound. At Rondout, home port, their Virginia-bred voices often could be heard well after docking time as the joy of singing inspired them. Known as the *Mary Powell* Singers, they became a tradition with the vessel.

One of the mourners at the funeral of Mate Bishop was Guernsey B. Betts, renowned pilot of the *Mary Powell*. He could have her going at full speed within two lengths after a landing. At Milton dock, it is said, he didn't even tie up, just paused long enough to drop a gangway for departing and boarding passengers; such was his knowledge of his boat's capacities and of the local tides and currents.

Although the *Mary Powell* had comparatively few accidents, one lad survived an ordeal aboard her that may well have been unique in side-wheeler history. Hoping to steal a ride away from New York's hot July streets in 1868, the boy swam out to his dream ship. He boarded her under the giant port paddle-wheel box and squatted in a spot next to the buckets. Hanging on to some iron grab bars, he probably thought himself well placed. Then the great wheel began to rotate, soaking him unmercifully with each passing wooden bucket. Two and a half hours later his faint cries were heard when the wheel stopped at the first landing. He was rescued, a half-drowned, bare-footed, frightened boy, lucky to be alive! What happened to him no one knows except that he dried out in the engine room and left the ship at Kingston.

The *Mary Powell* underwent many changes during her six decades. At one point in her career, when she passed out of the control of the first Capt. Anderson, her main saloon was almost doubled in size. It was embellished with solid walnut wainscoting. Blue velvet upholstered furniture of walnut and gilt added to the weight and majesty of its appearance. Three years after this transformation, old Capt. Anderson regained ownership of the vessel. Out went the walnut and gold saloon. In the captain's original decorating scheme a unique feature had been Brady photographs, on glass, of Washington Irving, James Gordon Bennett, John James Audubon and other leading citizens, most of them of the Hudson Valley. On one occasion early in her life the *Mary Powell* was cut in half and lengthened twenty-one feet. It materially increased her speed, as similar operations on several well-known modern liners have done.

Capt. A. E. Anderson brought the *Mary Powell* through what has been called the worst storm in man's knowledge on the Hudson River. The cyclone carried her broadside for some two miles to just above Haverstraw Bay in 1899. While lightning flashed, two storms seemed to join, striking the white lady as she moved up river. Her starboard funnel blew down, striking the paddle box. Then the other stack smashed down on the hurricane deck. She plunged on despite the spraying sparks. Some forty campstools were blown overboard, but none of the two hundred passengers was hurt. Repairs made overnight enabled the gallant vessel to sail on schedule the next morning at 5:30 A.M. for New York.

The Brady glass portraits and the walnut-gilt wainscoting of the *Mary Powell* had their match in the gaudy luxury of the Hudson's night fleet. We have the comments of one of South America's leading citizens, globe-trotting Domingo Sarmiento, describing this sumptuous mode of travel.

> They are floating palaces, three stories in height, with galleries and
> roofs for promenades. Gold shines in the capitals and architraves of the

thousand columns which, as in the *Isaac Newton,* flank monstrous halls capable of containing the Senate and the House of Representatives. Artistically draped hangings of damask hide staterooms for five hundred passengers, and there is a colossal dining room with an endless table of polished mahogany and service of porcelain and plate for a thousand guests.

The passengers' appearance was noteworthy to Sarmiento, writes William G. Mullins in a thesis on this traveler from below the border.

> Grandiose in itself because of the colossal forms of these traveling hotels, new luster is given to the spectacle by the cultured, polished and even ceremonious appearance of the passengers, since it is the general custom of men and women to wear their best clothes when traveling by water or rail.
>
> In these boats of the Hudson, there is a holy of holies into which precincts penetrates no profane eye—a mysterious dwelling: the delights of which one may nevertheless suspect because of the gusts of perfume escaping when its door is momentarily opened. This place is called the bridal suite.

When the *Mary Powell* was finally sold for scrap her owners made the condition that she was not to be burned or sunk as a setting for a moving picture. Souvenir seekers from throughout the country took parts of the famous craft before the junkers began. Parts of her engine were bought by Henry Ford for his Dearborn, Mich. museum. Two gilt balls from her masts went to one of her regular passengers, J. P. Morgan. He put them on his gateposts at his Highland Falls estate. Her steering wheel went eventually to the State Museum at Kingston. Her great iron bell, serving on into the present, is rung at Indian Point on the Hudson five minutes before the sailing of the last steamer to leave the amusement park each day.

A poem written in 1871 suitably drops the curtain on this lovely steamer:

Around the river's graceful turn
   The *Powell* appears in sight
She seems the water's side to spurn
   She glides along so light
Free waves her streamer on the wind
   She passes out of sight
Leaving the merry scene behind
   Her whistle cries, "Good Night."

The Colorado, *huge wooden paddle wheeler, opened transpacific steamship service*

PART SIX

Our Maritime Debacle

Confederate raiders played havoc with the North's ocean shipping. High insurance rates forced half our deep-sea merchant marine to go to foreign flags. A vindictive Congress prevented their return. All eyes were on the West and our brief experiment with ship subsidies before the Civil War was not repeated. The war marked finis to the clipper-ship era. Our great whaling fleet was never restored. Sail was fighting a losing battle against steam. With the few exceptions chronicled below, in America steam failed to take up where sail left off. Maritime progress continued, however, with zest on our busy lakes and rivers.

The COLORADO

THE Civil War was over, the Hudson's pride *Mary Powell* was only five years old, the Atlantic cable was laid and the reconstruction of the South had begun. American maritime enterprise had been all but wiped out from the Atlantic. All eyes were pointed westward as the rail link with California was nearing completion. Would our expansion stop at the Pacific?

The Pacific Mail Line had begun just as the gold rush made California the end of the rainbow for thousands. Despite fierce competition, many marine losses and the difficulties of overland travel at the Isthmus of Panama, the line prospered. On Jan. 1, 1867, it entered the transpacific service with the paddle steamer *Colorado*. She was the pioneer in steamship service between America and the Orient.

Built in 1864, the *Colorado* went to the West Coast via the Horn in the closing days of the Civil War. Confederate raiders were still abroad. It was rumored that the dreaded Southern cruiser *Shenandoah* was lying in wait for

109

the new $1,000,000 liner. Before taking up her service between San Francisco and Panama she was hastily armed with four large guns, two 20-pounders on her quarters and two 30-pounders forward. Her officers and men were supplied with revolvers, muskets, pikes and axes. These precautions, and the convoying of the *Colorado* by a Naval vessel may possibly have averted trouble, although the liner's speed would in all likelihood have saved her. She was the fastest steamer Pacific Mail had at the time. Her coastwise service saw no interruption and she was a popular vessel on the run. We do not know whether she ever carried full capacity, but if she did she would have had more than the peak load of America's second largest liner of 1955, the *America*. She could carry 1,500 in steerage and had fifty-two staterooms on her main deck for cabin passengers.

A great many changes were made to fit the *Colorado* for transpacific service. A new mizzenmast was stepped. Her two outside rows of staterooms were removed to make her superstructure narrower so she would ride better. Her water tanks and coal bunkers were made larger.

The maiden transpacific voyage of the *Colorado* was a humdinger from start to finish. San Francisco took note of the occasion with a great banquet. High expectations were held out for the China trade. Further public ceremonies at Honolulu and when she arrived at Nagasaki marked the run. Unfortunately Commodore Wilkins, one of Pacific Mail's leading executives, fell through an open hatch at Nagasaki. His death somewhat dampened the many parties staged. At Hong Kong the *Colorado* unloaded most of her 1,000 barrels of flour and the $560,000 in specie which she had carried across the Pacific. More and even more extravagant parties followed. Great significance was attached to the fact that mail and newspapers brought by the American ship were nearly two weeks fresher than those brought the other way around the world via Suez by British ships.

The entire Japanese Embassy staff boarded the great black-hulled liner at Yokohama, en route to Washington. Below, she had a full cargo. The round trip took seventy-eight days, the return passage being made in three weeks flat. So successful was the enterprise that four new liners were added to the run in rapid succession. They were the *China, Great Republic, Japan* and *America*. These were the last of the great wooden side-wheelers.

The *Colorado* soon returned to coastal service, making only an occasional China voyage. With the completion of the transcontinental railroad in 1869, the Panama route was doomed, and the ships it had employed became coasters or were laid up as spare boats. Built of unseasoned lumber due to hectic Civil War conditions, the hull of the *Colorado* deteriorated rapidly. She was scrapped in 1879. It is interesting to note that this great pioneer of the Pacific was shorter than either the *Western World* of Great Lakes fame or the Fall River queen *Metropolis*.

The PENNSYLVANIA

AN eight-line news story from San Francisco, Nov. 15, 1918, recorded the sad ending of a famous ship's life. The day after Armistice she burned in far-off Iquique, Chile. No lives were lost in the fire which gutted the 3,126-ton *Pennsylvania;* this was the report of the home office of the Pacific Mail Line, owners of the forty-five-year-old iron steamship. But a chapter in our maritime history had ended.

The *Pennsylvania* of 1870 and her three sister ships were the first important deep-sea iron vessels built in the United States. Financed by the Pennsylvania Railroad, these four ships made the reputation of Charles H. Cramp, Philadelphia shipbuilder. While not among the fastest, their steady thirteen knots drove them from the City of Brotherly Love to Europe in nine days. They could carry about a hundred in cabin class with 800 in steerage, in addition to some freight. It is reported that the Keystone Line or the American Line, as this company later became known, never lost a ship, a passenger or a bag of mail. But it continually lost money. It had no subsidy and operated against highly subsidized foreign lines.

It is strange to reconcile the lack of Congressional interest in transatlantic shipping at this time with the one subsidy that was paid about this time to the United States and Brazil Mail Steamship Company. It was a time in which foreign Atlantic steamship lines were booming. Their fleets were being restocked, so to speak, with new ships at frequent intervals. Changes and improvements in size, speed and luxury came so rapidly that the average service life of an Atlantic liner was about ten years. Not so with the Keystone Line's ships, the only American ships in the transatlantic run.

The line is the granddaddy of the United States Lines, one of America's greatest companies today. The *Pennsylvania, Indiana, Illinois,* and *Ohio* combined cost less than one twenty-eighth of what the newest ship of the United States Lines, the superliner *United States,* cost in 1952. It is hard to believe, but the *Pennsylvania* class were the only regularly operated American-built liners on the Atlantic between the Collins Line of the 1850's and the *St. Louis* of 1895.

Only two episodes stand out in the Atlantic careers of these liners. In 1877 General Grant began his celebrated world tour aboard the *Indiana.* In 1887, after the quartet had been given new triple expansion engines and been made into immigrant carriers, the *Ohio* was equipped with forced draft, a substantial innovation and improvement for Atlantic vessels. The famous "Keystone" emblem came off the *Pennsylvania's* single stack in 1884 when she was sold to the International Navigation Company, which eventually metamorphosed into the giant J. P. Morgan shipping combine, the International Mercantile Marine.

In 1897 these four old vessels were sold to Pacific coast interests. The

For decades the Pennsylvania, *and her three humble sisters, were the only American liners on the Atlantic*

Illinois, taken over by the Army, became the cargo ship *Supply* and was eventually scrapped in 1928, last of the quartet. During their Atlantic service they saw several major American-owned steamship lines started and prosper under foreign flags.

The era witnessed the decline in United States trade carried by American ships from 72 percent in 1861 to a mere 5.9 percent in 1898. The decline took place over a period in which trade as a whole increased substantially. Historians interpret the drop in our share of the carrying trade as reflecting the overwhelming drive of our economy to the West. Labor, capital and Congressional interest all followed this surge to assimilate the huge new areas added to the United States during the first half of the nineteenth century. Inland, coastal and lake shipping played a vital part in this expansion. Deep-sea shipping was largely left to foreigners. America was at this time largely an importer of goods and services.

This period saw our first merchant marine officers' training ship established by Admiral Stephan B. Luce. Boasting such famed schoolships as the *St. Marys* and the *Newport,* this school is now the New York State Maritime College. Other state schools sprang up in the years that followed in California, Massachusetts, Maine and Pennsylvania. In World War II, our national merchant marine academy was created at Kings Point, Long Island, N. Y.

The ALAMEDA

THE passing of the old side-wheelers on the oceans of the world meant the end of an era. For those accustomed to propeller-driven ships, the hulking, awkward paddlers would seem monstrous today. They were beamy and rolled frightfully, often lifting one spray-whipping wheel clean of the ocean while at the same time burying the other in a hill of green water. Engineers were on occasion badly burned as the wind back-drafted the flames down into the engine room during a particularly heavy roll. Yet never did the great walking beam stop its heavy seesaw motion high up on deck abaft the soot-caked stack.

The long narrow lines of the propeller-driven *Alameda* of 1883 must have been newfangled indeed to old timers who loved such ships as the *Golden Age,* the *Colorado* or the *Nevada.* But the new ships were a blessing to the passengers. Comfortable promenade decks, almost from bow to stern, and spacious public rooms high above the water, did much to make travel at sea the luxury it is today.

These changes introduced in American coastwise and ocean craft followed pioneer design developments of the White Star Line made in 1870 on the Atlantic. It was quite a wrench, for example, to bring the steering wheel forward to the pilot house. Seamen, since ages before the Vikings, had always steered aft. The *Alameda,* it might be added, was one of the first vessels to have the now

The Alameda, *of 1883, helped establish American shipping on the Australia run, later served to Alaska*

familiar bell-pull or jingle signal system to notify the engine room of speed changes. More powerful engines permitted less dependence on sails. Without sails, passenger space amidships rose tier on tier, resulting in today's classic outline.

The America of the *Alameda's* day was a rapidly changing world. While she was still on the drawing boards the first commercial telephone exchange was set up, and Woolworth's first "five-and-ten" store opened its doors. While she was building, DeLesseps began his ill-fated attempt to cut a canal through the Isthmus of Panama. The Brooklyn Bridge, spanning the East River suspended from noble Gothic stone towers, was opened the year the *Alameda* entered service.

Just as it had pioneered in the Orient trade, Pacific Mail was first to establish regular service to Australia from San Franicsco. Its first fleet of ships included the *Nebraska*, which inaugurated the run in 1871, the *Nevada* and the *Dakota*. Unlike the ill-fated *Titanic* of forty years later, these ships had lifeboats enough to carry every passenger and more. An iron pipe with fifteen hose connections extended the full length of each ship for fire fighting. Their best staterooms each had a window thirty-two inches square, quite a contrast to the auger-holes of their Australian competition. Two bridal chambers were forward of the 90-foot-long grand saloon. So much for the pioneers.

Their successors were the *Alameda* and *Mariposa*, famed Oceanic Line flyers built at Cramp's, the same yard which had built the *Pennsylvania* class liner a decade earlier for the Atlantic. The Pacific liners were to serve without interruption for sixteen years on their run.

The *Alameda* had a single propeller, and, for that reason, was still somewhat dependent on sails as an auxiliary in case of need. Her triple-expansion engines could drive her at a most respectable fifteen knots. During her life her original length of 314 feet was increased to 327. It is surprising how many ships have been so stretched out and how much faster they seem to be after the operation. After ten years on the Honolulu run the *Alameda* went to the Alaska Line which used her successfully until 1931 when she was finally retired. The Alaska Line, long a bulwark of passenger ship operations under the American flag, threw in the towel in 1955, when it sold the remnants of its passenger-ship fleet and turned entirely to freight service. The airplane put these ships out of business.

Charles H. Cramp, who built both the *Pennsylvania* and the *Alameda*, and whose masterpiece the *St. Louis* will conclude this part, described in succinct terms the distressing debacle faced by the United States at this time. In the period between 1870 and 1882, he wrote, some forty-one steamships for foreign trade were built in American yards. During the same time 714 steamers, averaging greater size than the United States ships, were built in British shipyards.

The CHRISTOPHER COLUMBUS

"McDOUGALL'S DREAM" would revolutionize ship design, or so Great Lakes enthusiasts of the last part of the nineteenth century thought. Of course there were those old-timers who refused to accept anything modern and called the cigar-shaped ships built by rugged Capt. Alexander McDougall, pig boats. Certainly their blunt bow did look like a snout. Today they are more commonly called whalebacks.

It is hard to conceive of an idea having such wide currency and such limited practicable application. Ship people the world over know what whalebacks are,

Whalebacks, like the Christopher Columbus, *were all the rage on the Lakes at the time of the 1892 Chicago Worlds' Fair*

although only some forty were ever built, all on the Great Lakes. Perhaps it was the very oddity of the rounded-hull design of these weird vessels which caught the public's imagination. Gordon Grant's inclusion of a whaleback in his boat books for boys may have had some influence in this direction; it did with this author.

Of all the whalebacks the greatest and most spectacular was the passenger ship *Christopher Columbus*. Lake historian Dana T. Bowen notes that this 362-foot, cigar-shaped vessel carried more passengers during her forty-four years than any other Great Lakes liner. She had the amazing passenger capacity of 5,600 on daylight trips.

In the year the *Christopher Columbus* was launched, 1892, two outstanding events took place which were to have great influence on the future of shipping. One was the successful operation of the gasoline automobile by Charles E. Duryea. In half a century this vehicle was to ruin many of our oldest short-haul passenger steamship services. The other was the invention by Dr. Rudolf Diesel of an engine which operated with pulverized fuel and air compression. The Diesel engine, although still not popular with American shipping, has been widely adopted, over turbine propulsion, throughout the world.

The *Christopher Columbus* entered service in 1893 between Chicago and the World's Fair site six miles away. She carried 2,000,000 passengers during her first season. She survived to be a feature of the 1932-1933 Century of Progress Exposition. At that time she was on the 170-mile service between Chicago and Milwaukee. Visitors to the fair were urged to travel on "this great Steel Steamship." Inducements listed were: "four broad and shady decks . . . a deck promenade one half mile long . . . excellent Café service and popular Lunch Room . . . High Class Amusements and Dancing entertainments."

Her eighteen-foot propeller, clean hull lines and 5,000 horsepower engine drove the *Columbus* at an eighteen-knot clip. A rapid turnaround was important to her owners, and they came to be adept at debarking passengers. She could, reportedly, discharge 5,000 passengers in five minutes. Her long life is a tribute to her passenger facilities. She survived until 1936. Her whaleback features, while they drew attention her way, did not provoke other lines to follow suit. She was the first and only whaleback passenger liner.

Whalebacks were designed to offer minimum resistance to wind and sea. They had round bottoms and trimmed easily, according to Capt. Earl C. Palmer, sailor-historian. They were good ships in their day, but the idea did not spread. Difficulty in unloading cargo and size limitations were serious handicaps. More conventional hull forms prevailed on the Great Lakes.

The PRISCILLA

A GENTLEMAN, whose name we shall not mention, was sailing to Fall River aboard the great white Long Island Sound boat *Priscilla*. His twin brother was with him. The gentleman wanted to stroll about the canvas-covered deck and watch the procession of Sound liners ahead and behind. His twin wanted to turn in early. So they compromised: he stayed up and his brother Francis took the big golden-colored key and headed for their two-berth stateroom.

Finally, after having had his fill of the blue silence of the forward deck and the gusty winds beside the rounded front of the pilot house bravely guiding the great 440-foot hull through the darkness, he decided to retire. He could hear his brother's heavy breathing through the wood fretwork set over the stateroom door, but he could not wake him, knock as hard as he would. His brother slept on, with the key lodged inside the door. Not wishing to rouse the whole boat, our friend finally decided to tip-toe down into the men's cabin, where one could sleep in any of the more-or-less open berths. These berths were for those who paid only their transportation fare. An extra charge was made for the stateroom. He was asleep in a moment, for only small lights illuminated the long, narrow semi-public apartment.

And then the dawn—and a horrible surprise awaited him! Hanging down from the bunk above were articles of apparel most certainly not worn by man. Fortunately, our subject had awakened early. No one else was stirring. Slipping out of the berth, he hastily made for an exit leading to the main deck. With shoes in hand he approached the door only to meet headlong the stout colored stewardess, matron of the ladies' cabin, whose sacred precinct he had invaded. She blanched noticeably, he later told the author, but made no effort to stop him.

This somewhat lengthy digression is a family story. Many other family stories live on about the Fall River liner *Priscilla,* most famous of Sound overnight boats. She served for forty-four years, over a span covering the Spanish-American War, the First World War and nearly up to World War II. A book by Roger McAdam honors her memory. Her interior design remains today a subject of much interest to the student. Costing $1,500,000 in 1893, she had 361 staterooms plus enough additional free bunks to sleep 1,500 persons. Her grand saloon is said to have been the largest room afloat in her day, measuring 142 feet in length, 30 feet in width and 24 feet in height. She was an institution. She was steamboat royalty. Passengers often reserved their staterooms weeks in advance, basing their summer vacation schedules on her sailing dates. Her polished-wood purser's stall and window, over which thousands upon thousands of keys have passed, is now a treasured memento at the Mariners' Museum, Newport News. Visitors to the museum often register through its portal.

The Fall River Line's contribution to a growing America came in its linking New England with New York and thereby the world. Ships carried the cotton of the South to New England. The Fall River Line brought the finished cloth to Gotham. Fish from Newport was another big cargo. Some say when the line lost to the trucks its contracts for supplying New York's Fulton Fish Market, its days were numbered. But the company was best known for its sumptuous cabins, public rooms and the luxury of its steamers.

A famed Boston architect was retained to prepare the *Priscilla's* interior layout. His name was Frank Hill Smith and he had previously designed the Fall River Line's *Puritan* and *Plymouth.* Gone was the black walnut styling of earlier boats. In its place were interiors more reminiscent of the delicate North Italian early Renaissance period.

The *Priscilla's* dining room was on the main deck. It was a work of art. Its windows looked out on either side, an innovation for the Fall River Line. Above the windows were leaded-glass panels with matching floral glass table lights. The red-and-green carpet, in pattern like an oriental rug, added to the color effect produced by the room's red woodwork.

Families planned their vacations to coincide with the sailing of the beloved Priscilla, of Fall River, famed overnight boat

Not quite as large as the *Commonwealth,* the last of the Fall River Line boats, nor as long-lived as the famed *Plymouth,* the *Priscilla* has always remained a favorite. She had a regal, feminine quality. Her career seemed charmed. Her most serious accident took place in a dense fog in 1902. The steamer *Powhatan* nearly severed the *Priscilla's* bow from the body of her hull, cutting almost to the keel. Her bulkheads held, and she was towed to Newport where a large wooden patch was put on the broken bow for the trip to a Hoboken shipyard.

Some twenty-two years later she raced at full speed to rescue 480 passengers from her newer competitor, the *Boston,* rammed in a thick fog by the oil tanker *Swift Arrow.* The *Priscilla's* thirty-five-foot paddle wheels, each weighing a hundred tons, are said to have made twenty-four revolutions a minute on this voyage of mercy. Her maximum was supposed to be twenty-two revolutions. The praise that was heaped on Capt. Fred M. Hamlen for this rescue was somewhat counterbalanced not too long after by a fifteen-day suspension handed him for grounding the *Priscilla.* No hull damage was sustained, although the great ship's port paddle wheel was badly smashed.

A relatively minor fire which flared up one spring evening not long after this, caused considerable alarm to the passengers. On board were some 400 Wellesley College girls. The fire fed on layers of grease and dust in the galley ventilator stack. It was quickly put out, but not before it had flamed twenty feet above the upper deck. A description of this fire in Roger McAdam's book, *Priscilla of Fall River,* caught the eye of Capt. Frederick Way, whose famed *Delta Queen* is the subject of one of our final chapters. Capt. Way wrote Mr. McAdam that this account of the galley-vent fire on the *Priscilla* had prompted him to have a similar vent on the *Delta Queen* "steam cleaned," so as to make such a close call less likely. And so it may have been that even after her long career had ended, the *Priscilla* was able to do a good turn for another boat.

The *Priscilla* was broken up in 1938 at Baltimore—but not before many of her furnishings, carpets, linens and pieces of silverware were auctioned off to take their place as treasured items in the collections of members of the Steamship Historical Society. The Society's former president, William King Covell, bought the whistle. He lent it to the ferry *Hammonton,* which runs on the Jamestown-Newport route past his beautiful Newport waterfront home. He hears it every day. At a meeting of the historical society in 1947, he distributed to all those present as table markers little pieces of wood from the outside rail and other supporting parts of the great ship's structure. The author still has his.

The ST. LOUIS

NOT SINCE the sea-green, shell-encrusted spittoons of the Collins liners of the 1850's had a real luxury liner been built in America for the Atlantic trade. But now things were going to be different. It was Nov. 12, 1894. President Cleveland

and 25,000 patriotic Americans were on hand. Mrs. Cleveland was holding a linen-wrapped bottle of champagne, American champagne, not French. She would soon smash it against the straight, American-style stem of a new 11,000-ton luxury liner to be named *St. Louis*. It had been twenty-two years since the *Pennsylvania* intermediate-class liners had been launched at the same yard, nearly twice that long since the *Adriatic,* last of the great Collins ships, had been built.

It was an era of nationalism. The Columbian exhibition in Chicago had stimulated our national ego as few other things have done. We were about to stretch out into the Pacific to annex Hawaii. And now Congress had finally roused itself to action following an era in which high foreign subsidies and discriminatory tactics kept our ocean fleet, with a few exceptions, in a stunted condition. The Postal Aid Law, passed in 1891, through mail payments, gave some stimulation to shipbuilding for nearby foreign routes such as those of the Ward Line to Mexico and the Red D. Line to Venezuela. Under a special enlargement of this act were built the transatlantic liners, *St. Louis* and her sister the *St. Paul*. Mr. Cramp, still going strong as our leading shipbuilder, boasted proudly before the Society of Naval Architects that "no foreign materials" went into the *St. Louis*. He went on to say:

> Since we began this work our English friends have had a good deal to say about it. They seem to think that it was impertinence on our part to enter the contest for supremacy on the North Atlantic. They deprecate the fact exceedingly. But they may as well understand that, after many years of practical expulsion from the ocean, the Yankees are coming again and coming to stay. The work we have in hand is only the beginning. It is a pretty fair start, but if they should ask you what the future has in store, you may tell them, in the words of our Paul Jones on a certain occasion, well remembered by Englishmen, that "we are just beginning to fight."

The *St. Louis* was a great ship. She was destined to serve heroically in the Spanish War and to do good work as a World War I transport. While never the largest or fastest ship in the world, she held many local speed records and had many firsts to her credit, some important, some not. She was the first American liner to run the gauntlet of German submarines in the First World War. She is said to have been the first to engage in target practice on icebergs, firing on one occasion thirty-two rounds, at 8,000 yards range. She may claim to have been the first to carry a cargo of apples to England, opening what has become a most promising commerce. Marconi's first wireless equipment installation was made on the *St. Paul*, her sistership. The operator was none other than a young man named David Sarnoff, to become head of the Radio Corporation of America.

A press release put out by her owners as the *St. Louis* was nearing completion noted details of her dining saloon amidships on the upper deck.

It is well lighted from the sides and above from a large dome, in one end of which is an organ, played from a keyboard placed in the saloon.

The release added that all of the 320 first-class passengers could be fed at one sitting. Six-foot six-inch beds in all the first-class cabins were another feature, as were the unusually good accommodations for 800 steerage passengers.

> The steerages are without doubt unexcelled on the Atlantic. They are lighted and heated by the same process as is used for the first and second cabin compartments. The berths are metallic with spring bottoms; and nearly all the steerages are fitted up in rooms. Tables and seats are provided in each compartment.

Modestly the company noted that special care had been given to ventilation and "it is believed that the system adopted is the most perfect in existence." Some 1,200 electric bulbs were used in the ship. Far better safety features were built into the *St. Louis* than went into the supposedly unsinkable *Titanic* of two decades later. Her watertight bulkheads had no doors or openings whatsoever up to the main deck. Perhaps more significant, in the light of the disaster that later befell the *Titanic,* the *St. Louis* had thirty-four lifeboats, more than enough for every soul aboard. Twin screws, first popularized on the British-built American Line steamers *Paris* and *New York,* eliminated forever dependence upon sail. Special provisions were made to fit the *St. Louis* as a naval auxiliary. These features were to prove invaluable only three years after her maiden voyage.

One of the great surprises of the military world took place on May Day in 1898. It was the destruction by Admiral Dewey of the Spanish fleet in Manila. "I will wipe it from the ocean," were the words of George Dewey, then Commodore, in response to the President's message to "capture or destroy the Spanish fleet." He did, and without the loss of a single American ship or seaman.

War clouds had hung low for some time. So close was the outbreak of hostilities that on April 15, the *St. Louis* was ordered to rush home from Southampton without passengers or cargo. She arrived at New York April 22 and sailed as an armed cruiser April 26, the same day Dewey left Hong Kong for his victory in the Philippines. The role played by the *St. Louis* was a stirring one. Early in May she cut the cable between the Virgin Islands and Puerto Rico. Her purpose was to disrupt all communications and thereby hamper the much-feared Spanish fleet in the Caribbean. An important cable connected Santiago, Cuba, with Jamaica. It had to be severed, although the cable was covered by the big guns from Morro Castle. It was a hectic affair as described by one of the ship's officers.

> The *St. Louis* steamed backwards and forwards across the harbor gradually getting closer to the forts. Shortly after the first exchange of shots, the grapnel was lowered over the port bow and 650 fathoms of line run out. About noon, when the *St. Louis* had reached a position about a mile from

With the St. Louis, 1895, America had a prestige liner on the Atlantic for the first time since before the Civil War

Morro Castle, our grapnel caught the cable. The Spaniards discovered our object and a battery to the east of Morro opened fire with a six-inch gun, the first shot falling about 200 yards short of the *St. Louis.* Capt. Goodrich thereupon ordered the fire to be returned by two six-pounders mounted on the starboard side, which were the only guns that could be brought to bear on the shore battery. Ensign Payne quickly fired the forward gun and Lieut. Catlin fired the aft gun, the shots falling thick and fast on shore. Another shell from the shore battery whistled over the *St. Louis.* . . . That was the last shot fired from that gun as the next moment it was destroyed by one of the six-pounders from the *St. Louis.*

Another mortar battery next opened fire from the brow of a hill and shells began to descend dangerously near. The fusillade was made more irritating because the mortar battery was far beyond the range of the small guns with which the *St. Louis* was armed. The guns of the *St. Louis* were then turned upon the signal station to the east of Morro, where the Spaniards had been signaling. A few shots tore away the roof and the men bolted without waiting to haul down their last signal. As Capt. Goodrich saw the mortar battery could not be reached with the guns at his disposal and that the other shore batteries had been silenced he took the *St. Louis* out of range of the mortars and then stopped to finish heaving up the grapnel. The cable was brought up and severed.

For nearly an hour the gallant American liner with her two tall smokestacks had been lying broadside to the Spanish batteries. Not an enemy hit had been registered unless we count one shell which came close enough to cut away some of the rigging. In return the vessel's two guns had fired 172 shots, doing considerable damage ashore. Most of the officers aboard the liner were her own peacetime men, hastily recruited into the Navy.

The *St. Louis* was then ordered to cut the cable off Guantanamo, forty miles away. Barely four hours after she had left Santiago, Cervera's Spanish squadron of four larger cruisers and two destroyers arrived at the Cuban port. The *St. Louis* was on hand some time later when Cervera tried to escape from Santiago and his fleet was destroyed. Meanwhile she cut other cables, took part in several bombardments and served as a trooper.

The *St. Paul,* her sister ship, survived what is described as the first naval action in which a destroyer was used. She was attacked by the 30-knot Spanish torpedo-boat destroyer *Terror* off San Juan. Speed could not save her. Her vast bulk was a perfect target for the onrushing *Terror,* built recently in Scotland. Good aim and guts did the trick, and before the Spanish vessel could ram the *St. Paul* she was pounded into a mass of wreckage by fifty-pound American shells. The military value of merchant ships has never been argued since these classic examples of service during the Spanish-American War.

Long years of peaceful operation followed. One of the most famous masters of the *St. Louis* was Capt. John Clark Jamison. He was short, only five feet two. Commodore Herbert Hartley tells a story about how Capt. Jamison cut down the mahogany weather rail on the bridge so he could look over it without standing on a box. This made it hard for the other officers who rigged up a canvas windbreak above the railing about a foot high. They removed it every time the Captain came on the bridge.

One clear, starlit night while the Captain was reading below, a young quartermaster was at the wheel. His name was Hartley and he was to rise to be master of the *St. Louis* and later the *Leviathan*. The canvas strip was up. Suddenly, who should appear but Capt. Jamison, blinking because of the darkness of the bridge. Approaching the rail, his pipe clamped between his teeth he paused inches from the canvas windbreak, which he didn't notice. Looking straight ahead right into the canvas he was quiet for a moment. Then he said something to the effect that it was a foggy night, wasn't it? Not caring to disagree, quartermaster Hartley said: "Aye, Sir." A pause followed. Then Capt. Jamison ordered that the fog warning be started. Every six seconds it wailed out over the clear dark blue night. Then the Captain's eyes grew accustomed to the darkness, but he never backed down an inch. He left the bridge with the quiet grunt: "Call me if it gets thick again."

It was Capt. Hartley who strode the *St. Louis'* bridge during her heroic World War I experiences. She was the first American ship to sail after the Kaiser had laid down a set course for American vessels and ordered them painted with red and white stripes from stem to stern. She accepted the challenge, made her own course, kept her regular colors and got through. The *St. Louis* was the first American ship to carry arms to Europe. She was the first American merchant vessel to be armed, receiving at the time a tremendous harbor send-off. Several attempts were made to sabotage her. On one occasion broken glass was mixed with the oil to be used in her engines. She had a twenty-five-minute gun duel with a U-boat on one occasion. Another time eighteen feet of her keel was found to be torn away suggesting she had run over and possibly destroyed a submarine. Still another narrow escape was once when thirty-five live high-explosive shells broke loose on deck during a violent gale. All but one were secured by the armed guard. The last one escaped their breathless clutching and dropped overboard near the twin churning propellers. It disappeared in the foam astern to everyone's immense relief. The *St. Louis* sailed as the *Louisville* during World War I.

Little remains to tell of the *St. Louis*. Her last years included a disastrous fire in New York after the war, efforts to rebuild her as an exposition ship, sale and resale to various speculators and finally a voyage behind a towline to an Italian scrapyard in 1925. Despite the predictions at the time of her launching, she did not commence a new and glorious era for American shipping. It was not until 1932 that the *Manhattan,* another luxury liner, was built for American-flag Atlantic service.

Men were men aboard the Edward Sewall, *one of the last of the windjammers, or quickly learned to be*

PART SEVEN

America Becomes A World Power

Between 1900 and the end of World War I our maritime scene underwent complete change. On the Lakes the cigar-shaped whaleback appeared like a comet and died as quickly. Along both the Atlantic and Pacific coasts railroad men went deeply into shipping. The Panama Canal doomed the few remaining windjammers. The LaFollette Seamen's Act prescribed new high living conditions on American ships, making the need for government aid imperative. And then war. With virtually no deep-sea ships we had to rely on seized foreign liners. We emerged victorious but with the greatest shipping hangover on record.

The EDWARD SEWALL

THE second mate had been a fine young man. He had never been to sea before on a sailing ship, but he had shown promise. And now he was lost over the side, carried over by a wave on the first day of the most horrendous gale ever experienced by the four-masted windjammer *Edward Sewall*. It was July 3, 1909. The ship was rounding Cape Horn from San Francisco to New York. The same wave that swept the second mate over into the swirling waters to his death injured the first mate. He was taken to his bunk. Four weeks later he went insane. The mind of one of the seamen snapped. He had to be confined in irons. Such were the terrors of the Horn in those last years of sail under the Stars and Stripes.

"I had my hands full for a while," was the way Capt. Richard Quick put the situation in his sea letter to Bath, Me., home port of the *Edward Sewall*. The storm continued three days. It was "the worst I ever saw in my life," he reported.

When the gale finally subsided not a sail remained! They had been torn to shreds. Sheets, blocks, braces and running gear were gone. The skylights were smashed, deck houses bashed in, stanchions broken off, the towing winch "all broken up," the pump damaged, deck rails washed away, lifeboats gone or smashed to kindling wood. The forecastle was washed out, and all the sailors had to live aft for three days. With one man lost overboard and two others confined, it is little wonder that the sixteen surviving seamen were uneasy.

"They started to get funny with me," Capt. Quick said, "because I was alone." But the Captain did not stand for any funny business. Waving his trusty "six-shooter" and putting on a "big bluff," he put a quick stop to any thoughts of mutiny. He walked the poop alone, waking the men at five every morning and keeping them on the go until 5:30 p.m. when they were only too willing to turn in.

With the ship's sewing machine they made new sails. They cleaned up the wreckage. Things again became shipshape. The wind kept strong and they finally reached New York to make what was for them a record passage of 110 days. Capt. Quick applied to the owners for a week or ten days' vacation. He said that he wanted "to go in the woods for a while."

The *Edward Sewall* was one of five steel ships and a schooner built at the turn of the century by A. Sewall at Bath. Arthur S. Sewall, who gave his name to the old company founded in 1823 by his father, was known as The Merchant Prince. He was a national figure, having garnered six and a half million votes in 1896, as Democratic candidate for vice-president, with William Jennings Bryan. At his death while the *Edward Sewall* was on her first voyage Arthur Sewall was described as follows by the New York *Sun:*

> He was one of the pioneer expansionists of the present generation of American expansionists. Few men of the present time saw earlier than Mr. Sewall did or appreciated more accurately the future possibility of American commerce on the Pacific. His ships were on every sea. He built and sailed them. He maintained tenaciously, and at the last almost alone, the ancient prestige and glory of the wooden shipyards of the New England coast.
>
> He was a man of that great industrial type of which New England furnished the earliest examples in this country. Much of the fame of his native state was due to the Sewalls, and many of the triumphs of American shipping on the seas have been won by the products of the Sewall shipyards.

Capt. Quick came to the *Edward Sewall* in 1901. Her first master, Capt. Joseph Sewall, a second cousin of the late Arthur Sewall, will be remembered largely for throwing a visiting Customs officer out of his cabin on the ship's maiden voyage and thereby incurring a $500 fine. Capt. Sewall was probably very well remembered by his mate, for he was forced to amputate this officer's injured thumb en route to Liverpool on a stormy 1901 crossing. Described in the Captain's sea letter as "not a skillful bit of surgery," the operation was at least a success to the extent that the mate lived.

Life at sea was not easy, to say the least. Of how little matter was the life of a seaman is shown in this statement by Capt. Quick after a 130-day trip from Philadelphia to San Francisco in 1904.

> The ship is in her usual good order, only a little mishap off the Horn. The big link in the fore upper topsail tie chain parted, letting the yard down. It struck the lower topsail yard, breaking the gooseneck and standard. Both yards fell on the foreyard, tearing the sails and making a bad wreck. At the time the yard fell we lost a man overboard. Could not save him. I cannot help telling you what a fine ship this is in heavy weather.

Hardly one month passed after this sea letter was written when a second man fell to his death from the yards of the *Edward Sewall*. With 1,200 tons of ballast aboard, she was nearly ready to start for Honolulu. It was afternoon. The Captain's report notes that the "rest of the crew heard him holler and saw him fall to the deck."

On one of the *Sewall's* sisterships a man fell ninety feet from a yard and survived. He not only lived, but he leapt to his feet, ran to the ratlines and climbed back up to his job of unfurling sail. Apparently when he fell he landed at the feet of a scowling ruffian of a mate for whom he had particularly great respect.

Although wages were a good $25 a month for seamen, the *Edward Sewall* frequently had trouble getting men. On one voyage in 1908 Capt. Quick described his crew as "the very poorest lot I ever had." They included six Japanese, seven Hawaiians, eight Americans, a Frenchman, three Filipinos and two Mexicans. Ten of his twenty deck men could not climb aloft to tend sails. There were no rules then requiring that seamen on American ships be American citizens. Capt. Quick wrote:

> Half a dozen good and tried seamen are among the crew, and it is up to them and the officers to make sailors out of the rest before the voyage is very old. Off the Horn is a pretty good section in which to learn seamanship, even against one's will.

Capt. Quick was a great sailor; a captain at twenty-five, he was to be master of the *Edward Sewall* for two decades, but he was tough! On the way home from her first voyage to the Orient, the *Sewall's* entire crew deserted at Honolulu. Of course the Hawaiian Islands were always a problem, because they attracted deserters. They were, however, one of the best places to get a full cargo of sugar for the States, and they needed coal from Hampton Roads.

Masters had to be tough in those days. Take the battle royal that enlivened the *Edward Sewall's* stay at Woosung, near Shanghai in 1903. Capt. Quick was returning to his ship aboard the launch of the USS *Oregon*, whose captain had offered him a ride. As they approached the stately windjammer sounds of tumult greeted their ears.

Knowing the temper of his men, Capt. Quick suggested that the *Oregon's* master might wish to bring his marines over to quiet things down. No sooner said than done. But as the first marine popped his head over the side of the *Edward Sewall* her crew forgot their own differences and united "to repel boarders." The *Sewall's* crew was rough, but the marines were rougher and after a while all was quiet. When the marines left, however, the battle was resumed. The *Oregon's* men returned. This time they left a guard of six to keep peace until the ship could reach Shanghai. There the ring leaders were turned over to the United States Consul. Much to Capt. Quick's irritation, the Consul let them all go, for "he always favors the seamen no matter what they do."

Capt. Quick took pride in running under more canvas than others thought wise. He relates with obvious relish how in 1907 while still off the Horn he came up "on an English three-masted ship under two lower topsails, reefed foresail, two staysails and one jib. At that time we were carrying six topsails, three courses with no reefs, three staysails and two jibs. We passed her in very short time but two hours afterward the two jib stays carried away and owing to the heavy gale of course the jibs were a total loss." But the jibs were back in place in less than two days. The British ship never caught up with the *Sewall*.

Late in 1907 the *Arthur Sewall*, slightly smaller than the *Edward Sewall*, was lost without trace. Suggestions of mutiny were discounted by her owners. One seaman showed up in Australia claiming to be a survivor, but his tale was full of holes. He dropped out of sight before he could be questioned. Many believed that the *Arthur Sewall* may have collided with the bark *Adolph Obrig*, which had sailed at about the same time and which was also posted among the list of missing ships. In the half century since this dual tragedy nothing has been heard from either ship.

Perhaps the most unusual episode in Capt. Quick's twenty years as master of the *Edward Sewall* occurred early in 1910 when she was carrying coal to Hawaii. His attention was called to a thin trail of smoke coming from the top or head of the steel foremast. The base of the mast was warm to the touch.

"Sometimes I get almost discouraged," the Captain wrote as he described how he ordered the hold around the base of the mast flooded. After flooding he set his men to shoveling out the coal. There was no evident fire, yet the mast continued to heat up. Suddenly to everyone's horror, the giant mast settled into the deck, dropping slowly, inch by inch, until it came to rest on the ship's keelson. It had dropped eighteen inches. Apparently the hot steel mast had burned away the heavy wooden chocks holding it firm in the ship's main deck.

> The ship was rolling some and as the rigging all slacked up, things looked pretty bad. We got all hands out of the hold and began setting up the rigging and getting the forward boats aft where we could save them. We then bored a hole in the mast above the deck and filled it with water, which cooled it off some.

Finally, with the mast secure, digging was resumed. Smoldering coals were found right at the mast's base after one night and two days of shoveling. The live fire area reached two feet up the mast and three feet away from it in the depths of the hold. Quick's sea letter ended with:

> One great mistake, I think, is to have the foot of the mast closed up with wood. That is the first thing that burns away and you cannot imagine the draft there is in one of those masts. I will close them with cement next time. I also found it a good thing to stop the top end of it. We tied canvas around the head, so stopped the draft.

"I burnt a pair of rubber boots off my feet," Capt. Quick said after reaching Honolulu with the coal still smoldering. It continued to trouble him. His wife and daughter, who often sailed with him, took up residence ashore. When the coal had finally been removed, the ship was put into shape again. Local riggers offered to re-step the mast, but Capt. Quick thought their price was too high and did the job himself. To hoist the giant mast he used 700 railroad ties, four fifteen-ton screw jacks and two twenty-ton hydraulic jacks.

Despite these valiant efforts, Capt. Quick knew that the days of the sailing ship were numbered. He frequently lost cargoes to big steamships which could offer quicker delivery. The projected Panama Canal would make ridiculous the lengthy voyage around Cape Horn. The high cost of canal transit would reduce to nothing the margin of profit then enjoyed by sailing ships over steamers. He got his master's certificate for steamship operation. Nevertheless he was still to have another ten years with the *Edward Sewall.*

A highlight of this second decade was his famous record voyage around the Cape in 1913. It was a record not for speed but for duration. The trip lasted 293 days, Philadelphia to Seattle. The passage began with trouble off South America. The ship's steel bowsprit dropped off, an unheard-of thing. He put into port only to have half his crew desert. A new bowsprit, and forty-odd days later, he was at sea. Before he had been gone many hours, the bowsprit broke off a second time. Capt. Quick was ready for the sick bay. Another month in port and a second crew deserted. But the worst was yet to come. It took the *Edward Sewall* sixty-seven days to get around the Horn. Once he was 300 miles to the west of the Cape only to be driven back to a point forty miles east of the Horn with the "white horses of the sea riding roughshod over his half-drowned ship," to quote from Mark W. Hennessy's book *The Sewall Ships of Steel.*

And then World War I came to put *finis* to the famous Sewall ships of steel. The *Edward's* sister ship *William P. Frye* was sunk by the German raider *Prinz Eitel Friedrich,* a converted passenger ship.

"It is the saddest thing I have ever witnessed," said the raider's Capt. Thierickens to a reporter later. "But I considered it in the line of my duty. It could not be helped."

This loss struck a tragic blow at the steel windjammer as a class. Only the *Dirigo* and the *Edward Sewall* were left. Late in October, 1915, the *Dirigo* was sold, leaving only the *Edward* in the Sewall fleet. A year later, Capt. Quick brought his famous ship into New York to complete her last voyage under the "S" house flag. She was sold to the Texas Company to carry oil in bulk. Capt. Quick remained with her for four more years.

In 1922 she was sold to the Alaska Packers who used her in Northern waters for twelve more or less uneventful years. Sold again in 1934 she was tied up in idleness until 1936 when she made her final voyage to Japan to be scrapped.

Capt. Quick, last of Maine's deep-sea sailing shipmasters, remained with the Texas Company for twenty-three years. He commanded several of their large steam tankers. Upon his retirement he returned to Bath to become a trustee of the Maine Nautical School, a member of the Board of Governors of the Propeller Club of Portland and President of the Kennebec Marine Museum. He died in 1947. Two of his officers aboard the *Edward Sewall* were present at his funeral. They were Capt. Soren Willesen, Executive Vice-President of the Sprague Steamship Co., and Vernon Mitchell, marine superintendent of the Texas Co. Both had been second mates on the famed windjammer, both loved Capt. Quick.

P.S.   Today's generation has moved far from the days of the windjammer. Paul C. Braynard, the author's three-year-old nephew, had this comment when he saw an old four-master in Hempstead Harbor in 1955:

"Look, Mommie, at the boat with the four television aerials."

The BRINCKERHOFF

FERRYBOATS, thousands of them, have populated our harbors and bays, our rivers and lakes. Few survive today. They are a fast disappearing species and yet their story is almost unchronicled. Presumably no one would think of saving a telephone pole, or weep at its passing to be replaced by underground wires. So have many people felt about the ferryboat. Ferryboats deserve more than this. Ever since the days when a young farm hand named Cornelius Vanderbilt ran away to pull an oar on one of the first ferries between Staten Island and New York, craft of this kind have helped make history. Ferries from the lowly raft type such as still link Edgartown with Chappaquiddick on Martha's Vineyard, to the great four-stacked *Solano* of San Francisco harbor, have had real appeal to the artist and social historian.

The thousands of Poughkeepsie-Highland ferry travelers who rode over and back across the Hudson on the little *Brinckerhoff* probably never dreamed she would be singled out to represent *the* ferryboat in the maritime hall of fame. Built in 1899 the little craft is now enshrined for posterity at the Mystic Seaport, Mystic, Conn. How she got there makes a story.

Principal actors in the drama of the *Brinckerhoff* were Freeman R. Hathaway, of Noank, Conn., and William H. Ewen, of Hastings-on-Hudson, both past Presidents of the Steamship Historical Society of America. Each was a devotee of steamboat Americana. Mr. Hathaway's specialty was Long Island Sound steamer history. Mr. Ewen was a Hudson River historian. They were equally interested in the *Brinckerhoff*, which after forty-two years had left the Hudson to serve on the Sound out of Bridgeport, Conn., as a link to nearby Pleasure Beach. In May, 1949, the old craft was laid up at Rondout Creek, not far from the last resting place of the *Mary Powell*. Her outboard paddle-wheel braces were found in need of replacement and Bridgeport city fathers decided against using her that year.

Mr. Hathaway entered the picture when he passed through Bridgeport in the fall of that year. Always eager for news about old steamers he took advantage of the occasion to call on Mayor Jasper McLevy. He explained the Historical Society's interest in the *Brinckerhoff* and inquired about her future. He mentioned Mystic Seaport as a desirable place to preserve the vessel as a relic, but departed, never expecting anything more to come of his visit. Some months later he was informed that his proposal had been accepted by the City of Bridgeport and the *Brinckerhoff* would be turned over to Mystic through the good offices of the Society.

Here Mr. Ewen came on the scene. Quickly grasping the possibilities of saving one of the last remaining Fletcher walking-beam engines, he rallied support of Society members up and down the Atlantic coast. The task was a formidable one for an organization whose total annual income went into the publication of a quarterly journal. Mr. Ewen estimated after a careful survey that it would cost $1,500 to reconnect pipe lines and tow or steam the *Brinckerhoff* to Mystic. Capt. Earl C. Palmer, then Vice-President of the Society and one of the nation's leading tugboat men, agreed to skipper the 140-foot craft to her final resting place. Ashby O. Reardon, a Society member from Alexandria, Va., volunteered to provide a ton of coal and to shovel it himself. Capt. Elwell B. Thomas, owner of a Stonington, Conn., boat yard, offered to bring a crew of workers down to paint or put the vessel in trim once she reached Mystic. Permission from the various maritime unions was requested for such volunteer work. The author, then a marine reporter on the New York *Herald Tribune*, described all these activities in a feature story launching an appeal for funds. Over $1,000 was raised, and then a New York tug operator, Joseph E. Meseck, offered to tow the *Brinckerhoff* to Mystic at no cost. There was jubilation in the Society's camp.

Plans were laid for turning the craft over to Mystic and New York City offered free docking space for the ceremonies at Pier 1, Battery Place. On May 3 Mayor McLevy came to New York expressly for the occasion. So did Mr. Reardon, from Alexandria, who commented: "I'm amazed at the show New York put

An odd one—the Brinckerhoff, *probably the only ferryboat that will ever be enshrined as a museum piece*

on for this old relic. I would never have thought we could get so much interest around here."

"It's a nice thing," responded Arthur H. Fletcher, of the Fletchers who had built the *Brinckerhoff's* famous engine. "There isn't much sentiment left in the world."

After the transfer the guests departed to historic India House for a luncheon in honor of the occasion, given by Clifford D. Mallory, Jr., head of the Marine Historical Association, operators of Mystic Seaport. At 2 p.m. the old ferry began her last voyage to Mystic under tow of the smallest of the Meseck tugs.

But the story had only begun. Monday night, five days after the *Brinckerhoff* had disappeared down the East River, members of the Steamship Historical Society were gathered for dinner aboard the Spanish transatlantic liner *Magallanes*. The conversation turned to the little ferry and the author was astounded to learn that she had not reached Mystic as of that afternoon. The voyage should have taken no more than twenty-one hours. The next day, when apprised of the situation, the *Tribune's* marine editor Walter Hamshar sensed a top news story and so informed the city desk. The great newspaper's own

airplane was dispatched to find the missing vessel, the Coast Guard was badg-
ered, Mystic Seaport was asked for the latest information. It was a front-page
story!

The log of the tug *Joseph Meseck, Jr.,* familiarly known as "Little Joe," told
the story. It would have been far less dramatic had there been a sending set
aboard the staunch little tug, for nothing really exciting happened. Fog closed
in at 11 o'clock on the first night of the voyage and the tow was not heard from
for twenty-seven hours. A Coast Guard rescue plane returned Thursday without
having sighted the ferry. A cutter from New London failed to find the *Brinckerhoff* on the following day, although a fishing boat reported her entering New
Haven Harbor under tow. The fog rose briefly and the ferry's Odyssey was
resumed. She reached Saybrook Point only to be fog-bound again. When the
fog lifted, high winds made the tow dangerous. Finally, Monday afternoon the
"Little Joe" and her charge pulled out of Saybrook Point and headed for New
London. After that it was smooth sailing. At noon on Tuesday the *Brinckerhoff*
arrived.

"It was the darnedest trip I've ever experienced," said Walter L. Meseck,
President of the towing company. Mr. Meseck spent an anxious six days while
the tow was in progress, making his headquarters at Mystic. He enjoyed the
hospitality of Charles Brooks, business manager of Mystic Seaport.

"Charlie's two children got to call me Uncle Walter," Mr. Meseck said.
"Talk about the man who came to dinner—that was me all right."

The *Brinckerhoff,* sad to relate, was not appreciated at Mystic and was allowed to deteriorate. Moved from one place to another in the Seaport area she
was eventually sold for $1 to a junk dealer who planned to put a restaurant on
her. Her priceless Fletcher walking beam engine, which many had urged be taken
out and preserved as a last resort, went with her. Still more months of neglect
and then a fire put an end to her career.

The MANCHURIA

TWENTY years is the average life of an ocean liner. Thirty years is rare. Forty
years of service is virtually unheard of and yet the *Manchuria* was to begin her
final and one of her most interesting "lives" at the age of forty-three.

We call her *Manchuria,* and yet she had three other names. Hers was indeed
a strange and interesting career. Built in 1904 by the New York Shipbuilding
Corporation she was to have been called *Minnekahda,* but was sold on the stocks
to Pacific Mail. After eleven proud years as flagship of this line's transpacific
run, she was sold for Atlantic service under the American Line's Blue Eagle
house flag. Her sister ship, the *Mongolia,* is reported to have fired the first Ameri-

A grand old Lady Liner, the Manchuria *was the oldest ocean passenger ship afloat when scrapped in 1952*

can shot in World War I. When the war ended the two graceful ships served briefly as immigrant ships and then went into the new intercoastal service under the now defunct Panama Pacific Line's standard. Both were sold to the Dollar Line and renamed: the *Manchuria* becoming the *President Johnson.* Her loyal friends always resented this name, feeling that there were many other Presidents she might have honored. They wondered why the name of the one chief executive who had been impeached was chosen for their favorite. She wore the name proudly, be that as it may, and did yeoman work in World War II.

The ups and downs of the *Manchuria's* long service parallel the fortunes of our merchant marine. As flagship of the Pacific Mail she served until driven out of the trade by low-cost Japanese competition. Her post World War I service on the Atlantic lasted only as long as there were virtually no foreign-flag ships to compete with. Her operation between coasts with the Panama Pacific Line was suffering even in her day from increasingly severe railroad and truck competition. That she lasted so long is a tribute to the optimism of her various owners, not to mention her Camden, N. J., builders, whose contract Number 2 she was.

The last chapter in her life began in 1947 when she was sold to Portuguese interests and renamed *Santa Cruz*. It was her new owners' plan to convert her to carry a few first-class passengers and many immigrants from war-devastated Europe to South America. The new owners' credit was not too good, as is attested to by the seven suits brought against the ship by jittery creditors. There was one for $550,000 filed by the repair yard, another of $11,058 for stores, and one for $4,212 for tobacco and liquors stocked aboard. All were eventually paid, and the old engines turned over merrily for the voyage to Italy. Flying the Panamanian flag, she carried thousands to a new life in Brazil and Argentina.

Soon the Italian Line bought her and spent more to make her first-class public rooms and cabins modern. She is shown to be perhaps more luxurious than ever before. Gone were the dark oak panels and white and gold ceilings, and, in their place, were put modern Italian furnishings. It would have taken a fine eye to discern any similarities between the Camden wonder-ship of 1904 and the rebuilt *Santa Cruz*. A close inspection, however, would reveal the same delicately fluted columns throughout the saloons and the double-circle decorations on her ceilings, there ever since her first days.

Finally in 1952, after completing some 2,500,000 miles under nine house flags, the gallant veteran was no longer needed, with the arrival on the scene of the new *Augustus* and *Giulio Cesare*. She was the oldest major passenger liner in operation when she was sold for scrap.

The OCTORARA

THE name "Octorara" often provoked questions. An old folder of the Great Lakes Transit Corporation, owners of the lake liner *Octorara*, explains the origin of the word. It was taken from the Iroquois Indian word Ottohehaho meaning either "where money or presents were distributed," or a place naturally long remembered. At least in one respect the ship was well named. She will be long remembered.

The *Octorara* offered Lake passengers deep-sea luxury. Built in 1910 she and her two sisters were ocean liners in miniature. Except for having their single smokestack at the stern, as was Lake custom, she had much in common with ocean-going coastal liners. She could accommodate 594 passengers with an

The Octorara, *with stack aft, was a familiar sight on the Lakes. Later she served in the Pacific as a transport*

additional 150 in her crew. She boasted a double bottom, a daily newspaper, barbershop, soda fountain, library, newsstand and "modern system of ventilation." Her surprisingly large dining saloon occupied about one-quarter of her length on the promenade deck. This deck was described as 375 feet long on each side, in a company folder, raising something of a question, as the ship herself was only 361 feet overall. Since the deck extended from prow to stern the curve inward fore and aft could account for the seemingly extra fourteen feet.

The 2,952-mile voyage from Buffalo to Duluth and back, via Chicago, cost only $98.50 in the 1930's. Stop-over privileges were available on all tickets. The only cargo carried were the automobiles of passengers. Shore excursions, special admission to golf courses at ports along the way, dancing every afternoon and evening, deck games and bridge tournaments with "prizes awarded," were a few of the inducements offered.

Very real luxury was available, at an extra price. Most expensive were two observation suites under the pilot house. Included were a bedroom with twin beds, wardrobe, electric fans; a drawing room with couch, dressing table; a private bathroom and an observation room with day bed, davenport and easy chairs. Each suite could accommodate a party of five.

One cannot suppress an occasional chuckle at some of the fine-print paragraphs under general information for prospective passengers. For example:

> *The particular attention* of hay-fever victims is called to the well-known curative climate of the Upper Lakes. There hay fever is unknown and there are many well-authenticated cases of permanent cures from this distressing malady by a few weeks' sojourn in this district.
>
> *Exercise at sea*—One of the many advantages of water travel is the opportunity to exercise by walking. Eight laps around the promenade deck equals one mile—a breakfast appetizer.
>
> *Fish dinners*—The Epicurean who enjoys a fish diet will appreciate the delicious lake trout and white fish which, when procurable, are included in the menu.

The depression of the 1930's put travel managers up to all sorts of tricks. One practiced by the *Octorara* people was the luring aboard of casual diners at ports of call.

> If you are in Buffalo, Chicago or Duluth when our ships are in port come over at the dinner hour and treat yourself to the novelty of dining aboard ship. You'll find the cuisine unparalleled, the service faultless and the prices reasonable. Have dinner amid luxurious surroundings comparable to those of the finest hotels ashore, while the enchanting strains of the ship's orchestra are wafted gently to your ears.

When war came the *Octorara* was hastily remodeled into a Coast Guard barracks ship. When the need for tonnage reached a fever peak in 1943 she was taken down the Mississippi, rebuilt for ocean service and became an inter-island transport on the Pacific. With her in this service were two small overnight boats which had served on Long Island Sound. They were the *Arrow* and the *Comet,* built originally as the Maine steamers *Belfast* and *Camden,* and mentioned earlier in the chapter on the two *Bangors.* While far from suitable for the service they played their part. When the war ended the *Octorara* was laid up in Suisun Bay, finally to be scrapped in 1952. From Lake luxury liner to Pacific veteran, hers had been a strange and useful career.

The YALE Glamor Ship of the Coastal Fleet

THE *Yale*, known and loved on both Atlantic and Pacific coasts, may rightly be called one of the merchant marine's most illustrious ships. A veteran of both the First and the Second World Wars, she was the fastest ship in the merchant fleet when new in 1907. Shortly before being scrapped in 1949, she reached the depths of ignominy for a ship, being listed by the American Bureau of Shipping as a hotel!

From the very beginning the *Yale*, and her sister ship the *Harvard*, were marked as special ships. They were the culmination of a century of coastal ship design dating back to the *Clermont*. The *Yale*, especially, became known as the glamor ship of the coastal fleet. She had style. She was rakish and clean-cut even in her last days as a barracks ship in Seattle. Her twin, well-proportioned smokestacks, jauntily raked, made her seem in motion even while she was tied up at a pier. Her tall, sharp bow, somewhat reminiscent of big Great Lakes overnight boats, gave her the lines of a greyhound. Perhaps that is why she was renamed *Greyhound* by the Navy during part of her service in World War II. And finally, that last touch that set her apart, the *Yale* was painted white, from boot topping to bridge.

The *Yale* was built for service between New York and Boston around Cape Cod. The Cape Cod Canal, now such a boon to coastal freighters, was yet to be built. Her owners were the Metropolitan S.S. Co., a part of Charles W. Morse's vast shipping empire. Built by John Roach & Son, Chester, Pa., the *Yale* was engined by Andrew Fletcher, of Hoboken. Her three propellers were each driven by a turbine engine, the *Yale* being the third turbine-propelled ship built in the United States.

The New Haven bulldog motif played a conspicuous part in the interior decoration of the 407-foot-long vessel. Yale-blue decorations were a feature of her interior, with the letter "Y" carved here and there amid the plush surroundings. Her 311 staterooms, located on the two lower of her three passenger decks, could accommodate 987 overnight travelers. The cabins were grouped in two rows, back to back, on port and starboard sides, with the outside rooms opening on a narrow, open promenade and the inboard rooms facing on long passageways. Twenty-two extra large "luxury" class cabins were forward on the upper deck. There was no stateroom No. 13.

The *Yale's* preliminary trial was a short run down New York Bay on June 27, 1907. Two days later she made a run to Boston, with an elapsed time of 13 hours, 48 minutes. Held up to await completion of the *Harvard*, the *Yale* set out on her first regular run Sept. 18, with a full passenger list. Making the 330-mile voyage in an easy 15 hours, the *Yale* and her sister proved real competition to coast railroad lines. They averaged twenty knots on coal fuel, their twelve Scotch boilers generating 12,000 horsepower.

A coastal speed queen, the Yale *was noted for her ability to literally rock over the sand bar at San Francisco*

Three prosperous years followed and then events took place that were to completely alter the careers of the *Yale* and her sister ship. The Morse shipping combine collapsed and the Metropolitan Line was sold to the New Haven railroad interests. At the conclusion of the 1910 season the *Yale* and *Harvard* were chartered to the Pacific Navigation Co. and sent to the West Coast.

The trip to the West Coast was interesting. The twin white flyers, only recently converted to oil burners, were temporarily rebuilt to burn coal, because of the difficulty of obtaining oil fuel on the voyage around South America. Sailing together Oct. 17 they made calls at St. Lucia, Rio de Janeiro, Montevideo and Punta Arenas before transiting the Straits of Magellan. The twins reached San Pedro, Cal., Dec. 16. It is said that they steamed within sight of each other all the way.

Running all year around with the regularity, if not quite the speed of an express train, the *Yale* and *Harvard* made four trips weekly in each direction between San Francisco and Los Angeles. San Diego was added to their schedule in 1911. Passing through several hands, the *Yale* and her sister continued on this route until called to war service in 1918. Rebuilt as transports with added bridge and crow's nest the twins reached Southampton, England, on July 24, and immediately went to work as cross-channel ferries. They each made over 200 trips and carried over 368,000 troops. Returning a year later they were laid up at the Philadelphia Navy Yard.

The Los Angeles Steamship Co., known as Lassco Line, bought them at this point and restored the two sleek sisters to their now familiar San Francisco-Los Angeles-San Diego route. Between 1921 and 1935 the *Yale* made 1,330 voyages, traveling 1,270,000 miles.

A contemporary Lassco Line folder shows that the *Yale* and *Harvard* maintained sailings every Tuesday, Wednesday, Friday and Saturday from San Francisco, leaving San Diego every Tuesday, Thursday, Friday and Sunday. Southbound the voyage commenced at 4 p.m. with arrival at Los Angeles at 11:30 a.m. the next day and at San Diego at 8 p.m. that evening. Northbound the trip began at 9 a.m. at San Diego and at 3 p.m. at Los Angeles with a 10:30 a.m. arrival at San Francisco.

Flying huge name pennants, the *Yale* and the *Harvard* became immensely popular on this 18-hour "overnight trip de luxe," as the folder described it. "First-class passage only" was sold "on the *Yale* and *Harvard*, no second, intermediate or steerage," the brochure added. "The fare is graded according to the location of the stateroom chosen, whether standard or de luxe, inside or outside room, upper or lower deck, etc."

A quaint feature of this folder was the warning which ran as follows: "Unnecessary delay will be avoided by bearing in mind that a BERTH is a bed or sleeping accommodation for one person only. A STANDARD STATEROOM contains two berths. Reservations should be secured in advance."

Under the Lassco house flag the *Yale* and *Harvard* were rebuilt to accommodate 500 passengers. A large glass-enclosed veranda café and ballroom was built aft on the upper or "B" deck. Two chevrons, for the two years of war service, were on the forward stack. The stacks were painted black as they had been originally with the Metropolitan Line. A thorough engine overhaul by Lassco in 1921 had raised their horsepower to 14,000. The *Yale* was said to be the faster of the two, and could make almost twenty-four knots. As rebuilt by Lassco, an added 275 tons of steel in the form of a new deck and structural stiffening practically eliminated the excessive vibration which was formerly so objectionable.

One early morning in 1931 a rancher in a field overlooking Point Arguello, a notoriously bad bit of coast near Santa Barbara, heard the whistle of a ship in distress. Twenty years earlier, almost to the day, the same rancher had heard the whistle of a ship in distress—the *Santa Rosa*—which had become a total loss. Since this spot was known as the Cape Horn of the Pacific this was not too unusual a coincidence, but the more he heard the whistle that 1931 morning the more he was positive that it was the very same whistle he had heard back in 1911. And he was right!

The *Harvard* was the ship in distress. She stranded at twenty knots on a clear night but not one of her 490 passengers and crew of sixty was lost. It was her 972nd voyage. The man who heard *Santa Rosa's* voice twenty years later must have had a keen and retentive memory, because—according to the *Harvard's* people—he actually heard the whistle of the long-vanished steamer. It seems that on the *Harvard's* forward stack was the whistle which was installed when she was built, back on the East Coast. On the after stack was a second, auxiliary whistle—and this whistle, which sounded at the time of the wreck, was one which had been salvaged from *Santa Rosa!*

Although the Clyde liner *Iroquois*, miniature ocean steamer, was brought out to run with the *Yale*, the loss of the *Harvard* seemed to doom the service. The *Iroquois* became the hospital ship *Solace* in World War II and after that was sold to Turkey for use in the Mediterranean as the *Ankara*.

The *Yale's* career, however, was far from ended in July, 1935, when she was withdrawn from the San Francisco-San Diego run and laid up at Antioch, Cal. Two years later on the East Coast the even more famous Fall River Line was to discontinue, after just short of a hundred years of operation. Coastwise overnight boats were through. In fact the entire domestic merchant fleet, long the backbone of American shipping, seemed about to disappear. World War II administered the coup de grâce. Today, thanks to the truck, not one passenger ship operates between two American ports except the three ships of the Old Bay Line, which connect Baltimore, Norfolk and Washington. That line, it might be noted, is generally accepted as the oldest American ship company—and one of the world's oldest steamship lines.

The *Yale's* service as a hotel began in 1941. She was bought by a contracting firm and taken to Sitka and later Kodiak, Alaska, for use as a floating dormitory for her owner's employees who were doing defense production jobs. Her active career, however, was not quite run. The *Yale* served during the final days of World War II carrying passengers between the Aleutian Islands.

Then there was a brief stretch as a barracks ship in Seattle. On Jan. 5, 1949, the Maritime Commission offered her for sale with the proviso that she be "completely scrapped, dismembered, dismantled or destroyed, within the continental limits of the United States" in eighteen months. She was at that juncture resting in the Olympia, Washington, reserve fleet.

The *Yale*, which in her busy lifetime had made one voyage through the Straits of Magellan and two through the Panama Canal, was to make one more intercoastal trip, but this time as scrap steel in railroad flat cars. She was junked at Stockton, Cal., and her steel sent overland to a Pittsburgh mill.

The LEVIATHAN

THE story of the *Leviathan* could begin half a dozen different ways. It could start at her launching with all the pomp of the Kaiser's Germany. It could begin with her stupendous war service, during which time she carried one twentieth of the entire American Expeditionary Force. Or it could begin with her decade after World War I as the world's largest liner. From 1914 to 1938 the *Leviathan* was the best-known ship afloat. Tales of her vastness, of her difficulties and her achievements are legend. If she grounded it was front-page news, with the follow-up stories about how the press was conspiring with England to destroy our merchant marine. If a rat was sighted aboard her during one of her frequent periods of idleness, the story was exaggerated and compounded until it would provoke a Congressional inquiry. If she lost $70,000 a voyage, mid-western papers would make it $700,000 and comment editorially upon such ghastly waste. She was in many respects the world's greatest ship. She was also the biggest white elephant in America's maritime history.

Let's begin, instead, at the end, in 1938. Can you imagine an old British sea-dog sitting down in his cottage named The Crescent, at Maghull, Lancashire? He is Capt. J. M. Binks. His lot would have been a much happier one had he not been master of the *Olympic* on that foggy day she sliced the Nantucket Lightship completely in two with the loss of seven lives. Although he was still hearty he had retired immediately after the incident. We are with him in our mind's eye as he takes pen in hand to write a friend about a recent assignment. It was a jinx voyage, with troubles, ghosts and a mutinous crew the whole way across. It was a heart-breaking curtain for the great *Leviathan*. It was her trip from New York to shipbreakers in Scotland.

"We got away on Tuesday from Pier 4, Hoboken, about 4:30 p.m.," he wrote, "and we certainly put some smoke over Lil Old New York and kept that up all the way across the ocean."

The great ship anchored off Staten Island for fuel. No sooner had night fallen than one of the boilers burst, the first of many accidents. Four hours after getting under way the next morning the surgeon reported to Capt. Binks that there were no medical stores on board.

"I returned to anchorage, awaiting these stores, which were being sent out by tugboat," the Captain calmly reported. Weighing anchor again the chain parted and the anchor plummeted down the rusty bow into the sea, accident number two.

"Anyway we started on our journey at 3:32 p.m. wondering what the next accident would be. About two hours later a phone message from the engine room asked for the surgeon to be sent down, as one of the engineers had fallen down a ladder and broken his jawbone—accident number three," wrote the doughty mariner.

The crew was awful, except the American senior engineers, Capt. Binks said. He added that he was continually afraid of fires in the vast, empty passenger spaces. Seven fires did start, but all were in the boiler rooms and were easily put out.

The first of two ghostly episodes took place one day when one of the few who could steer kept the wheel over too long one way.

> The liquid (in the hydraulic steering cylinder) ran out over the side so that she wouldn't steer, so we tried to turn her around the other way, but nothing doing. For over an hour she wanted to go back to New York. Then everything got all right and back on our course we went.
>
> The same night the fog whistle started blowing for some reason every minute, although it was a clear night. We searched 'round to find out what happened, but it stopped on its own. We never really knew what was going to happen next.

Despite having been laid up for four years she averaged over seventeen knots on the seven-day run to Scotland. The morning after they had dropped anchor it was blowing a gale. The crew were all packed up and refused to move a finger since their articles had specified that they were to be paid off either at anchorage or at dusk. The situation looked critical for "there was no steam in the main engines when the ship dragged her anchors and we drifted nearly on the rocks of a small island named Yaystack." [The saga continued as printed in the November, 1938 issue of *Atlantic Monthly*:]

> A few British engineers ran below and got a little steam up so that we were able to weigh anchor and just managed to save the ship, and in time had enough to steam up to the anchorage again.

"We had nothing to eat that day," Capt. Binks added, reporting that some cooked food and a few cases of beer were brought out from shore and tided them over until a new crew and more supplies arrived the next day. The matter of food had been critical all the way over. Capt. Binks, in his gentle way, summarized the problem by writing that one of the cooks was probably really a "plasterer." The bread he baked was so bad that the Captain was forced to eat the biscuits of the lifeboats all the way across.

Now Sunday the 13th arrived to take her into dock. We weighed anchors and on turning the ship round to go under the Firth of Forth bridge an oil pipe burst and we lost all our steam. The ship was heading right across the Firth. I couldn't go ahead or astern, so I lost the tide and had to anchor until Monday, which cost another 1,000 pounds sterling. She was a hoodoo ship all right. I was glad when we docked.

So there you have the last voyage of your greatest merchant ship of America.

Everyone who has had anything to do with her since she first came out lost money. Now she will never go to sea again, as we flooded her No. 1 hold to sink her in the mud in Rosyth Dock so she won't blow around the dock while they cut her up for scrap.

So much for Capt. Binks' account of the end of the *Leviathan*.

She had a glamorous beginning. Launched at Hamburg as the *Vaterland*, on April 3, 1913, she was without question the world's largest ship. Some 1,500,000 rivets, weighing two pounds each, had gone into her hull. Her double bottom and watertight bulkheads were especially designed in light of the *Titanic* disaster of a year earlier. Her great length of 950 feet posed severe strains which were to lead to at least one serious crack in later years. She was the second of three mammoth Hamburg American Line passenger ships designed to give Germany undisputed rule of the seas. War ended her career under the German flag after only three voyages to the United States.

Then began a period of idleness at Hoboken. Darkened were most of her 15,000 electric lights. Unused were her 160,000 pieces of linen, quiet was her candy shop, her flower shop, book store and drug store, her Roman swimming pool, gymnasium and Ritz-Carlton restaurant. Most of her 1,200-man crew were sent home. On April 5, 1917, four years and a day after she had been launched, American bluejackets swarmed aboard, surprised the small crew that had remained below and took over the great ship.

Mrs. Woodrow Wilson was asked by the Shipping Board to select a name for the *Vaterland*. She probed through dictionaries, studied mythology and otherwise racked her brain for weeks. Finally she went to her husband at his desk. Without a second thought he said: "*Leviathan* . . . monster of the deep. It's in the Bible," he added. Years later Wilson's successor, President Harding,

Some say the Leviathan *was the most famous ship ever built. Can you spot the* Dalzell *tugs pushing her?*

modestly agreed to permit the great vessel to be renamed in his honor. A few weeks later, not long before the Teapot Dome scandal broke, he changed his mind.

When World War I ended the *Leviathan* was on the verge of being sold to the great J. P. Morgan shipping combine. Because this vast fleet included many foreign flagships, William Randolph Hearst started a crusade to prevent the sale. He succeeded, dooming the *Leviathan* to years of poor management and failure. Had she been operated in company with other great liners and by an established firm she might have at least fared as well as the *Berengaria* and *Majestic*, her sister ships.

Instead the *Leviathan* became a political pawn. She was owned by the United States Shipping Board. This body was charged by Congress with seeing to it that we became a great maritime nation. They divided up our vast fleet of shiny, new war-built vessels and established a socialistic maritime empire. Using private operators as agents, they organized lines on every ocean, to every principal area. Business recognized the need of the protection of at least one American line on each trade route. The public clamored for it, and the Shipping Board did its best. The case of the *Leviathan* shows the Shipping Board at its most inept. She headed a fleet of three pre-war German liners and two new transports, none of them finished in time for war service.

Was the *Leviathan* the largest or second largest ship? The *Majestic*, originally the *Bismarck*, was third of the (famed) pre-war German trio, the *Berengaria*, built as the *Imperator*, having been the first. Had the *Leviathan* been restored after the Great War on the original plans there would have been no question. But she was altered and re-measured. In 1922 it was announced that she was 59,956 gross tons, making her nearly 5,000 tons greater than the *Majestic*. Both ships claimed the title: "world's largest ship." The battle raged until in 1931 the depression forced the *Leviathan's* owners to economize in every possible way. To the horror of *Leviathan* rooters it was announced one day that the big ship had been re-measured and was now 48,943 tons. This meant a saving of $40,000 a year in port tolls. It meant also a substantial loss of face, for the *Leviathan* fell below not only the *Majestic*, but the *Berengaria*, *Bremen* and *Europa* in gross tonnage.

When the *Leviathan* made her first voyage as a luxurious American passenger ship in 1932, Prohibition was in force. It was the practice then to sell liquor aboard American ships outside the twelve-mile limit. St. Louis brewer August A. Busch made a national issue of the fact, pointing out that drinks could be sold on government-owned ships but not on American soil. As a result of the publicity the United States Shipping Board, which owned the *Leviathan*, took the pledge. The absence of alcohol aboard the *Leviathan* is claimed by some to have been one reason why she was not as popular as it was thought she should have been. However, the widely-hailed resumption of liquor sales outside the twelve-mile limit effected in 1929 when private interests bought the big vessel failed to lift the white elephant out of the red.

As the depression became more intense the *Leviathan* turned to short cruises in between her regular Atlantic voyaging. One was advertised as a "week-end house party" to Halifax and back. Four days for as low as $35 if you went tourist class. First-class fares were from $65 to $1,000, depending on your choice of cabin or suite. The cruise folder ran in part:

"Come! Put a paperweight on care and sail bracing Northern seas. Judge these four days on the world's most famous ship for what they are worth to you. A chance to recuperate from the petty trials of daily living . . . four whole days . . . time short enough to steal away from an office desk, time long enough to renew spent energy or to spend pent-up energy. . . ."

All was to no avail. The *Leviathan* became a permanent citizen of Hoboken until the saga of Capt. Binks returned her to the front pages for one last fling. On April 15, 1955, as this book was being put together, a column of city briefs in the New York *World Telegram and Sun,* had this to say:

"U.S.S. *Leviathan* Veterans Association—32nd annual reunion of men who served aboard the *Leviathan* during World War I will be held at 6:30 p.m. tomorrow in Dunhall's restaurant, 40th St. and Broadway."

The *Leviathan* represented the F. Scott Fitzgerald Roaring Twenties. In the words of her most famous master, Commodore Hartley, she was "the glamor ship of the age." Celebrities crowded her passenger lists. There were Will Rogers, Queen Marie of Roumania, General Pershing, Richard Byrd, Sir Thomas Lipton, Mrs. Woodrow Wilson and Gloria Swanson. Just as the *Leviathan* took on a completely new character under the American flag, so America was a new and different land in the twenties. As the title of André Siegfried's book *America Comes of Age* suggests, the United States had matured fast in those hectic years. Ours was a new international responsibility.

In one huge bound we had become a world power. It was too much for our head, and we grew giddy until brought back to reality by the depression. Our operation of the *Leviathan,* world's largest ship, was a play in the same character. After all, Germans had built the ship. Perhaps we were not yet ready for such a champion. It would take another decade and another war for our economy to produce a true American standard bearer of the superliner category. But she would come, and, strange to relate, it would be William Francis Gibbs who would design her. Mr. Gibbs was responsible for rebuilding the *Leviathan* in 1922-1923. He designed the *United States!*

The GREAT NORTHERN

"BACHELOR DECK FOR TIMID TOURISTS," said the headline of a New York paper January 8, 1915. "Will Be Novel Feature on Trips Through Panama

Built to compete with coastal railroads, the Great Northern *was America's fastest ship for years*

Canal," read the second part of the headline. The article, now a faded clipping, heralded the maiden voyage of a vessel that remains to this day the finest example of coastal ocean liner to fly the American flag—the *Great Northern*.

The bachelor deck idea may have had some slight news angle, but it was strictly a gimmick, as press agents say. As the new craft was built on the East Coast for service between San Francisco and Portland, her first voyage would be through the new Panama Canal. It was for this trip that her owners are reported to have advertised a special "bachelor deck" for men only. A similar novel feature was announced for the first run of her sister ship, the *Northern Pacific*. On these decks "the timid tourists will be perfectly safe" the imaginative reporter wrote. The *Great Northern* was to quickly prove that she did not need such press agentry to win her place among the most famous American ships. She lived to see yeoman service in both world wars in addition to having a highly successful peacetime career.

Just four weeks after the *Great Northern's* maiden voyage was announced, Germany proclaimed the waters around the British Isles a war zone. Five months later the Cunard liner *Lusitania* was sunk, with the loss of 1,198 men, women and children. With the destruction of British shipping by submarines, America was never in such need as then for ships of the size and speed of these two new coastal ocean queens to brave the submarine danger and keep the lines of communication with our future allies open.

Originally part of a great transportation dream of railroader James J. Hill, these two crack liners were 524 feet long and had a tonnage of 8,225. Each could carry 856 passengers in great luxury. It was the boast of their owners that they made the same time between San Francisco and Portland as did the railroad. They were billed as the twin palaces of the Pacific.

After heroic service in the World War I, during which time she made eighteen voyages to France, the *Great Northern* again returned to the West Coast. She was bought by H. F. Alexander who promptly renamed her after himself. She was the fastest ship under the American flag at that time and had made a world record round-trip voyage to Europe during the war of 12 days, 1 hour and 35 minutes. The *Leviathan* was a faster ship but was not in active operation in 1922.

Two crashes marred her first year with Alexander's Admiral Line but they only helped to establish the ship's reputation as unsinkable. Her sister had burned in February, 1922, and was a total loss. The old *H. F. Alexander* went on to become extraordinarily popular on the Coast. She was described in company folders as "one of America's truly great ships, the super ship *H. F. Alexander*. Telephones in every cabin, an orchestra which played during lunch and dinner and for dancing each evening and a children's play room were among her special features. "Ordinary clothing is recommended as it is not customary to dress for dinner," the folder added.

Renamed the *George S. Simonds* for her term of service in World War II as a transport, she operated in the North Atlantic, Mediterranean, around Africa and between Hampton Roads and Jamaica. The American Legion in its *Merchant Marine Bulletin* for July-August, 1954, referred to her as "one of the prettiest and best-loved small liners in the whole history of the American Merchant Marine and one of our most seasoned war veterans." She was scrapped at Philadelphia in 1948.

Built as a troopship, the President Harrison *became a world cruise liner, was finally captured by the Japanese*

PART EIGHT

We Become Merchant Marine Minded

Then with a rush we built the world's largest merchant marine. Of course none of the steel ships were ready in time for World War I but we were now really big time. New services branched out on all foreign trade routes including around the world. Coastwise shipping on the other hand was beginning to feel the competition of better roads for trucks and automobiles. Ships built in this period played vital parts in World War II, for which we were better prepared due to the 1936 Merchant Marine Act. This act recognized the need for subsidies for building and operating ships on overseas trade routes.

The PRESIDENT HARRISON

THREE hard-to-believe events took place in 1924 in connection with the opening of the first regular around-the-world steamship service by an American line.

The liner *President Harrison* inaugurated the run under the famed Dollar Line house flag. She was one of a large fleet of transports completed during World War I, but too late for service, and converted for passenger use. First, it was found that American officers who had circled the globe were not available for the maiden voyage. Second, maps of the Mediterranean and Indian Ocean had to be obtained from the British consulate in San Francisco. Third, when the American liner reached her first French port of call, the port officials there refused to accept American tonnage measurement and would have delayed the voyage had not our State Department intervened. American merchant ships were almost unknown in the Mediterranean. To such a low ebb had our merchant marine fallen since the Civil War, but it was rising again.

Ships were our "bridge to victory" in the first great war. Their construction was one of the production miracles that astounded Europe. Although we had sev-

153

eral major shipyards able to build large vessels, Uncle Sam was forced to build from scratch the giant shipbuilding plant at Hog Island, Pa., for the great effort. And none but a few wooden and concrete ships were ready in time. The concrete ships, particularly, created a great stir. They were failures. The wooden ships made excellent breakwaters after the war. Many of the steel ships rusted in laid-up fleet sites around our coast. Some were put to work, a few lasting to see duty in the second war. The *President Harrison,* built by the New York Shipbuilding Corp., was among the largest and best of this war-built armada.

Our experiment in government shipping operation was a failure, but it did lead to the establishment of a wide variety of privately-owned American lines, including some of the most important now in operation. Among the companies formed or given a big push in this era were American Export Lines, American Mail Line, Farrell Lines, Moore-McCormack Lines, Lykes Bros. Shipping Co., the Mississippi Shipping Co. and the United States Lines. Among the older companies which expanded rapidly were the Grace, Munson and Dollar lines.

The Dollar Line, now known as American President Lines, had begun in 1892 when its founder, goateed Capt. Robert Dollar, bought a little wooden steam schooner named the *Newsboy.* The line expanded steadily, first spreading across the Pacific and then in January, 1924, opening its around-the-world service, which it has maintained ever since.

Television star Art Linkletter made two voyages on the *Harrison* as a merchant marine cadet. He described his job as a combination quartermaster and seaman. He washed decks when he wasn't standing watch. One of his strongest memories is the midnight to 4 a.m. stint in the crow's nest.

"I'm afraid I went to sleep a lot," he remarked years later, "and every time I awakened, it seems I'd see a ship lit up like a Christmas tree only a few hundred yards away. It wasn't easy explaining," he added. Mr. Linkletter is now one of the owners of American President Lines.

A Japanese warship stopped the *Harrison* the day before Pearl Harbor, and allowed her to go on only after learning she was bound for China. A few hours after the attack on Hawaii had taken place she was run aground to avoid seizure by the Japanese. Two of her stewards fell from a lifeboat as they were leaving their ship and survived an ordeal that few have lived to tell about. Swept toward the ship's stern they were carried for three complete revolutions by the still-moving propeller.

The *Harrison* was later salvaged by the enemy only to be sunk in the China Sea by an American submarine. She was the largest American vessel to fall under Japanese control in World War II.

The AMERICAN BANKER

THEY had nothing to eat but a case of salmon and nothing to drink but whiskey. Their schooner, the *Pioneer*, had sprung a leak and was foundering. For two days they tossed in an October gale on the Atlantic. Then a big Japanese cargo liner hove into sight.

"If I'd had a rifle I would have taken a shot at those Japanese on the bridge of their ship," said the schooner captain later as he told reporters how the big freighter looked them over and went on her way without even notifying the Coast Guard of their plight.

"We were lashed to the rigging for a whole day after that, before we were picked up by the *American Banker*," he added. "It was lucky for us that an American ship came along, with an American captain who wasn't afraid and had some humanity."

The *Pioneer* had been flying the American flag upside down, her "I am in distress" code flags, and her code flag Z meaning "immediate help needed" when the Japanese ship passed her by. It was midnight when the lights of the *Banker* blinked into sight. To make sure he was seen, the schooner captain soaked a bundle of blankets in gasoline and hauled them into the rigging. Capt. Alfred M. Moore of the *Banker* saw the fire and changed his course to investigate. Once staff captain on the *Leviathan*, Capt. Moore proved his skill on this tricky occasion. Approaching as close as he dared, he dropped a lifeboat which picked up the five salmon-and-whiskey-sated seamen from the near-sinking schooner. Fluffy, the *Pioneer's* cat, was saved too, but got a soaking inside a laundry bag.

Countless other rescues seemed to fall the way of the *American Banker* and her six sister ships. All had been built as transports for World War I when we were caught with virtually no merchant marine in ocean service. All had been converted later into highly successful one-class passenger ships operated by the American Merchant Line between New York and London. Of the lot the *Banker* led a charmed life. At this writing, she is enjoying a new career as a Swiss luxury liner in North Atlantic service.

It could only happen on the *Banker* or one of her homey sisters. Imagine the passengers on a great luxury liner turning to during their crossing to decorate the smoking room and lounge with murals. Tony Sarg, Hubert Ripley, J. M. Hewlett, George Wharton Edwards, C. H. Walker, Philip H. Chadbourne were among the party which had chartered the entire ship. She could only carry eighty-five passengers. They were former students of the Ecole des Beaux-Arts and were returning to Paris for a reunion. Their artistic efforts have been hidden by the more modernistic decorations of the *Arosa Kulm*, the name which the sturdy *Banker* acquired in 1952.

Charles Lindbergh and his wife used the *Banker's* sister ship *American*

Importer to escape the sorrows that their home in America had for them after the kidnaping and murder of their son. Admiral Giles Stedman made his now-famous statement: "Plenty of oil and one big prayer did it" aboard the bridge of another sister ship, the *American Merchant*. He said this about the twelve-hour rescue of twenty-two British seamen from the sinking *Exeter City*. Another sister ship, the *American Shipper*, accidentally speared a whale in 1939. To disengage herself she had to reverse her engines and steam backwards. But it was the *Banker* whose life seemed to be charmed.

When World War II came, American ships were barred from the war zones by our Neutrality Act. A quick paper transaction gave them all new names and put them under the Belgian flag. With cargo popping out of every hatch and carrying huge deck loads these seven sisters sailed forth to face the German U-boats at their most ferocious worst. Six were sunk, several with large loss of life. Renamed *Ville D'Anvers*, the thinly-disguised *American Banker* sailed on. In October, 1943, she was hailed as the holder of "what may be the record for performance of a single ship in the battle of transportation." She had made thirty-eight crossings in the war zone without a scratch.

Once she was dogged by a submarine for twenty-four hours. Her master refuses to explain how he escaped, except to say he had just sailed in circles. Between 1940 and 1943 the 8,000-ton craft carried 100,000 tons of cargo, enough to supply 12,000 soldiers overseas for a month. She brought 25,000 tons of material home to support the war effort.

Little did the World War I equivalents of Rosie the Riveter know what powers of endurance they were building into the *American Banker*, launched as the transport *Cantigny* in 1920 at Hog Island. With two careers under the two names, *American Banker* and *Ville D'Anvers* behind her, she still had at least three more names to go in 1946 when the war ended. Sold to the famous Isbrandtsen Line, she hoisted the Honduran flag and operated a while as a freighter. Her fourth name was *City of Athens*. She won it to popularize a new service to Greece, this time under Panamanian flag, for Italian owners. Rebuilt to carry several hundred passengers, she passed through a most unsavory period. Eventually, she was libeled in Philadelphia and sold on auction block for $400,000 to cover claims of more than $1,000,000. What she did under her fifth name, *Protea*, is shrouded in obscurity, but she was finally picked up by an able and ambitious Swiss shipping man named Nicolo Rizzi. Mr. Rizzi founded the Arosa Line with the *American Banker* as his first passenger ship. Arosa is a resort town in Switzerland.

Originally the *American Banker* carried twelve passengers. This was increased to sixty-five, to eighty-five and then to 300. Under her new name of *Arosa Kulm* she was completely rebuilt in Germany to carry 982. In contrast to the simplicity of her days as an American Merchant Line ship, her public rooms were luxurious. She had a fancy bar, a veranda café, a knickknack store and even an outdoor swimming pool. Owned by a Swiss, flying the Panamanian flag,

A famed European leader christened her. Some say this is why the American Banker *leads a charmed life*

rebuilt in Germany, catering largely to Canadian immigrants, and with a mixed German-Italian crew, she was indeed a cosmopolitan.

She was more than that. Throughout her long career a strange association seemed to link this ship with Belgium. There was her somewhat unexpected transfer to Belgium registry. Then there was her positively charmed life under the great square black, gold and red flag. Finally there was the selection of the ancient Belgian city of Bruges as a port of call when the *Arosa Kulm* began her transatlantic service under the Arosa house flag. Zeebrugge, the ocean seaport of Bruges, had not been on the route of an Atlantic passenger ship service for decades.

This historic little liner would not serve for long under the Arosa house flag. The company went out of business in 1959 and the *Arosa Kulm* was scrapped.

Perhaps there is an answer to this string of links with Belgium. Paul E. R. Scarceriaux, President of the Belgian Nautical Research Association, recently unearthed what may be the source of all these coincidences. It so happened that when the *American Banker* was launched in 1920 she had a very special sponsor. He was a foreign war hero. He was making a triumphant tour of the United States and by chance happened to be in the area of Hog Island, where most of our vast World War I fleet was built. He was asked to officiate at the launching. He did. His name: Albert, King of Belgium.

The DORCHESTER

THE custom of naming ships with standard suffixes or prefixes is common practice. One famed American coastwise company had a naming system we think must have been unique. It was their habit to have one ship's name begin with each letter of the alphabet. All were named after counties in states served. For example in 1927 they had the *Alleghany, Berkshire, Chatham* and *Dorchester* as the first four ships in their fleet. Since they had only twenty ships they skipped a few letters, but the pattern was there.

The *Dorchester,* one of the three newest of the Merchants and Miners fleet, was destined to figure in one of the Second World War's sagas of heroism. She is the ship on which the four chaplains joined together as she was sinking, gave their lifebelts to others, and went to their death arm in arm. Two were Protestants, one Jewish and the fourth Catholic.

The *Dorchester,* new in 1926, was the last ship built for the famous Boston to Baltimore service founded in 1852. She was similar to the "City" boats of the Savannah Line, large, comfortable, reasonably fast. French telephones were in every cabin. Felt-lined windows eliminated the "annoying rattle often experienced with windows on board ship," it was stated. A berth light, thermos bottle and electric fan were in each room. All rooms had running hot and cold water, quite an innovation for her day. Three rooms and the four suites had private tub baths, while sixteen rooms had shower baths.

The sinking of the Dorchester *set the stage for the drama of the Four Chaplains in World War II*

With virtually every other coastwise liner, the *Dorchester* was taken over for the war effort. Her identical sister the *Chatham* was the first American troopship sunk in the war, going down en route from Nova Scotia to Greenland with the loss of twenty-seven.

The sinking of the *Dorchester*, February 3, 1943, was much more costly in human life. Of the 904 on board, 605 were drowned or froze to death before rescue came. The loss would have been even greater had not Coast Guard volunteers jumped into the icy waters in heavy rubber suits. Secured with lines from their ships these heroes helped the survivors to safety as many of them were too numbed to hold on to lines from rescue boats. Those of the *Dorchester's* naval guard who survived are convinced that their guns made the U-456 pay dearly for her conquest.

Government indifference, competitive factors such as the truck and airplane and the trebled cost of shipbuilding when the war ended, forced the *Dorchester's* owners to throw in the sponge. The line had no ships, could not afford new ones. It was liquidated along with many other famous old American coastal concerns. Gone were the colorful house flags of the Morgan Line, the Mallory Line, Clyde Line, Puerto Rico Line, Savannah Line, Eastern Steamship Lines, Colonial Line, Old Dominion Line and the Merchants and Miners Transportation Company.

Gone were most of the shipyards which built ships for these famous companies. A technological revolution had taken place of great significance to our pattern of transportation. Our coastal water routes were not empty, however, for as passenger liners went to the boneyard or were sold to foreign operators, more and more oil tankers entered the service. In 1955 one out of three ships in our merchant marine were tankers. No other ship type contributed more to our victories in World War II. No other vessel class means more to our daily economy in peace. Oil tankers circle our coast on all sides, inconspicuously but with the regularity of a fine watch. In never ending procession they distribute the wealth of our oil wells in the form of gasoline and petroleum products without which our economy would quickly rust to a halt.

Today the *Dorchester* and her four heroic chaplains are remembered by a wide variety of memorials. A swimming pool in the Bronx, an interfaith memorial plaque in Wakefield, Mass., another in Falls Church, Va., and a 3-cent United States postage stamp have all done honor to their sacrifice. Rep. Peter W. Rodino, Jr., of New Jersey, is seeking Federal recognition of the day the chaplains were lost as *Dorchester* day.

Guiding spirit in the construction in Philadelphia of the most extensive memorial, the Four Chaplains Chapel, was the Reverend Daniel A. Poling, editor of the *Christian Herald*. A letter to him by President Truman in 1947 was used in the campaign for funds. It began:

> The death of the four chaplains on Feb. 3, 1943, when the transport *Dorchester* was sunk by enemy action in the North Atlantic is an heroic event without a parallel in the American annals.

Father John P. Washington was the Catholic chaplain among the four. Rabbi Alexander D. Goode was Jewish. George L. Fox was Methodist. The fourth, a minister in the First Reformed Church, was Clark Vandersall Poling, Dr. Poling's son.

The DELTA QUEEN

HER maiden voyage, or so it was advertised, began June 2, 1948. It was a ten-day run from Cincinnati to Muscle Shoals on the Tennessee River and return. Fares ranged from a modest $112.50 to $200 for the voyage, remarkably economical in an era when ocean liners were getting from $20 to $70 a day for cruises. Later, cruises all the way to New Orleans and back were to be priced at only $225, and up. The *Delta Queen* was bound to be a success, and that she was. She still is today, for that matter. The *Delta Queen* is at this writing the only overnight passenger ship on the Ohio or Mississippi, a sharp contrast to the booming, prosperous horde of Diesel towboats (they actually are pushers) that have given our inland waterways new life in the past few years.

In a strict accounting of things one may say that the *Delta Queen* had had at least two other earlier maiden voyages. For example her hull had been put together on the River Clyde between 1924 and 1926, knocked down and sent by steamship to California. This was in effect her maiden, maiden voyage although she had yet to taste water along her keel. Her German-built wheel shafts and cranks were assembled upon her Scotch-built hull in sunny Stockton, Cal., where her four wooden passenger decks were added. And then another maiden voyage between San Francisco and Sacramento for the $875,000 sternwheeler. But life was only beginning. During the depression the great white queen and her sister, named *Delta King*, remained idle for a spell; then had several years of war service as ferryboats in San Francisco Bay.

The saga of the *Delta Queen* and how she was picked out of the drab idleness of a laid-up fleet after the war, taken around through the Panama Canal to New Orleans, up to Cincinnati and rebuilt preparatory to her maiden voyage under the Greene Line house flag is an epic of maritime courage. It has been told with all the enthusiasm of a true riverboat captain, the art of a writer of a best seller and the perspective of an historian by Capt. Frederick Way, Jr., who is in real life all three. His story is entitled *The Saga of the Delta Queen*.

It recounts with true relish how his friend Capt. Tom Greene sent him to California to prepare the 1,800-ton *Delta Queen* for her voyage. More than that, he was to have been her master on the 5,000 miles around. This phase of the saga is one of the most remarkable. The *Delta Queen*, despite her four decks of luxurious public rooms and cabins, was flat-bottomed and drew only seven feet of water. She made the voyage at the end of a towline, to the keen disappointment of Capt. Way. At the last moment he had been displaced by a union crew of ten officers and men. His story, somewhat bitterly describes how

With German engines, Scotch hull and California deck housing, the Delta Queen *is today pride of the Mississippi*

the union required him to hire, among others, a chief engineer at $1,260, an assistant engineer at $997.50 and a second assistant engineer at the same salary. All this despite the fact that the *Delta Queen* did not use her engines at all on the voyage.

When she reached New Orleans Capt. Way resumed command.

"When I signed on as captain at the New Orleans Custom House I harbored a curious feeling of becoming a custodian or curator rather than a river master," he wrote. As planked up for her ocean voyage, the *Delta Queen* looked like a huge piano box, cased two decks high with unpainted lumber. But this heavy protective layer all came off, and the *Delta Queen* was made ready for her trip to Cincinnati. This time his crew was hand-picked and of a completely different nature.

"A stranger crew of deckhands never ringed a timberhead on the Father of Waters," the saga goes on, for Capt. Tom Greene had invited all his big business friends to join him on the voyage. "A boiler explosion would have set the financial affairs of Cincinnati back on its heels for our generation," Capt. Way joked as his crew was continually augmented with big brass.

"Once when our paddle wheel broke down I counted $5,000,000 worth of talent scrambling around between the bucket planks armed with nuts, bolts and wrenches." But Capt. Way's greatest moment came as he walked ashore to inspect the mooring-line knot tied around a cottonwood tree.

"You Capt. Fred Way?" asked a farmer who stood nearby. "Been watching the papers since this boat was in California, like everybody else."

Later Capt. Way, in a letter to Fall River Line author Roger McAdam, told how he had profited from reading McAdam's book about the famed *Priscilla*. The conclusion of his letter links these two great river queens.

> What we have done, to all practical purposes, is to rescue the *Priscilla* of the Sacramento River and pump some new life in her and prolong her usefulness. Dismissing all sentiment in the matter, as a plain statement of 1948 facts, we couldn't have built nor procured a better steamboat than the *Delta Queen*. The combination of a steamboat company having ample finances and ambitions to excel in construction and accommodations doesn't happen every day on our rivers—when it does the result is a *Priscilla* or a *Delta Queen*. They're impossible to beat, by modern standards.

This fine vessel was still in service as the Second Edition of this work was issued, having survived a nationally-publicized battle over safety regulations between her operators and the Coast Guard. A much larger, and super-safe companion vessel, the *Mississippi Queen* was added to the service in 1976.

The PRESIDENT WARFIELD

WHEN the cool spring water from the sponsor's bottle splashed over the sharp white bow of the *President Warfield* on that sunny day in 1928, who could imagine what was in store for the sturdy little overnight boat? Within a year she was to be shelled by our own Coast Guard in a comic opera engagement. Within fifteen years she would be zigzagging in deadly seriousness with German subs all around. Finally she was to be the central figure in one of the most disgraceful episodes of violence and human misery, in Britain's resistance to the Jewish efforts to establish a nation in Palestine.

Her name, often confused with that of President Garfield when she was front-page news, was in honor of one S. Davies Warfield, President of the Baltimore Steam Packet Co., her owners. This gentleman, whose niece was to become the Duchess of Windsor, died before the vessel was completed. Instead of becoming the *State of Florida* as had been expected, the new craft was named after him.

Her melodrama with the Coast Guard took place in 1929. When she failed to heave to after a warning siren from a cutter, two blank shots were fired and finally a solid shot across her bow. The Coast Guard had been tipped off that contraband whiskey was aboard. It is said that 123 gallons of gin were found aboard in the rumble seat of an automobile. Another six gallons, labeled lobster and herring, were uncovered in lockers.

She was built as a coal burner but converted in 1933 to oil. A 1929 company folder describes how her boilers and engine "are enclosed in a steel wall to the hurricane deck, preventing any possibility of fire from this quarter." She was a sturdy ship, a fact that was to be emphasized in her last days by none other than a newspaper owned by Britain's Aneurin Bevan, then a member of Attlee's Cabinet. She was a fast ship, too, attested to by the song her engine-room crew composed during her World War II service. It was sung to the tune of "MacNamara's Band." It went in part:

> Oooooh, we call our ship the
> *Warfield*
> She's the finest in the fleet,
> And when it comes to making time
> She simply can't be beat.

After fourteen years of useful service on the Chesapeake Bay with two brief spells on Long Island Sound, the second and more violent phase of her career began. She became a part of the now-famous "skimming dish" convoy of coastal boats. The British desperately needed ships and they would take anything, even ferryboats. In the hectic passage that ensued three of the convoy were lost to the enemy. The *Warfield* got through. One torpedo missed her by only thirty feet. She had the pleasure of getting in several shots from her 12-pounder at one of the attacking wolf pack.

"The defense was so fierce that it could not be observed whether two or more of the transports hit, sank or not," Berlin radio reported. The Nazis later claimed to have sunk three ships of the *Queen Mary* class. Britain's King George decorated the *Warfield's* master, Capt. J. R. Williams, and her chief engineer for their heroic conduct on this crossing. Only five years later British warships were

The President Warfield, *as an overnight boat (top left), a Normandy invasion craft, and a damaged Israeli refugee ship*

to attack the same vessel and British sailors were to kill her First Mate, an American. But we are ahead of our story.

There was quiet before the storm. For several months the *Warfield* recovered from her perilous Atlantic voyage, serving as a training and barracks ship in an English harbor. Then she returned to the American flag, becoming the U.S.S. *President Warfield*. Thirty days after D-Day she ploughed across the Channel to Omaha Beach as a station ship. A spell of trooping on the Seine and her war days were over. Back home she came. She was a prime subject for the busy cameras of members of the Steamship Historical Society who in 1946 visited the fleet laid up in the James River, as guests of the Mariners' Museum at Newport News.

She was not idle long. She was sold to a shipwrecking firm for $8,028. Next and very secretly she was bought by Hagganah, the Palestine underground agency. The Zionists were openly fomenting revolt of the Jews in British-mandated Palestine as part of their campaign to create what is now the state of Israel.

After extensive repairs the *Warfield* set out for sea. Her destination was China, via Suez, it was reported. Unfortunately she ran into heavy weather, strained her seams and had to be rescued by the very Coast Guard cutter that had once stopped her with a shell, reports Alexander Crosby Brown.

"This unwelcomed spotlight increased the mystery surrounding her departure," Mr. Brown wrote in an article for *The American Neptune*.

Nevertheless she was soon off again and a curtain of darkness dropped around her movements. The British Government watched her closely, and warned France not to permit her to take on refugees for Palestine. She reached Marseilles in April, 1947, moved to La Spezia, Italy, and then back to Port le Bouc, France. Her French papers allowed her to sail in fine weather only and prohibited her carrying freight or passengers. Despite this and probably with sympathetic if unofficial approval of the French authorities, she proceeded to the French port of Sette where she took on board 4,554 Jewish passengers, more than twice the capacity of the *Queen Elizabeth*, world's largest ship.

The matter had now reached the highest levels of diplomacy. British Foreign Secretary Bevin wrote French Foreign Minister Bidault expressing his dismay, and protesting strongly at the French facilities given to the *President Warfield*. Mr. Bevin added that he intended to make an example of this ship by obliging her to return to the French port with all her passengers. The matter was headlined throughout the world. British warships followed the *Warfield*, which had been renamed *Exodus 1947*. Their frequent challenges were answered only by a blaring record of Elgar's famous British march "Pomp and Circumstance" played over the *Warfield's* loud-speaker system. It must have galled the British who doubtless had nothing but distaste for their job.

As the creaking *Exodus* approached within sight of the "promised land," five British destroyers and a cruiser closed in. The world watched. A special

United Nations committee on Palestine was in Jerusalem at the time. What happened is not a credit to the British Navy. As all attempts to make the *Exodus* stop failed, two British destroyers were ordered to come alongside and seize the ship. In doing so they rammed her, smashing in large sections of her main deck. Using tear gas, lead-tipped truncheons, strings of firecrackers, and, it was charged by her master, machine guns, the British seamen clambered aboard. The terrified Jews, well over half of whom were women and children, fought back with milk bottles, tin cans, sticks and potatoes. The British sailors forced their way into the pilot house and struck First Mate William Bernstein, a 24-year-old American. He died that night in a British hospital at Haifa. Two others were killed and over fifty wounded in the melee.

Had not the *Exodus* had a sturdy steel hull this pounding by two British destroyers might well have sunk her. How many of the helpless Jewish immigrants would have been saved in such an event can only be guessed. It was with this in mind that Mr. Bevan's newspaper noted that "a major tragedy was averted only because the *Warfield* was a strong ship and had exceptionally strong pumps."

The deed brought a wave of violence in Palestine. For days front-page stories described fanatical attacks on British police, bomb episodes and the like. A dusk-to-dawn house arrest was ordered for the 90,000 Jews in Jerusalem. Nights of panic followed as the underground capitalized on the despair of Jewish moderates over the return to France of the *Exodus's* passengers. Eight died and fifty-six were injured in a week in Jerusalem. A British troopship was sunk in Haifa.

"Why the British, intercepting the *Exodus*, failed to divert its passengers to Cyprus, as they had done in previous cases, remains a mystery," the New York *Times* wrote in an editorial two months later. Instead they were returned in several tortured stages to concentration camps in the one country they most loathed as the prime author of their misery, Germany.

As for the battered *Warfield*, she remained a revered hulk in Haifa harbor long after independence had been won for Israel. She was there long enough, an Israel steamship official told the author, to see "every one of her original passengers" who had survived, eventually reach Jerusalem after the British shackles had been thrown off.

Like the first *Bangor*, scrapped in Turkey in 1888, and the *James Baines*, which burned in Liverpool, the *Warfield* was never to return to the land of her birth. In fact she never sailed again, being tied up in Haifa until she burned to the water's edge in 1951. A beautiful model of the *President Warfield* was placed on exhibit in the Baltimore headquarters of the Old Bay Line, operators in 1955 of the only overnight passenger boat service on America's Atlantic, Gulf and West Coasts.

The war which brought such adventures to America's coastwise merchant ships proved the catalyst which more than anything else was their undoing. The great industrial surge which war production stimulated, inflated prices to such an extent that postwar replacement of the coastal fleet proved impractical. There were no new *Yales, Great Northerns, Dorchesters* or *President Warfields.* Fortunately for the United States the nation had become merchant marine minded as never before. The 1936 Merchant Marine Act had established a system of government aid for ships on ocean services. A nucleus fleet of new tonnage was on hand when World War II came. America emerged from the war with the world's largest deep-sea merchant marine.

The *Exodus 1947* burned in Haifa harbor and her hulk was still there as the Second Edition went to press. It is hoped that some day it will be refloated and rebuilt to serve as a monument, for she is one of the world's most famous ships.

The URUGUAY

AS the United States grew bigger, individual ships played a smaller and smaller part in our history. No longer were there outstanding names as *Mayflower,* such a basic part of our heritage, or *Columbia,* so important in our territorial development. The nation's merchant marine as a whole continued to serve our economic and social advancement. There still were ships, nevertheless, which took their turn as leading actors on the stage of America's history. One of these was the *Uruguay.*

> And see! she stirs!
> She starts,—she moves,—she seems to feel
> The thrill of life along her keel.

This snatch of a Longfellow poem was fixed permanently in the author's mind in 1927. It was used as a series of captions under pictures of the launching of the *California,* later the *Uruguay,* at Newport News, Va. The new liner was the first passenger ship built to have turbo-electric propulsion.

Electric drive was a refinement of the turbine. It provided a more economical method of connecting the high-speed turbine unit with a necessarily slow-moving propeller shaft. It also gives superb maneuverability. Following successes with the *California,* electric drive was fitted on many ships, including the great French superliner *Normandie.*

The *California* was not the largest merchant ship ever built in America, despite reams of publicity releases to this effect, by Winfield M. Thompson, of the International Mercantile Marine, her owners. Her original name and the trade route she was built to serve, in fact, even her external appearance were to change before she really found her place in history. Although she served successfully on the run between New York and San Francisco for a decade,

Christened California, *this great liner became famous as F.D.R.'s "Good Neighbor Fleet" flagship* Uruguay

she is best remembered during this era as being the ship on which labor leader Joseph Curran rose to fame as founder of the National Maritime Union.

Curran's strike, a shift in government mail policy and a visit of state to

South America by the late President Franklin D. Roosevelt were to mean an entirely new career for the *California*. The President was startled to find American prestige at a low ebb in the lands below the Equator, in South America. He learned, too, that very few South Americans came to the United States as tourists and that South American business men looked to Europe for their raw materials and finished goods. What we needed to change all this was, in his own words, a "good neighbor fleet." Government mail payments had gone a long way toward making the intercoastal service of the Panama Pacific Line a success. When the basis for these payments was altered so as generally to exclude the *California* and her two sister ships *Virginia* and *Pennsylvania,* the line took them out of service. Labor strife also played a part in this decision. The ships were available. At the President's direction, they were renamed, rebuilt and turned over to Moore-McCormack Lines for operation as the Good Neighbor Fleet to South America's East Coast.

As the *Uruguay,* the *California* lost her two short smokestacks and gained a giant streamlined funnel. She was a beauty. Along with the *Brazil,* formerly the *Virginia,* and the *Argentina,* originally the *Pennsylvania,* the *Uruguay* rapidly fulfilled the President's dream. Then came World War II.

No more useful troopships operated in World War II than this trio of fast liners. They served on every ocean.

One of the war's strange accidents took place aboard the *Uruguay*. She was in collision with a Navy tanker near Bermuda in 1943. The tanker, a part of the *Uruguay's* convoy, zigged when she should have zagged. Thirteen lives were lost, the only fatalities that marred the war careers of the three Moore-McCormack liners. At the time of the crash one of the *Uruguay's* soldier passengers was asleep in the sick bay. He never knew what hit him. He awoke to find himself shivering and damp on the fore deck of the Navy oiler. She was slowly backing away from the gaping hole made in the big liner's side. He was uninjured.

Reconverting the *Uruguay* after the war was no small problem. Much larger crew quarters and a completely new standard of safety features were placed in concentric circles. A bronze piece of sculpture, entitled "Spirit of the colored colonial interiors of the *California*. The rebuilt dining saloon was a com- required. Passenger spaces were modern, completely different from the prune- bination dining room, moving picture theater and night club. Tables were North Star, Guardian of the Seamen," was the room's focal point. A large, round, removable smorgasbord table was located in the center of the room. It could be removed when the space was needed as a dance floor.

The success of the *Uruguay* in the postwar years was due in part to the growing awareness of the place of South America in our sun. Mooremack's James F. Roche said in 1955 that one of his chief aims as publicity director for the line was to sell South America as a place to travel. No effort was spared, at the same time, to make the passengers happy. "Give them more than they expect," was the motto.

An illustration of how this thinking was used to make capital out of what would have been a bad break is seen in an episode that happened in 1952. The *Uruguay* with 322 passengers struck a submerged object and bent one of the propellers. Excessive vibration forced her to turn toward the Newport News shipyard, place of her birth. The whole event was turned into a special treat for the passengers. Rows of quickly-hired busses met them at the pier and they were whisked off on a tour of historic Williamsburg. Although their ship was in drydock, the evening was spent on board with a special vaudeville show and the customary moving picture. On the following day another excursion was arranged, this time to Yorktown. The ship sailed the next day and was able to make up the lost time, returning to New York on schedule after her thirty-eight-day cruise.

In 1954 the *Uruguay* was taken out of service. Still looking modern, the big ship made a lonely passage to the fleet of idle ships in the James River, Va. Well beyond the average twenty-year life of a ship, she was anchored side by side to a row of red-leaded *Liberty* ships held in reserve for a future emergency. Queen of the James River fleet she was pushed around a bit by Hurricane Hazel in the late summer of 1954.

This gallant steamship and her two historic sister ships were laid up in 1960 and scrapped shortly thereafter!

The CITY OF NEW YORK

SHE had sailed in peace, but was returning in war. She was the *City of New York,* of Farrell Lines, or, the American South African Line as it was known in 1942. And then a torpedo struck.

The *City of New York* was doomed. Her wound was a vital one and there was no time to lose in abandoning ship. It was March 29, 1942. They were off Norfolk, but far out of sight of land and alone. On the ship's slanting deck was a pregnant woman and her two-year-old daughter. The expectant mother had been of much concern to the ship's surgeon, Dr. Leonard H. Conly. Capt. Sullivan and Dr. Conly had a plan, however, for just such an emergency. Mrs. Desanka Mohorovicic had been assigned a special lifeboat place and Dr. Conly would go in the same boat.

But the best-laid plans go awry at times, particularly aboard a great liner which was to sink in nineteen minutes. As the lifeboat was lowered a wave smashed it against the ship's side. Dr. Conly was injured. Mrs. Mohorovicic had fallen while leaving the ship and hurt her legs. Capt. Sullivan stayed at the bridge until the last, finally swimming off as the vessel disappeared beneath him. He swam to the lifeboat that had Mrs. M. in it and from then on personally navigated the craft with its precious cargo. It was noon; the survivors were huddled in lifeboats scattered about on the debris-littered sea. Their home for the past weeks had disappeared below the waves. They were happy to be alive. Yet for the moment their own fears were forgotten. All eyes followed the captain's boat.

They saw gallant sailors hustle to raise a sail to protect Mrs. M. from the spray which made constant bailing necessary. The doctor might have been seen taking his instruments out of the boat's well-stocked first-aid kit. A strong young seaman supported Mrs. M. as her hour approached. She was a Yugoslavian, the wife of the consul from that nation in New York. She was more than that, she was a Spartan, in the words of James A. Farrell, Jr., President of the Farrell Lines. Night fell, but few slept.

We can imagine the emotion that must have been in the hearts of those in nearby boats when the new baby's first cries floated over the lonely waves at 2:30 a.m. March 30. It was a boy, healthy and normal in every way. He was quickly wrapped in a turban offered by another woman passenger in the boat. For sixteen hours the child was kept warm under his mother's life jacket. Mrs. Mohorovicic's absolute faith in God saved her during these hours, she said later, and kept her from becoming panicky. How great her joy must have been, however, when over the wave crests loomed the gray outline of a United States destroyer.

A warm bed and the best possible care were quickly given the mother, her little daughter and the tiny new passenger. When the mother had recovered enough to sit up, the destroyer's captain paid her a courtesy call. Her first question surprised him. She wanted to know the name of his ship, she wanted to name her baby after the destroyer. And so it was that the baby became Jesse Roper Mohorovicic. At this writing, in 1955, he is a growing, towheaded and perfectly normal Brooklyn lad.

"He wants to join up with us," reported Walter McCormick, passenger manager of Farrell Lines, owners of the *City of New York*. "He wants to go to sea as a cadet on a Farrell Lines ship."

The *City of New York* was America's first Diesel passenger ship. She was a comfortable ship, the first American vessel built for foreign trade with a construction loan under the 1928 Jones-White Act. This act recognized the importance of restoring the American flag to the high seas. The lessons of World War I had not been entirely forgotten. The millions wasted on Hog Island-type ships, none of which were finished in time to serve, were constantly called to the public's attention by the acres of laid-up shipping. We could not count on having giant enemy ships like the *Leviathan* to be seized as transports. Neither could we expect coastal ships like the *Great Northern* or the *Yale* to fill the bill. New ocean ships were needed to link our farms and industries to foreign markets. The 1928 law began a revival of our deep-sea shipping which was to culminate in the momentous 1936 Merchant Marine Act, known as the Magna Carta of the merchant marine.

Farrell Lines began their service to Africa shortly after World War I. They represented one of the new shoots of our reborn maritime enterprise. No foreign ship lines had brought goods directly on a scheduled basis to the United States

Shown off Capetown, the City of New York's *sinking in 1942 produced one of the war's great human interest stories*

from South Africa since the turn of the century, when an American sailing ship operation had ceased. Instead, cargo had to be shipped first to England and then here. Since America was changing from a debtor to a creditor nation, it was vital that we have every facility for direct trade to foreign areas. This Farrell Lines provided.

The *City of New York* was their crowning achievement in their first decade of service. She was America's first passenger ship to Africa. As war clouds gathered three new luxury liners were built, only to be taken over as transports when war came. Today the Farrell Lines house flag is carried on a large fleet of modern freighters and on two passenger liners, named appropriately, *African Endeavor* and *African Enterprise*.

The *SANTA CLARA*

FORMED in 1894, the Grace Line has one of the longest and most illustrious histories of America's steamship companies. The twin-screw, electric-drive *Santa Clara* was one of the company's most successful ships. Her unfortunate loss off Normandy on D-Day plus one was a heavy blow. The fact that it did not turn out to be a great tragedy is a tribute to her able captain and to the British and American navies as well as to her sturdy construction. She was built by the New York Shipbuilding Corp., Camden, N. J.

South America's increasing importance to our economy and security is nowhere better illustrated than in the expansion of the Grace Line. Its green smokestack, with white band and black top, has become a familiar sight throughout Latin America. The Grace Line today is the oldest American steamship line in ocean service offering passenger and freight service under one continuous management.

A medium-sized luxury liner, the *Santa Clara* was nine years old when World War II came. She had established a reputation for service on the run between New York and South America's West Coast, via the Canal. After Pearl Harbor she was quickly taken over by the War Shipping Administration and converted in jig time into a troopship. Instead of 200 passengers lolling in luxury on her decks she was re-equipped to carry 2,074 troops. The Government renamed her *Susan B. Anthony*, in honor of the famous suffragist. One round trip to Australia and return to New York with one stop at San Francisco found her taken over by the Navy. She participated in the North African invasion, in which two of her slightly larger sister ships, the *Santa Elena* and the *Santa Lucia*, were sunk. Two other Grace Line Santa ships were part of the mammoth African invasion flotilla.

A year and a half later, she was off Normandy with dive bombers, flying shells and smoke creating an inferno all around her. Aboard were 2,317 troops, a full load. Her master was Capt. Thomas L. Gray, a former Grace Line skipper.

Grace Line's luxury liner Santa Clara *when new, and just about to disappear off Normandy beachhead after hitting a mine*

She was approaching occupied France under a hail of enemy fire. Suddenly with a dull thud she struck a mine.

It was a crippling blow. Capt. Gray knew his ship was doomed. He maneuvered the troops from side to side as she settled, using them as counter-flooding weight to keep the transport on an even keel. As told to the author some years later, the fact that not a single soul was lost was largely due to the bravery of British and American rescue craft. They came alongside moments before the *Santa Clara* sank and took all sorts of risks getting the troops off.

The last few men aboard the sinking liner, including Capt. Gray, dove off as she slowly rose at the bow and began to slip under the waves. A photograph taken at the last moment shows her forward funnel top, inches from the water's edge, still blowing forth columns of white steam and smoke. Fifty feet of her keel at the bow are out of water. Capt. Gray, who received high Navy commendation for his handling of this affair, served briefly after the war as labor advisor to the Grace Line. He has since retired to a farm, the goal of ninety-five per cent of all seafarers.

The Grace Line has a new *Santa Clara*. She is one of nine sleek new sisters, each of which carries fifty-two passengers and a large cargo of freight. With the *Santa Rosa* and *Santa Paula*, big passenger ships, this gives Grace the largest fleet of passenger liners under the Stars and Stripes.

The latest *Santa Clara* has already made a name for herself. In 1947 she reported having struck a forty-five-foot sea monster with an eel-like head. The animal, whose body was about three feet in diameter, was said to have been wounded or killed by the collision. It was last seen thrashing "in a large area of bloody water and foam," according to Chief Officer William Humphries.

PART NINE

Today's Beauties

World War II demanded more ships than any other war. The merchant fleets of all our allies put together were not enough. Our small new fleet was only the beginning. We built about three new ships for every four that existed when war started. Our expanded postwar economy has put many of these ships to good use. No longer is America self-sufficient. Ships, American ships on every ocean, are needed to insure our exports and imports. Without them the products of our farms and factories might pile up on our docks, freight rates might skyrocket. America has again resumed her rightful place among the maritime powers of the world.

The LURLINE

NEWS of the Japanese attack on Pearl Harbor was rushed to the bridge at 10:15 in the morning as the great white luxury liner *Lurline* was homeward-bound from Honolulu. Watertight doors were closed, a blackout was organized, plans for security were made and then the ship's passengers were called together in the lounge. Captain C. A. Berndtson, Commodore of the Matson Line, explained the situation to his tense guests. His ship's powerful turbines were pushing the 631-foot liner through the Pacific at her maximum speed of twenty-two knots. It was a race for life, for reports of Japanese submarines were being picked up on all sides.

Hours later as the *Lurline* sped through the moonlit night, passengers clad in life jackets strode her broad wooden decks. They prayed silently for the protection of fog or rain. Neither came. Word that the *President Harrison* had been captured by the Japanese came in over the wireless. The American carrier *Langley* was reported damaged in Manila by a Japanese air attack. An Army transport was torpedoed. The Rose Bowl game was shifted from Pasadena, Cal., to Durham, N. C., and real Rose Bowl roses were quickly transported to the

Duke University stadium to give authenticity to the occasion. The *Lurline* raced for home.

Built in Quincy, Mass., in 1932, the *Lurline* was flagship of the Matson Line whose famed West Coast service linked Continental America to the Hawaiian Islands. With her sister ships *Mariposa, Monterey,* and the slightly smaller *Matsonia,* the *Lurline* flew one of the proudest house flags in American shipping. She was especially designed for tropical travel, and boasted a cork lining as insulation along her hull. An unusual feature was a men's club room, whose confines were prohibited to women.

Three days after Pearl Harbor the *Lurline* slipped silently under the Golden Gate Bridge. It was 2 a.m., but no formalities held her up in the outer harbor. She docked shortly afterward and her passengers were whisked through immigration at top speed.

"We turned her around to replenish the garrison at Honolulu," wrote Hugh Gallagher, Matson Vice President. "We did the job in six days, ripping out all the fancy stuff and making her into a troop transport. If you want any material on this, I can give you plenty."

The *Lurline's* war service demonstrated to perfection the value of government aid in her construction and of her operating subsidy. Without large liners of this type our war effort in the Pacific would have been gravely handicapped. There simply were no foreign ships to use. The principle underlying both her building and running subsidy was a simple one, evolved after years of debate and argument. It was to the effect that if an American shipowner is willing to accept the burdens and expenses of American-flag operation, the Government will compensate him for the difference in cost, American vs. foreign. Both American shipbuilding and ship-operating cost factors are substantially higher than foreign, due to our higher standard of living. Keen foreign competition at the same time requires that American ship lines charge the same passenger fares and freight rates as do their foreign rivals.

The *Lurline's* gleaming whiteness was soon covered with admiralty gray. Her sumptuous fittings were removed or boarded up. Great overstuffed chairs were replaced with tiers of bunks. Galley equipment to feed thousands was hastily installed, and, in less than a week, she was under way again. Aboard were 3,292 troops, as well as bombs, ammunition and supplies. With her steamed her running mates *Matsonia* and *Monterey,* both of which had been taken over for war service even before Pearl Harbor. Her wartime experiences, largely in the Pacific, would fill an exciting book. Her great speed enabled her to go it alone without convoy and she seemed to lead a charmed existence.

When peace came, the *Lurline* was reconverted at the astonishing cost of $20,000,000. She had cost only $8,000,000 to build at Bethlehem Steel Company's Quincy, Mass., yard. Raymond Loewy was in charge of recreating her interiors. Loewy, who has designed everything from fountain pens to airplanes, was called

The great white Lurline, *whose name is synonymous with the last word in luxury, flagship of Matson Lines*

America's foremost industrial designer. He has described his *Lurline* job in this way:

"We translated the gay, relaxed atmosphere of Hawaii into the ship's design so that a passenger's island vacation begins the minute he steps aboard the *Lurline.*"

Real beds which recessed into the wall during the daytime, air conditioning, private baths in every first-class cabin and a generous splash of modern furnishings and color combined with fireproof construction to make for the utmost in luxury and safety.

The *Lurline's* master, Captain Harold Gillespie, was made Commodore of Matson's fleet in 1955. Known as one of the best in the business, "Handsome Harold" has become a legend on the Hawaiian route.

His favorite answer to the query as to why ships are called "she" is the familiar line: "Because their rigging costs more than the hull." He can alternate this with, "because they require a lot of paint." The following brief yarn, which we credit to Bennett Cerf, might well be listed under the title, "Why Captains Grow Gray." A timorous lady passenger is the heroine. She boarded the *Lurline* hours before sailing time. Wandering around in a daze in the magnificent and ultramodern surroundings, she accidentally walked off the vessel without realizing it, into the equally sumptuous pier waiting room. Thinking she was aboard, she waved cheerily when she saw the great white hull moving slowly, believing the passengers crowding the rails were seeing the ship off. When, at long last, she realized her error, she became hysterical. However, alert company officials soothed her and quickly amended matters by escorting her out to the *Lurline* in a small power boat.

The *Lurline* was sold in 1963 to the Chandris Line, a Greek company, re-named *Ellinis*. As of the Second Edition she was still in service, carrying American cruise passengers and others.

The SEATRAIN TEXAS

SOME chapters back we said that single ships were not playing quite as out-standing parts as did such craft as the *Mayflower* and the *Columbia*, which almost singlehanded helped to shape our history. If there is an exception to the rule, the story of the *Seatrain Texas* fits the bill. Under extraordinary circum-stances and against great odds she delivered a cargo which stopped Hitler's advance in Africa and marked the beginning of the end for the Third Reich.

It was July, 1942. General Bernard L. Montgomery's British forces were battered and reeling. Tobruk had fallen and Field Marshal Rommel was ad-vancing triumphant. Radio Berlin crowed with confidence, "Cairo will be ours within a month." Winston Churchill appealed personally to President Roosevelt. Every effort was made to produce the vital tanks and armor-piercing weapons that Montgomery must have. In ten days American labor and capital strove side by side producing, as never before, these vital war goods under an emer-gency order labeled "ZZ-2." A convoy of six freighters, loaded to their marks and below, set sail July 13. This was less than two weeks after the cry for aid flew across the Atlantic from 10 Downing Street to the White House. In the center of the convoy was the *Fairport*, loaded with the most vital cargo of all—new tanks. Six days out a single enemy "sub" broke through the destroyer screen and fired four torpedoes. One hit. It hit the *Fairport* and she went down like a rock, carrying the precious tanks. Without them the convoy, which reformed and went on toward Suez via Capetown, was a dagger without a point. Some-thing had to be done, and quickly, too.

Again the wires between London and Washington buzzed. More tanks, and fast, or all Africa might be lost. There was a ship riding at anchor in New York which upon close examination seemed ideal for the mission. She would have to be large. She would have to be fast. She would have to have cargo booms which could lift the heaviest cargoes. All these the *Seatrain Texas* had; she had been built only two years before for the New York to Texas coastal service. In 1929, the original *Seatrain* had shocked the American shipping world with her revolutionary construction for carrying on tracks in her hull, full-loaded rail-road freight cars. Some men thought the idea was so good it was unfair com-petition. The company prospered and built new ships. The newest was the *Texas*.

The *Texas* had already performed heroic war service. Her giant holds were ideal for tanks. On one of her missions she had rescued the only three survivors

She helped throw Rommel out of Africa. The Seatrain Texas, *forerunner of a new type in coastal ships*

from the sinking of the *City of Atlanta,* old Savannah Line steamer which took forty-four down with her to their death. This was one of those ghastly episodes of the war, with the U-Boat surfacing and coldly playing its small searchlight over the tortured faces of the drowning American seamen for ten minutes. Capt. Kenneth G. Towne, master of the *Texas,* was rushed to conference with Navy officials. It would be his job to get 250 tanks to Montgomery in time. He would proceed at top speed and go it alone.

"Roosevelt is issuing the orders on this himself," one Admiral told him in confidence.

It took eighteen days to get to Capetown, but her sixteen and a half knots was probably twice the speed of the original convoy, and to Capt. Towne's pride and surprise he found its five surviving ships at anchor beneath the towering platform of Table Rock. They had left Brooklyn over two weeks earlier than the *Texas,* which had been named "Treasure Ship" by British code masters.

A corvette flying the Free French flag escorted the hulking *Texas,* the like of which had never been seen before in that area, up through the dangerous Mozambique channel. In parting, seamen from the *Texas* loaded a wooden raft with matches, candy, magazines and razor blades, and let it drift back to within reach of the French craft.

"Thanks. We never expected to find a Santa Claus this far from home. God be with you!" came a message by flag signal.

Near the mouth of the Gulf of Aden another message came through. It was by wireless, and it was so badly garbled that no one could make head or tail of it. "Forget it," the Captain said, fearing to break radio silence. Another vessel, an Italian submarine, heard the message, however, and decoded it with a captured code book. The submarine immediately changed her course and moved to a spot outside Socotra Island. Meanwhile the *Texas* proceeded through a narrow channel between Cape Guardafui and the Island. She was safe. Later Capt. Towne was told what the message had been. It had warned him to change his course and pass the island on the outer side to avoid the submarine. By its failure to come through clearly, the message was a success. The enemy had missed by a hair his last chance to destroy the ship which was to cost them the African campaign.

Thirty-five days out of Brooklyn, and way ahead of the original convoy, the *Texas* reached her destination. British stevedores were on board before her lines were secure. Her great 70-ton booms were swinging the tanks onto the broiling sand-strewn dock of Port Taufiq in a matter of minutes. Three days later, while the original convoy was still out of sight, the tanks went into battle. They spearheaded the attack which was to destroy Rommel and turn his advance into Hitler's first retreat of the war.

At this writing the *Texas* is back in her customary peacetime role. Her black funnel, placed aft as on tankers, boasts its customary white band with red railroad track, symbolic of her service. She is one of six seatrains serving between New York and Savannah, New Orleans and Texas City. Three others of the fleet also saw heroic war service.

No longer do shipping men wail at the competition from this new type craft. Many plans are being laid to copy the basic idea developed with the seatrain. Combination railroad-car and truck-trailer carrying ships are on the drawing boards of a dozen companies. The word "seatrain" is now a regular term used to describe a well-accepted ship type.

Here is a postscript. One of the Army gun crew aboard the *Texas* on her epic voyage was Arthur G. Suss, of Maspeth, Long Island. He is the son-in-law of Mrs. Margaret Meyer. "Marge" Meyer did most of the typing of this book.

The PRESIDENT CLEVELAND

EVER since the tiny *Enterprise* made her historic voyage to Canton right after the Revolution, American ships have been a leading factor in Pacific shipping. The first steamship to cross the Pacific was an American liner, the *Monumental City*. Our Pacific Mail initiated the first regular transpacific liner service. American ships have been important instruments in our Eastern policy. The opening of Japan was accomplished by our Navy with the aid of merchant vessels. Trade with the Orient has long been a magnet engaging the interest of all phases of

Queen on the Pacific, the President Cleveland, *standard bearer of American President Lines' Oriental service*

American enterprise. That the highest hopes have not yet been altogether fulfilled is not the fault of shipping. Today we lead on the Pacific as in no other maritime sphere. We have more ships, finer ships and deeper roots in shipping services in this vast region.

In point of size our flagship on the Pacific is the *President Cleveland,* featured in this chapter.

> We welcome you with sincere pleasure as a guest of the American President Lines, and assure you of every effort on the part of the officers and crew to make your voyage comfortable and one which you will long remember with pleasure and satisfaction.

So begins the red-and-gold brochure passed out to each passenger aboard the beautiful *President Cleveland* and her sister, the *President Wilson.* The only regular passenger liner service under the American flag across the Pacific, American President is in a sense the direct inheritor of the traditions of the great Pacific Mail, proudest of all American deep-sea lines. Just reading the colorful literature put out by the line makes the most confirmed landlubber long for the sea. Generations of experience have made APL well aware of what the traveler needs. A brief description of the ship's officers with their different armbands, a page of nautical terms "to add to the fun of the first-voyager," and a table showing how time is kept by the ship's bell are also included in the "Guest List" brochure.

Do you play bridge, or canasta, or even cribbage? A special member of the ship's entertainment staff is assigned for each of these games. So there are also specially designated instructors for mahjong, ping-pong and shuffleboard. Although a steady schedule of sports, horse-racing games, concerts and dancing is programed, the passenger is reminded in a chatty sort of way that he may ignore them all and just relax in the sun to his heart's content. Twelve times around the promenade deck make a mile.

Surprises await the new voyager at every turn. The menus will probably stagger him. Menu art has been highly developed on today's passenger liners. Bright colors, classical or modern designs of museumlike beauty match the truly fabulous selection of foods on the business side of these menus. A scrutiny of the six principal entrees offered on five successive days aboard the *President Cleveland* showed only one duplication. Fifteen types of cheese, thirteen varieties of dressings, over sixty different appetizers make the most seasoned epicure pause.

Largest vessel ever built on the West Coast the *Cleveland* went into service late in 1947. She had been laid down as a giant P2-type transport but altered at the shipyard to be the nation's first major postwar luxury liner. A novel feature which attracted wide attention was the use of aluminum. Her twin modernistic smokestacks were aluminum as were her topmost deck houses, lifeboats and decorative trim. All this improved stability. Two separate engine rooms, a feature demanded by the Navy, make the *Cleveland* less vulnerable to torpedo attack. Like all other modern American liners, national defense features were incorporated into her design from the keel up and paid for by Federal government grants to enable rapid conversion into a transport.

To serve her passengers' needs the *Cleveland* employs some sixty in her deck department, eighty engineers, about 200 stewards and cooks, some twenty in the purser's department and half a dozen concessionaires.

Harbor boats tied down their whistles on Dec. 27, 1947, when the sleek *Cleveland* re-established steamship travel to the Orient on her maiden voyage. It was a great day. Six years of wartime sailings and troopship austerity had whetted the appetites of San Franciscans for a bang-up confetti-and-colored-serpentine streamers-type old-time sailing. They got it. Escorting planes roared overhead. Thousands jammed Pier 44 to wish the new queen of the Pacific *bon voyage*. Bands played. The crowd sang "Auld Lang Syne" and "Aloha." Never before had the great red- and blue-smokestacks with their white eagles looked so proud.

George Killion, President of the line, called the maiden sailing "an event of national importance for America's postwar merchant marine, symbolizing as it does the hope for many new such liners necessary for national defense and to transport our overseas commerce." More than 4,000, including then Gov. Earl Warren, had been wined and dined at three sumptuous functions aboard the new liner before the sailing. This resumption of transpacific service came just eighty years after the *Colorado* inaugurated regular steamship service from San Francisco to the Orient under the American flag.

The *President Cleveland* and *President Wilson* were sold to the Orient Overseas Line and renamed *Oriental Empress* and *Oriental President*. The oil crisis caused them to be laid up and the *Oriental President* was scrapped in 1974. The *Oriental Empress* remained laid up at this writing, but was not thought to be long for this world, a sad ending for two fine ships.

The DEL NORTE

SPANISH explorer Cabeza de Vaca first saw the mouth of the great Mississippi in 1528. DeSoto traveled it in 1542. Bienville from France founded New Orleans, 110 miles above its mouth, as its great seaport in the year 1718. And yet it was not until World War I that regular American-flag services out of this great Mississippi Valley area were commenced. In 1919 five New Orleans men pooled $50,000 to form the Mississippi Shipping Co. and to begin two-way service to Brazil and South America's East Coast. They were a warehouse owner, two river barge men, a coffee merchant and a banker.

By 1947, their company, best known as the Delta Line, had become a large

The Del Norte, *Delta Line's streamlined coffe liner. Ultramodern from bow to stern she has the new look in ships*

and successful corporation, both in operations and financial strength. A year before that this company had put into service the *Del Norte*, first of three ultramodern, new passenger-cargo liners costing over $7,000,000 each.

Ever since the Ark, ships have had sheer, that is, they have curved down from the bow to a low point in the center of the hull and then up again toward the stern. Ever since the *Savannah*, smoke has come out of smokestacks. But ship designer George Sharp held nothing sacred. As he had done with the three government-owned passenger liners *Panama*, *Ancon* and *Cristobal* before World War II he did again on the new Delta ships. He designed the *Del Norte*, *Del Sud* and *Del Mar* without sheer except for their bow sections. This gives the public rooms an almost perfectly flat deck. With these Delta ships he went even one step farther. Although they are steamships and have the normal amount of smoke that all oil burners have, their great tear-drop aluminum smokestack is one in name alone. Inside are the living quarters for the radio officers, the radio rooms and an emergency generator. The smoke is carried away through two tall, black-tipped pipes just behind the stack. They look like king posts, as the stubby cargo boom masts on modern liners are called.

The *Del Norte* is the first major liner with no upper berths. In her larger cabins there are two beds and a couch which may be opened to become a double bed. Widespread use of aluminum and glass presaged the techniques used in the superliner *United States*. Air conditioning even throughout the crew's quarters make for comfort in tropical travel. Regular casement windows illuminate every stateroom in place of the customary port holes. Some 119 passengers can be carried, in addition to 7,500 tons of cargo.

The sleek craft gains further streamlined appearance from her forward semi-circular house which encloses two decks of radial cabins around a core in the form of a stairway, which descends four decks to her dining saloon. An elevator pampers the taste for luxury. Sand-colored tile and Lido beach umbrellas surround a large outdoor swimming pool. Rates vary from a minimum of $900, for the 42-day cruise, to $3,240.

The 60,000,000 inhabitants of the Mississippi Valley have reason to be proud of New Orleans, their outlet to world markets. They are proud also of the Delta Line luxury liners, largest American passenger ships using the Louisiana port. New Orleans grew in leaps and bounds between 1919 and 1955. It became a serious rival to New York. It is home port to the three largest United Fruit passenger ships; the three Alcoa passenger ships, to be described below, and the three Delta passenger ships, as well as Delta's large fleet of freight vessels. It is also the base of operations for the fabulous Lykes Bros. cargo fleet, largest under the American flag.

With certain place name substitutions, the following Delta Line advertisement could stand for the credo of the entire Amerian Merchant Marine:

> Delta Ships are unofficial envoys of the United States. They carry, as part of their cargo, friendship between the Americas. When a Delta vessel docks at a Latin American port, trade contacts spread out like the ripple caused by throwing a stone in a quiet pool. Merchants buy and sell. Our goods are removed and their products loaded for the return trip. Business relations and friendships are developed. With each recurring voyage, the ties between our peoples grow stronger. Our vessels are taking their responsibilities for building the commerce and cordiality between the Americas with great seriousness. As ambassador to the Americas it is our job to exchange ideas as well as transport products.

The three lovely Delta liners were scrapped in 1972.

The ALCOA CAVALIER

THE *Alcoa Cavalier* and her two sisters, the *Alcoa Clipper* and *Alcoa Corsair*, are the aristocrats of the Aluminum Company of America's fleet of merchant ships. Each carries an average of seventy passengers who enjoy every convenience of luxury travel. Below decks there is a great variety of general cargo southbound to the Caribbean, and 8,500 tons of light pink bauxite ore northbound to the Gulf.

Lush shore excursions and beach picnics in Trinidad go on during the cargo-loading period. The trim liners are washed from stem to stern before smart limousines bring the passengers back to their air-conditioned quarters. The Alcoa Steamship Company's campaign to lower the cost of hauling bauxite by carrying ordinary cargo southward and by providing space for passengers has meant cheaper aluminum for countless homes and industrial users.

On the second voyage of the *Alcoa Cavalier* following her construction in 1947, one of the happy passengers was artist Boris Artzybasheff, whose covers on *Time* magazine have made him famous. It was his assignment to study the people of the lands touched by Alcoa ships. From this voyage came a startling series of composite portraits that gave eye-appeal to Alcoa advertisements.

Just before this series of pictures was used, Alcoa had run a light-hearted set of "Girl in Red" shipboard scene ads, featuring an attractive young lady passenger, her "Lord Plushbottom"-type father and a young man, the romantic interest. Three other clever advertising projects assured full passenger lists for these liners. One stressed the historic background of the Caribbean; it was known as the pirate series. Another was a group of flowering-tree reproductions, so popular that over 50,000 were bought by the public to frame. A third, on Caribbean dances and music generally, added to the lure of the area as a tourist Mecca. At this writing a new device is being used. It is an art contest. Some 1,300 paintings were submitted from the citizens of the fifty-odd ports visited by Alcoa ships. Good will by the cartload is being generated in the Alcoa-served areas, which are important to the whole of America as our second largest market.

More about the *Alcoa Cavalier*. In a sense, she is much like a private yacht. In off season it is not uncommon to charter her entire passenger space to a single group booking. Staterooms on the ship fit the best Hollywood idea of what a liner's cabin should look like. Disappearing beds give the appearance of a living room in daytime. Soft pastel tones, deep wall-to-wall rugs and plenty of luggage space make for living at its best. Life aboard the trim little liner generally centers around the swimming pool aft of the bar and lounge on the promenade deck. Her sixteen-day cruise begins at New Orleans and ends at Mobile. Stops are made at LaGuaira, under the shadow of the Andes Mountains, Guanta, Puerto Cabello, Trinidad, Jamaica, and on alternate voyages, either Curaçao or the Dominican Republic.

Throughout its literature and advertisements, the Alcoa Steamship Company points out with tact and charm that the itineraries are "designed primarily to provide fast and efficient service between Gulf ports and the Caribbean." Passengers are reminded that "the carrying of freight is always the main purpose of this service." Nevertheless, and despite the fact that Alcoa by no means caters to the low-price cruise market, a year-round record of near capacity has been achieved for the *Alcoa Cavalier* and her sisters. This success is a tribute to the company. It bodes well for all America, in a sense, for during World War II some sixty per cent of the bauxite made into aluminum in the United States came from the Caribbean and Surinam.

The Alcoa Steamship Company's penetration into this area and the deep stakes it has driven there are not unlike the commercial pioneering of the merchants of Salem in the days that followed the American Revolution. Our new state in world affairs has produced a new dependence on foreign lands for raw materials. As in years gone by, American ships are playing their part as links in this chain of national development.

Although the trim Alcoa Cavalier's *basic duty is carrying bauxite, she has sumptuous passenger accommodations*

Alcoa went out of the passenger ship business in 1960, and her three fine little liners were laid up and scrapped.

The INDEPENDENCE

OUR train left Grand Central at 5 p.m. Saturday. It was a cheerful gang of reporters that occupied the last cars of a special. We were going to Boston to board the new American Export Lines steamship *Independence*. The author was then assistant ship news editor for the New York *Herald Tribune*. It was January, 1951.

We had special New Haven Railroad menus printed for the *Independence* party. A short wait in the narrow aisle of the dining car and then a meal of roast turkey. Not long after, we were at Commonwealth Pier, Boston, a dingy old structure. What a contrast to the gleaming newness and beauty of the *Independence*, fresh from her speed trials on which she had demonstrated herself the fastest ship in America's merchant marine.

It was our second visit since the keel laying of March 29, 1949, at the Bethlehem Steel Company's Quincy, Mass., yard. Another special train had brought us up to the launching June 3, 1950. And now the great, new 1,000-passenger, 29,500-ton luxury liner was ready. We boarded her with keen anticipation, for not only was she one of the world's largest ships, but she was the fulfillment of a long-cherished dream—a top-flight luxury passenger service to the Mediterranean flying the American flag.

Costing about $25,000,000 the *Independence* was designed for quick conversion into a troopship. As such she could carry 6,000 men and their equipment on a continuous voyage to any port on the globe. The theme in her construction was "Modern American Living At Sea." Her decor highlighted America's great maritime history. Henry Dreyfuss, noted industrial designer, produced everything aboard from the paper bar napkins and ash tray styling, to a new shape and color-marking pattern for her two smokestacks.

A far cry from the *Leviathan* of older days, the *Independence* had no double- or triple-deck public rooms, no giant main staircase, no palm court. Instead, she had low-ceilinged lounges, soundproofed to give quiet restfulness, and with many-colored walls, and a night-club atmosphere in her saloons and restaurants. Air conditioning throughout, circular aluminum showers, a glass-enclosed soda bar adjacent to the main swimming pool, these and other modern touches set the *Independence* up as a model for all future liners. Her deck chairs were light as a feather. Made of aluminum with plastic matting of many colors they were a novel innovation. Many staterooms had polarized glass in their windows, which, with the turn of a switch, could be altered to straight glass.

We slept aboard at Boston preparatory to sailing at 8 a.m. for New York. It was gusty and cold outside, but the quintessence of comfort inboard. The specially selected guest list of 500 seemed particularly appreciative of the decorations and styling of the Boat'n Bottle Bar. Forty hand-blown bottles hung from the walls, each with a miniature model inside. The models depicted the history of sailing craft. Also on the walls were six panels showing decorative and useful knots used at sea. The knots were made by a young girl, working under the guidance of an old tar.

Particularly attractive hand-done watercolors of fish hung in four super de luxe suites on the topmost deck. The leisurely voyage from Boston had hardly begun before the loud speaker announced in a somewhat embarrassed way that one of these choice watercolors was missing. "Would the passenger who has absconded with it please return it, for it was especially done to fit the decoration of the room?" Some hours later the ship's scuttlebutt had it that not only had the painting not been returned, but a companion piece in a room across the way was now also missing!

The ship's huge air-conditioning plant was putting out 184,540 cubic feet of cool air per minute as the noontime sun brought hungry dignitaries into the dining room. All three dining saloons for the three classes were on B deck. The first-class saloon had a depressed central section with terraces on three sides. A forty-foot mural showed the entrance to Boston Harbor from the sea. On the outer bulkheads were open screens of metal, illuminated by fluorescent lights. Leather banquettes lined the two outboard bulkheads and the edge of the dropped-deck level. Amber mirrors and walnut flexwood panels covered the other bulkheads.

"American living goes to sea" is the by-word aboard the Independence, *one of the world's largest and fastest liners*

On deck the great stacks were warm. Wisps of brown smoke curled from their tops. If laid on their sides, ten modern automobiles could pass through either stack at the same time. No water was in the big swimming pool, or the smaller one for tourist class. An offshore wind gave the great new liner a slight list to port. It was not evident unless one checked the horizon on either side and noticed that the landward side seemed to be lower than the sea side. After lunch the author went to the bridge to inquire where we would be at 3 p.m. so that a *Herald Tribune* airplane could find us for pictures for Monday morning's paper. Capt. Hugh L. Switzer estimated that we would be thirty-six miles due East of Sankaty Light on the eastern tip of Nantucket. With this information we went to the radio room, a marvel of the latest equipment, to relay the news to the flying cameramen. As it turned out, no pictures were taken because of the bad weather.

The maiden arrival in New York was a dandy. Airplanes, helicopters, a Navy escort, fireboats and the "works" contributed to making the entrance of the *Independence* a sight to remember. Mayor Vincent R. Impellitteri and staff climbed aboard from a cutter. They unveiled a great framed replica of the Declaration of Independence, central feature in a niche called the "Shrine of Democracy" on the forward bulwark of the lounge, then went up to the bridge where the Mayor posed with Capt. Switzer. The great whistle was roaring almost continuously, in answer to each greeting. A high point was reached as the *Independence* passed American Export's Jersey City freighter piers. A burst of salutes from each cargo-liner added to the din.

As the trip ended the passengers clustered on the promenade waiting for the gangplank to be swung up from Pier 84.

"What's holding us up?" joked Mrs. Norman Stabler, wife of a prominent New York newspaperman. A burly longshoreman on the pier, who overheard her remark, shouted back: "Water!"

The *Independence,* and her sister ship *Constitution,* which was her junior by six months, have proved highly successful ships. Her crew and their families were paid $13,000,000 in wages out of the ship's earnings of $29,000,000 for her first hundred Atlantic crossings. Another $4,000,000 went for labor in other categories, from travel agents to stevedores.

Can you imagine how many spoonfuls were in 234,000 lbs. of sugar consumed during her first three and one-half years in service? Or how many cuts were taken from the 1,250,000 lbs. of beef used? American farmers sold American Export 265,000 dozen eggs, 650,000 pounds of poultry for the *Independence* alone in this period.

Said John Slater, company President:

> Ships are national economic assets. Nevertheless there is an alarming lack of public understanding and support for our maritime industry. Our shipping needs such understanding and support to remain strong and virile. It can keep open essential trade routes. It can fulfill its assigned destiny as an ever-ready auxiliary to the armed forces in time of war.

The *Independence* and the *Constitution* were sold in 1974 to Orient Overseas Line, and because of the oil crisis, laid up in Hong Kong. The chance of either of them resuming operation is slight, although there always remains a possibility. The *Independence* was renamed *Oceanic Independence* and the *Constitution* became the *Oceanic Constitution.*

The UNITED STATES

WHETHER you think in terms of the seven wonders of the world, or whether you prefer to examine things in their microscopic detail, the *United States* is indeed the world's most wonderful ship!

The *United States* in her first three years of service steamed nearly half a million miles at sea while carrying over ninety per cent capacity without once slowing due to mechanical defect, and her shower valves are thermostatically regulated so the user cannot be scalded.

The *United States* has the greatest power of survival against sinking or burning of any merchant ship ever built, and the dresser drawers lock when closed in her staterooms and cannot rattle.

Powerful engines of the most advanced design thrust the *United States* through the ocean at an average speed of thirty-five land miles per hour, and each aluminum rivet used in her superstructure was first heated to 1040 degrees and then kept in a deep freezer at 40 below zero until used.

The man hours required to build the *United States* would have been suffi-

The United States, *a ship without a peer, the world's fastest, safest and most modern liner*

cient to construct 6,000 average-size homes, and there is not a spot on the ship where you could not stand a coin on end, so perfectly has vibration been eliminated.

By whatever yardstick you select, the *United States* is America's greatest maritime achievement since the days of the clippers, perhaps in all time. She is probably the most remarkable single moving unit ever designed by man. For a nation that had for so long turned its back on the deep blue ocean, her construction and achievements are truly indicative of a return to at least potential maritime leadership.

"Well, of all days, last Saturday had to be pretty miserable, but despite that I had a grand time," Stephen Gmelin, a friend, wrote me about his experience photographing the *United States* several months after her maiden voyage.

"There's one thing I wish I had done. As the ship backed out, I noticed a man sitting near me on the bulwark. This man, a wide-brimmed hat pulled low over his head, watched her back out. His head was in his hands. He had a sort of dreamy expression. Well, a little later, as he moved away, I realized that it was none other than Mr. Gibbs himself. . . . What a picture it would have been, the *United States* in the background and her creator looking at her from land."

William F. Gibbs has been compared to John Ericsson, who designed the *John S. McKim* and the ironclad *Monitor*. His influence on naval design cannot be measured. During World War II his firm designed half the ships of the new United States Navy. Ever since he was charged with rebuilding the *Leviathan*, it had been his ambition to build a truly American superliner. In 1944 he began his masterpiece. Four years and several million dollars later the tentative design was accepted by the United States Lines and real work began. The Navy was a close partner as was the Maritime Commission, for both were to subsidize the great ship's construction.

"Certainly not!" Mr. Gibbs said when asked whether he designed the *United States*. "About half of the marine-engineering brains of the country have been applied to this ship. A great ship is the most complicated structure man creates. Topflight American manufacturers produced important refinements in design especially for her. She is the product of a prodigious explosive power—American industry."

Throughout her construction secrecy was a guiding principle. Many features of the great liner have never been revealed: her exact horsepower, her hull design, details of her staggeringly-powerful engines. One picture of her under-water lines slipped past the careful Gibbs & Cox censors and was published in a trade magazine. The entire edition was destroyed. Competitive factors played a part in this censorship, but topflight Navy secrets pioneered in by Mr. Gibbs were basically at issue.

The marriage of Navy requirements with commercial needs is wonderful to observe aboard the *United States*. Her galleys, plumbing and air conditioning, for example, serve some 2,000 passengers and another 1,000 crew in peacetime. In war these facilities can handle 14,000 troops. Her size was limited by the requirement that she be able to transit the Panama Canal. Although her 3,000-mile Atlantic crossing does not require it, she has fuel capacity to cruise to San Francisco and back without refueling. Her cost: $70,000,000.

"She made twenty knots . . . going backwards," was the comment of Walter Hamshar, of the *Herald Tribune*, describing one feat at her trials. "She is a Navy ship, but no passengers will be aware of it," Mr. Gibbs said as quoted by George Horne in the *New York Times*. Besides the press there were many among the 1,700 on her trial run in June, 1952, who represented the 800 companies from forty-eight states whose products went into the 53,000-ton giantess.

The next chapter after her trials was the triumphant voyage from her Virginia birthplace to New York, the home port whose name she bore below her own on her great spoon stern. Three special trains brought 1,200 guests to the Newport News Shipbuilding & Dry-Dock Company. They trooped aboard by searchlight, for it was night when they arrived. The yard was lit up like daylight. For miles around the gigantic red-white-and-blue smokestacks of the *United States* could be seen towering above cranes and machine-shop chimneys. Soon she would be gone, and it was going to be a wrench for the vast shipyard community. Since that cold keel-laying ceremony in February, 1950, the new superliner had been chief subject of conversation. Would she break the record, not broken for a hundred years by an American-built ship? Would she be completed instead as a troopship, as was actually the plan for a brief period in 1951 when the Korean War was flaming?

To while away the hours en route to New York the guests were treated to first-run moving pictures, *Pat and Mike* and *Walk East on Beacon Street*. Those who cared to, cavorted in the swimming pool whose code-flag wall decorations read: "Come on in, the water's fine." A fully equipped gymnasium, luxurious dog kennel, three libraries with 2,291 volumes, not to mention her various bars, attracted keen interest. There were a few who climbed the aluminum ladder within the battleship-like aluminum radar mast forward of the smokestacks on top of the pilot house. We wonder if any realized that even at its topmost point, 175 feet above the keel, the proud *United States* was overshadowed by the ghost of Donald McKay's magnificent clipper—the *Great Republic,* whose 200-foot masts were truly cloud scrapers.

The arrival in New York was breath-taking. The author stood on top of the broad pilot house, observing the reactions of Walter Jones, publicity director of the United States Lines. We were barely twenty feet from the great whistle which blew continuously.

Barely two weeks later, the *United States* was again to receive a boisterous welcome—this time on her return from Europe with both the Eastbound and the Westbound speed records tucked away.

"At no time since the days of the clippers has so much interest been generated by the general public in an achievement of American shipping," said Walter E. Maloney, the then President of the American Merchant Marine Institute. "The *United States,* her owners and crew have placed the entire merchant marine in a new position of importance to the country at large," he added. The shipping trade association head said that the margin of 3.90 knots by which the *United States* beat Britain's *Queen Mary* was the greatest ever achieved in the history of steamships on the North Atlantic. Her time between America's Ambrose Light and Britain's Bishop's Rock was 3 days, 10 hours and 40 minutes. This is 10 hours, 2 minutes faster than the *Queen's* best.

"Congratulations on your magnificent achievement," came the word from Prime Minister Winston Churchill by radiogram to Commodore Harry Manning. All Britain followed Churchill's lead. The reception at Southampton was warmer, those who saw it say, than that given in New York a few days later. Thousands turned out to greet her in everything that would float as she steamed into the British port. Overhead were British jet planes. Six thousand people had applied to be admitted to the Southampton dock, whose capacity was two thousand. British and American destroyers escorted her by sea. A local police band struck up, "Anchors Aweigh," then played "God Save the Queen," and ended up with "The Star-Spangled Banner." Both anthems were echoed by the ship's band aboard the *United States.* A new song was also specially popular on this gala occasion.

Just as a song was written to commemorate the Atlantic flight of **Lindbergh**, and Gertrude Ederle's swimming the Channel, not to mention the **death of** Rudolph Valentino and the double-crossing of Jesse James, a ballad was born honoring the new superliner. The chorus goes in part as follows:

> She's got New York's style,
> California's grace,
> The Mid-west's strength,
> And Texas' space,
> The South-land's charm,
> And the Nation's pace,
> She's got Freedom's form and
> Liberty's face
> So salute the *United States*.

No one can rightly take more pride in the extraordinary successes which have come to the superliner *United States* than Major General John M. Franklin, President of United States Lines. To him belongs the credit for bringing the great vessel into reality. We can well imagine that the day the *United States* was delivered to United States Lines was probably one of the proudest of his life. The remarks of the Secretary of Commerce of the United States, Charles Sawyer, on this occasion, are worth remembering.

> This is the proudest day in our maritime history. For this ship is truly the First Lady of the Seas. No other passenger ship ever built is so beautiful, so fast, so safe, so useful!

The saddest postscript of all must be added to this ship's story. The magnificent *United States* was laid up in 1969, and has remained idle in Norfolk, Virginia, up until this writing. Her sales price dropped repeatedly until in 1977, it was only $5,000,000. Many schemes were proposed to restore her to service, or to rebuild her as a floating hotel or a gambling resort. She remains in excellent condition and it is hoped that her career is not really over. I am writing a book about her as this new edition goes to press.

EPILOGUE

WHAT will the ship of the future look like?

Would there be anything recognizable other than the same old waves and clouds?

We can assume that ships will have much the same general shape as they now do. There will be a bow, designed to throw aside the waves. The hull will probably remain more or less cucumber shaped. Anti-rolling fins, now becoming standard equipment, may become larger. The chances are slim that speed pat-

What the cruise ship of the future may look like, with funnel aft and heavy plastic-covered superstructure play areas

terns of the future will call for such basic hull alterations as the Marilyn Monroe shape now popular in supersonic jets. The stern may change radically if some form of jet propulsion is found feasible.

With propulsion all thinking leads to some form of atomic power. How this will affect routing and speed no one can tell. Some surmise that it may permit speeds not believed possible today for surface vessels, that it may make ships competitive with planes. With jet aircraft, however, it would seem likely that atomic power would not be directed toward super speeds.

One thing would appear certain. Atomic power should make it possible to eliminate the smokestack, so long the proud trademark of steamships. The space saved could well be used as a sun deck. The stack, however, has great lasting power. It may be retained even with atom ships. Fully a generation ago it was thought that the Diesel engine would doom smokestacks. A few stackless ships of that era are still around, looking very odd. It was a good fifty years before tall, sailing-ship masts were abandoned on steamships.

Before the stack vanishes it will probably be moved aft. This is the way we show it in the accompanying drawing. The placing of engines at the stern has long been feasible. Tradition is largely responsible for keeping the engine and stack halfway between bow and stern. The farce of a dummy stack amidships and smoking king posts aft is surely a transition step.

Our sketch shows roll-back glass or heavy plastic coverings facing the bridge front. A similar all-weather roll-back covered deck would stretch from pilot-house to smokestack far aft on the top deck. Glass-enclosed Lido beaches, tennis and handball courts will make for mass appeal. The areas will be heated to permit their use even on the North Atlantic. All-aluminum superstructures will save enough weight to allow swimming pools on the highest decks. Mechanical ventilation will eliminate air funnels. Internal supports will remove the need for mast and stack guy wires and stays. Cargo hatches, where necessary, will be flush to the deck. Fore and aft decks will be swept clear of bitts, anchor chain and bollards. The long promenade deck may be dispensed with as the need for larger public rooms becomes evident. Lounges, smoking rooms and ballrooms will extend from port to starboard. Rows of many picture windows will overlook the ocean.

The artificial custom of having a few first-class cabins so that a lower tourist rate may be charged for the rest of the ship will probably be abandoned. Increased air competition may force all-tourist ship styling, except for a few luxury-cruise ships. The long-projected cafeteria ship may be the answer to competition from airliners. Such ships will offer a five-day crossing or less with a minimum of frills and feathers. Passengers will pay only for their modest cabin. Meals will be extra. Enormous public rooms and acres of deck for all will appeal to new strata of the public. Two 100,000-ton, 35-knot ships are projected for such a service. Each would carry 6,000 passengers. Winter cruises out of New York and other ports might keep such ships sailing on the North Atlantic throughout the slack winter season.

New liners now building will give a foretaste of these trends. Sky lounges in a glass-enclosed smokestack top are a feature of new American President luxury liners for round-the-world service. Twin new Grace Line liners will boast an open-air tiled swimming pool, a Playa (beach) deck, Techo (roof) bar and recreation center on the top deck. Moore-McCormack Lines' sister ships building at this writing will have styling reminiscent of the great superliner *Normandie*, still probably the most modern ship in outline. Matson and Farrell Lines have announced plans for new luxury passenger ships for the Pacific and African runs, respectively. A sister to the *United States* is projected. It is understood that serious thought is being given to making her atom-powered.

Eight years after the first edition of this work came out, the Home Lines brought out their magnificent *Oceanic*, which in many particulars was a dead ringer for the sketch I made (see above) of the cruise ship of the future. My caption predicted the "heavy plastic-covered superstructure play areas". It was one of the chief features of this new cruise ship. It was called "Magradome", and could be opened and closed as the weather required. The huge single stack aft and the general outline shown in my sketch, all came true in the *Oceanic*, which has since come to be regarded as the most perfect and the most successful of all cruise liners of the era.

PART TEN

Twenty Years Later

The changes in only two decades show at what a frightening pace the world is proceeding. Virtually all the liners of the 1950's are gone. Airplanes have replaced passenger ships on most of the long-distance liner service. The cruise ship, however, is rapidly taking the place of the point-to-point ocean liner, and a bright future for ocean cruising is assured. But America has been left almost completely out of the cruise liner picture. The twenty years since 1957 have seen the complete elimination of the American flag from the world's passenger ship scene.

As this edition went to press the last two full-sized American passenger liners on the seven seas were just retired—the Pacific Far East Lines' Mariposa *and* Monterey. *Only four combination passenger-cargo ships remained under the Stars and Stripes, the* Santa Magdalena *class ships. Built for Grace Line, they sailed for some years with their limited passenger space sealed off as strictly cargo vessels, but were re-instated to carry some 90 passengers each under the ownership of the Prudential Line. In 1978, they were sold to Holiday Inns and it was proposed that they be operated by that company's maritime subsidiary, the Delta Line.*

The American contribution in these two decades has been in the container ship, the LASH-type barge carrier, and in the large tanker and bulk carrier area. It is here that the modern-day "Famous American Ships" are to be found. They are the ships that will be remembered.

N.S. SAVANNAH

IN 1957 when the first edition of this book was published, the couple of pages it contained on the S.S. *Savannah*, of 1819, started a chain reaction. At the instigation of Captain Hewlet R. Bishop, of the Maritime Administration, I began a search for the wreck of the old vessel. With help from many people, the search was a three-year effort. I had trips in Navy blimps over the wreck site on Fire Island, as many as 50 skin divers in the water on several occasions, 24 separate expeditions to the area and tremendous fun. A prime goal was to bring up a piece of the historic craft to fit into the world's first nuclear merchant vessel, just authorized by President Eisenhower. A secondary goal developed during the effort, and that was to have the new nuclear ship named in honor of the first ship with a steam engine to cross any ocean. While the search for the wreck was not successful, the effort to name the nuclear ship *Savannah* did succeed. She was to be built by the New York Shipbuilding Company, at Camden, N.J., and the day I learned of the decision by the President to call her *Savannah* I called the yard and urged them to lay her keel on May 22, National Maritime Day, the day in 1819 when the first *Savannah* began her first and only Atlantic crossing. This happened.

Sad to relate, the careers of the two ships had much in common. While the first was a magnificent success mechanically and did serve to introduce steam to the oceans of the world, as the charter of the Savannah Steam Ship Company stated its basic purpose to be, the ship was a failure economically. The new *Savannah*, built with an equally high purpose, was mechanically magnificent— most successful! She was intended to be our proof to the world that America, which dropped the first nuclear bombs, was determined to use nuclear power for peace. In line with this high goal, no phase of her construction was secret. The whole world was invited to come and watch, and specialists from many nations did.

The most serious kind of problems that could be imagined dogged the vessel, however, and her brief career has already ended. At first she was assigned to States Marine Lines to operate, the idea being that she would carry passengers and commercial cargo all over the world as our ambassador of nuclear good will. Her completion was hailed around the world as the opening of the nuclear age for shipping, although the Soviet Union had beaten America with the first non-military nuclear ship, the icebreaker *Lenin*. But just as she was ready to sail a jurisdictional battle between unions developed which idled her for an entire year. A new operator was finally found who could draw on deck officers and engineers from a union that had not been involved in the hassle. It was American Export Lines. By this time the nation had forgotten its high goals for the *Savannah* and the vessel was operated like an ordinary ship. Her excellent passenger quarters were substantially cut down because they became too expensive to maintain and eventually eliminated altogether, but not before I had a trip on her from New York to Philadelphia.

Although American Export Lines was given the ship to operate at the cost of only $1 a year, the unreal safety requirements of the Atomic Energy Commission and the fact that she was forced to carry two and three times as many crew as was necessary made her operation economically impossible. She was also handicapped by the refusal of some ports to permit her to enter, notably those in Japan. Nevertheless she sailed every ocean and made many visits in the Orient, Europe, the Mediterranean and South America. She had never been intended as anything but a show ship and so economically she could not possibly succeed. Eventually American Export Lines turned her back to the Maritime Commission.

The Savannah, *world's first nuclear powered passenger-cargo liner*

She was laid up in Galveston, Texas, and her atomic fuel removed. She had used only a thimblefull of uranium in her five years of cruising. She could not continue, however, without losses that were too large for the government to accept. Like the original *Savannah*, she was mechanically most successful, but economically must unsuccessful. Offered to the City of Savannah for possible use as a museum, the beautiful craft lay there for two years. Unfortunately, the city fathers in Savannah were unable to raise the funds that would have been needed to create a maritime or a nuclear museum in her. She was then taken up to Charleston, where she lies at this writing.

I have not given up on the plan to find the bones of the original *Savannah*. The three-year effort taught me many things, particularly the things not to do the next time. In all likelihood her hulk is close to, or even perhaps under, the huge sand dunes at a point where an old inlet had years ago broken through the narrow strip of sand. One day she will be found, and perhaps a piece of her sturdy wooden hull can be put aboard the new *Savannah*, which, by then, will be properly financed and secure as a museum to the safe use of nuclear power on the high seas.

SANTA MAGDALENA

THIS SHIP and her three sisters, the *Santa Mariana, Santa Maria* and *Santa Mercedes* were built in 1963 by Grace Line. Bought by the Prudential Steamship Company, they were at this writing being turned over to the Delta Line, the maritime arm of the great Holiday Inn conglomerate, which has acquired them. This quartette is significant because they are the last deep-sea passenger ships in the American Merchant Marine. They are also most interesting ships and in their relatively brief lives have gone through much.

As first designed, they were powerful looking vessels with a huge amidships superstructure and no traditional smokestack. A tall, thin pipe rose where the stack should have been and Fred Sands, Grace Line's public relations man dubbed it a "smoke stalk", to the amusement of ship news reporters. In my *A Tugman's Sketchbook*, published in 1965, I included a number of pen sketches

The Santa Magdalena *going through the Panama Canal*

of the *Santa Maria* and made several joking references to this smoke stalk. I was disappointed that Grace Line never showed any interest in that book and eventually concluded that their feelings had been hurt. A year later the company, at great expense and to the detriment of the overall appearance of the ships, installed a little smokestack over the smoke stalk on each ship. It was a most unusual operation and actually done with a helicopter hoisting the new stack up and letting it down in place. Since then people have become accustomed to the new silhouette.

The *Santa Magdalena* was built first and her interior decor honored Colombia. The *Mariana* was dedicated to Ecuador, the *Maria* to Panama and the *Mercedes* to Peru, all nations which the ships have served in their careers to date.

With a gross of 14,442 tons and a length of 547 feet on a 79 foot beam, the four smart sisters were among the first vessels with built-in container cargo cranes. As first designed they were capable of carrying 175 twenty-foot containers. Constructed by the Bethlehem Steel Company at Sparrows Point, Maryland, they could carry up to 125 passengers in fully air-conditioned luxury.

When they were sold by Grace Line to Prudential they were put on a purely cargo route and their passenger spaces closed off. Their home port was changed from New York to San Francisco. The popular demand for passenger space was so great that three of the four sisters were restored to their original liner status and did very well. Only the *Santa Magdalena* continued as a purely cargo ship, but then, she too was reconditioned to carry about 100 passengers and once again the four operated together.

The purchase by Holiday Inn of these four vessels was seen by many as a most happy development, in that it assured the continuation of American-flag passenger service on the high seas. It came just as the *Mariposa* and *Monterey*, of Pacific Far East Lines, were ending their service following the end of their government subsidy. The departure of these two fine Pacific liners marked a low point in the 200 year history of American passenger liners. They were the last full-fledged passenger liners in the American Merchant Marine.

JOHN W. BROWN

A UNIQUE service has been performed by the Liberty ship *John W. Brown*, one of some 2,700 standard-type vessels built for World War II. She is a school ship for those seeking to serve on merchant vessels, and has been since 1946. As the years go by it seems that she may well become the last surviving ship of this type, a most famous American ship. The Liberty ship was developed as an answer to the shocking success of the German submarine effort in the second war. In order to deliver the goods, first to Great Britain, and then to our own forces, a bridge of ships was necessary. Whereas in the first great war our tremendous shipbuilding effort had been too late, in the second war we were more prepared and the Liberty ship can well be said to have been our single most useful weapon.

The story of the Liberty is well told by L. A. Sawyer and W. H. Mitchell in their book *The Liberty Ships* published in 1970. The design was British and the very first ship of this design was actually built in Britain. She was named the *Empire Liberty* and completed in 1941. The glory of the design was its simplicity. The rounded bow, shown in the sketch, and the carefully thought out simplicity of all components made possible the production miracles in this world's greatest shipbuilding effort.

Naming so many ships was a problem. The first of the strictly American Liberty ships was the *Patrick Henry,* naturally. Frank Reil, a well-known ships news reporter from the *Brooklyn Eagle* who had gone to Washington to help the Maritime Commission, remembered a story about the early naming plan. It was proposed to name the vessels after dead Congressman, and Frank, doing some research, discovered that quite a number of Congressmen had committed suicide. To name a Liberty after a suicide seemed ridiculous so he proposed that more care should be taken in the selecting of names and that all should be of men, or women, who had contributed in some way to Liberty. And so the naming system was begun.

The *John W. Brown* was built in 1942 at Baltimore, Maryland, by the Bethlehem-Fairfield shipyard. She was completed in 41 days, not a record by any means. The *Robert E. Perry* had taken only 4 days and 15 hours to be launched. The *John W. Brown* was named for a West Coast labor leader, a carpenter in fact. After war service she was loaned by the government to New York City for educational use, becoming an annex to a vocational school. Her wartime log, it might be noted, still exists and gives a day by day account of service in the European war zones which included bombings, depth charges going off and a ramming by a landing craft. She was rebuilt to carry troops and landed men on the Anzio beachhead during the invasion of Italy.

Her service as a school ship has been long and worthy. Laid up at a very decrepit old East River pier, she was the scene of many ceremonies and graduations in the immediate post war years, with the author participating as a member of the advisory board. Moved to the Hudson, she currently is tied up to Pier 42, at the foot of Morton Street. She is very much a living creature, with a slight haze drifting from her stack and crews working on deck and exercising alongside in lifeboats. Her propeller does not move, however, as it was long ago uncoupled from the engine. But her bakers cook real food, serve real meals, and her other trainees get the feel of a real ship. Many good seamen have graduated from her decks, some going on to become officers and ship line executives.

The *Twin Falls Victory,* renamed *John W. Brown II,* lies next to her, an

The John W. Brown, *right, and* John W. Brown II *in New York*

example of the more than 500 Victory ships built in the later days of the war. One day, when funds are available, she will be rebuilt to take the place of the *John W. Brown*, which by then, it is hoped, will have been preserved as a most important part of our nation's maritime heritage.

C.V. LIGHTNING

NAMED after one of America's most famous Clipper Ships, this fine container ship is one of five operated by American Export Lines between New York and the Mediterranean. The letters preceding her name—"C.V."—refer to the fact that she is a Container Vessel, a new way the company has of setting her apart from ordinary freighters.

The *Lightning* is 610 feet long and has a beam of 78 feet. Her design draft is 27 feet. The good-looking vessel has a displacement tonnage of 26,670 long tons.

Her deadweight is 16,343 long tons. A service speed of 21 knots makes her one of the world's fastest cargo liners. Her bale capacity is 952,000 cubic feet and she can carry 1,070 standard 20-foot containers, or an equivalent combination of standard 40's, 40-foot refrigerated vans and gondolas.

The large single stack shown in the sketch below has the same red, white, blue and buff colors of the stacks on the magnificent *Independence* and *Constitution*, operated for so many years in the passenger service to the Mediterranean by American Export. An interesting feature of the *Lightning* is the "cut-off" look of her stern. This style stern is a modern one, and originated with a wish by naval architects to offer the largest possible internal cubic area for cargo carrying. The older style counter sterns so long popular on American Export ships were beautiful, but offered considerably less money-earning space.

The *Lightning* and her sister ship, *Stag Hound* have made a fine reputation for themselves on the route pioneered by American Export since the years immediately after the end of World War I. Three newer container ships of the *Export Patriot* class are of identical dimensions. Two newer ones of the same class are expected to be added to the American Export Lines fleet shortly. The company was recently sold to the Farrell Lines, but is expected to maintain its identity on the Mediterranean run because of the excellent reputation that has been built up over the past half century.

American Export Lines' container ship C.V. Lightning

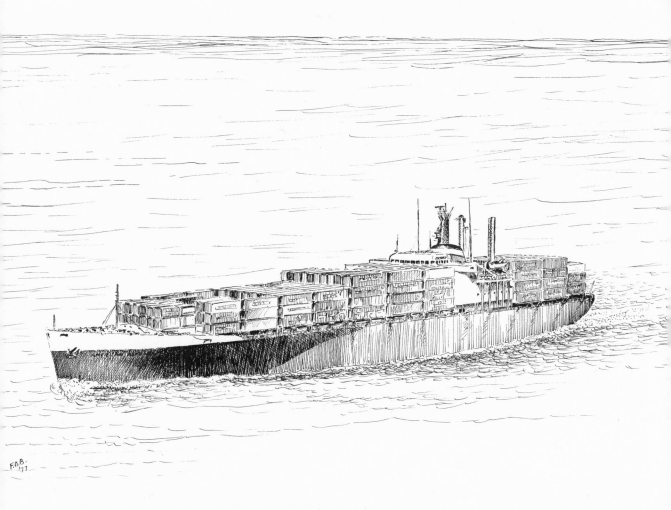

The American Astronaut *loaded full and down*

AMERICAN ASTRONAUT

THE EVOLUTION of the container ship was so rapid that it actually caught ship designers and shipyards flatfooted. Old style pier complexes were rebuilt at great expense only to find that they were out of date and had to be abandoned immediately after their expensive reconstruction. New container ships, half built and still on the way, were seen as too small even before their launching, and were cut in half and new mid-bodies installed. The *American Astronaut* belongs to a class of eight vessels, the first two of which went through such major surgery before completion.

The container revolution began in 1955 when Malcolm McLean, Southern trucking man with no previous maritime experience, bought the Waterman Steamship Corporation. He converted four tankers into container ships and put them into service between Gulf and East Coast ports in 1956. Then he did the same to two war-built C-2 cargo ships, operating them under the new trade name Sea-Land. In 1958, he rebuilt four more C-2's this same way and was moving ahead fast. The Grace Line did the same to two of its C-2's, but was prevented from being another very early container operator by a labor dispute in South America. Sea-Land obtained these ships and continued to earn highly valuable experience as the first major container carrier.

In 1964, the United States Lines, seeing the writing on the wall, ordered five general cargo vessels with hydraulically operated container guides within the holds and fittings for stowage of containers on deck. Two were under construction when work was halted. They were cut in half and new, wider midsections built to be added, with a wider hull wrapped around the older portions. They became the *American Lancer* and the *American Legion*. Nicholas Bachko, Senior Vice President of U.S. Lines, noted in a recent historical summary of the container ship, that "one can go into the engine room and see the original hull inside the wider new hull" on these two historic ships.

The next three were wider and larger from the outset. They became the *American Lark* class. Finally, came the *American Apollo* and the *American Astronaut*. New U.S. Lines container ships are on the drawing boards.

The *American Astronaut* has an overall length of 704.6 feet, an extreme beam of 90 feet and a full load draft of 32 feet, 9 inches. Her full load displacement is 33,400 tons. When passing through the Panama Canal, her tonnage would measure 15,146 net. Should she ever use the Suez Canal, her measurement would be 15,887 tons, while her U.S. net tonnage is 13,621 and her gross tonnage is 19,127. No wonder the tonnage admeasurement field is a complicated one.

The *Astronaut* can carry 1,342 containers of the 20-foot type at a speed of 22.25 knots. Her maximum shaft horsepower is 26,000 and she has a 10,000 mile cruising radius, with a normal consumption of 147 tons of oil per sea day.

In the accompanying sketch her red, white, and blue smokestack can barely be seen behind the containers stacked on deck four high. This is the same stack marking arrangement that was made so famous two generations earlier on the great liner *Leviathan*, although she had three 64-foot tall smokestacks. But the traditions of the *Leviathan* and other earlier U.S. Lines vessels are still very much alive on the modern U.S. container ships: in fact some of the old liner's cadet officers later served as masters on some of the first of this company's container carriers.

The U.S. Lines piloted container service in the North Atlantic-Europe trade on March 18, 1966 by converting the *American Racer* class of vessels, delivered in 1964 and 1965, into container ships. These operated in 1967 when the *American Lancer* and *American Legion* began the United States Lines' full Tri Continent Container Service.

A trans-Pacific container ship, the President Madison

PRESIDENT MADISON

SO RAPID has been the development of the container ship that this fine American President Lines ship, the *President Madison*, new only five years ago, is at this writing one of the smaller of the modern container ship fleet flying the American flag. A $22,000,000 vessel, she has three sister ships, the *President Jefferson, President Pierce* and *President Johnson*. All were put into service in 1972-73.

The *President Madison* has an overall length of 669 feet, a beam of 90 feet, a draft of 33 and a deadweight of 18,995 tons. Her displacement is 30,300 tons. She carries a crew of 40 plus 2 cadets. She has a capacity of 1,484 containers of the 20-foot type. She and her three sisters were called "Pacesetters" when they were new, and rightly so. They serve from the United States West Coast across the Pacific. Other American President services link the Orient with the U.S. Their company traces its origins back to 1848.

In addition to building the four "Pacesetters," the company spent millions in the conversion of its Seamaster, Master Mariner and Searacer classes of cargo ships to carry more containers and in the construction of new container terminals from New York to Hong Kong, not to mention the acquisition of nearly 19,000 containers. The familiar red, white and blue flying eagle insignia may be seen on many of the containers shown aboard the *President Madison* in the sketch of this vessel that accompanies this short reference.

On the *President Madison* the containers can be stacked six high below deck and four or five high above deck, a total height of 86 to 95 feet above the waterline. She and her sisterships have facilities to carry refrigerated containers on deck.

One cargo area is especially equipped with dehumidification systems for the protection of climate or weather-sensitive cargo. Large dockside container cranes at the various American President container terminals can stow 30 containers an hour.

Other automated features aboard the *President Madison* include bridge and engine room systems for speed control and constant monitoring of the steam turbine power plant. The ship's fully cellular design and automated lifting equipment on the piers are so perfected as to permit complete loading or unloading within 36 hours.

The first *President Madison* was built in 1921 for the U.S. Government and subsequently acquired by the American Mail Line, one of the APL's predecessors across the Pacific. She was one of a famous class of passenger/cargo liners known as the "535s" because of their overall length. Originally named the *Bay State* and renamed the *President Madison* in 1922, the ship was sold to Philippine shipping interests in 1939 and was eventually lost by grounding off the Coast of Japan in 1940.

EXXON SAN FRANCISCO

ONE OF THE newest and finest of the Exxon Company's fleet of tankers, the *Exxon San Francisco* can carry over 600,000 barrels of oil. She is 810 feet long and has the modern silhouette. All her accommodations are aft in a massive and highly functional deck house. The bridge is supported on two thick structures that bend forward as they descend in a massive and moving manner. The clean cut lines of the hull show this craft as an extremely functional piece of maritime art, a famous American ship.

With a deadweight of 75,600 tons, she has two sister ships, the *Exxon Baton Rouge* and the *Exxon Philadelphia*. All three are propelled by steam turbines with 19,000 shaft horsepower and a speed of 17 knots. Each vessel is a marvel of modern automation. One man can supervise the centralized control room, directing the oil transfer to or from the 21 cargo tanks. Over 100 cargo valves and six cargo pumps can be handled by one man from this control room. Remote reading tank gauges can be read on a master panel. Draft gauges are also tied in to this control panel and the trim and stresses of the ship can be calculated for all loading conditions. The ship is so huge that direct contact with the crew on deck is maintained by a walkie-talkie system.

Remote control of the anchor windlasses and mooring is available at the rail of the ship. Deck officers navigate and control the main engines from the bridge. Also on the bridge are two true motion radars and controls for a 1,300 horsepower bow thruster to help in maneuvering. The engine room is designed so that it can be operated by one man. The huge vessel has only one boiler, with a completely automatic combustion control system, one main steam driven

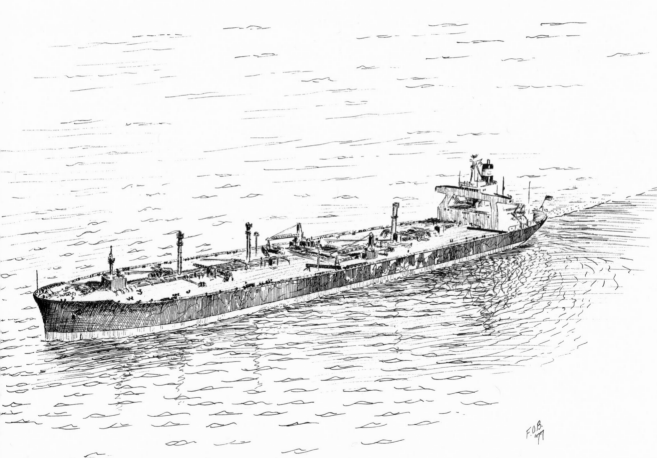

The large American-flag tanker Exxon San Francisco

electric generator, one auxiliary Diesel generator, as well as the emergency Diesel generator. A "stick" control is featured on the command console, instead of the conventional forward and astern throttle valves. The console also features remote digital readouts and continuous printouts of "bell book" and rough log information. The ship's propeller is 26.9 feet in diameter. It has four blades and turns 80 times per minute.

Exxon's marine department has its headquarters in Houston, Texas. Products from the two Exxon refineries at Baton Rouge and Baytown are carried to eastern ports. Exxon tankers also carry crude oil from the Gulf of Mexico to the New Jersey refinery. Crude oil and product deliveries are also made on the West Coast. The 17-ship fleet represents about 11% of the total U.S. tanker fleet.

The *Exxon San Francisco* and her sisters provide ultra modern living quarters. An elevator connects all decks from engineroom to bridge. The crew's private accommodations are designed for comfort, with carpeting, paneled walls, fluorescent lighting and air-conditioning. Officers' quarters include a lounge and messroom and are described in a company folder as being "among the best and most comfortable afloat in today's merchant vessels."

ARCO JUNEAU

THE DISCOVERY of oil in Alaska was one of the great events in recent American history. The sketch shown here is set in Alaska. The magnificent mountains in the background are a fitting setting for one of America's largest merchant vessels, the Atlantic-Richfield Company's *Arco Juneau*. She is indeed one of America's most famous ships.

The *Arco Juneau* lifted the first load of North Slope Crude from the Alaskan port of Valdez. The vessel has a summer deadweight capacity of 120,585 deadweight tons. Built in 1974, she is 883 feet long, overall, and has a beam of 138 feet and a summer draft of 51.75 feet. Her 20,000 shaft horsepower gives her an average speed of 16 knots. Her gross tonnage is 57,692 tons and her net is 49,807 tons. The different tonnage categories represent different ways of measuring her capacity and do not mean her weight, as such.

The *Arco Juneau* is typical of the very large American oil tankers in basic design. She has no forward deck house and her superstructure aft is very high to make it possible for her officers to navigate from her bridge and pilot house. The elimination of this forward bridge and house was a drastic and major change in world tanker design, and is one of the offshoots of the burst in size phenomena of the last two decades. The consolidation of all accommodations in the one tall structure aft has meant a substantial increase in efficiency. It also represents a major step forward in personnel safety, as the walk along the catwalk from bow to stern during heavy weather was always a most dangerous part of life aboard a tanker. On a tanker trip down the United States Atlantic Coast the author was surprised to have the master warn him to remove his glasses before making such a walk one day. "If you don't", he said, "they may blow off your face and then where will you be."

The wide bridge with its two long bridge wings stretching some 30 feet out beyond the central deck house on either side is an identifying feature of the *Arco Juneau* and her two sisterships: *Arco Anchorage* and *Arco Fairbanks*. Two smaller tankers also serve under the Atlantic-Richfield houseflag on the Alaskan run. They are the *Arco Prudhoe Bay* and the *Arco Sag River*. Two new tankers of 188,500 deadweight tons were building at this writing, one to be delivered in 1979 and the other in 1980.

"We have equipped our fleet with the most modern navigation, safety and environmental protection equipment available," said Captain Charles M. Lynch, Vice President, Marine Transportation. "Satellite communication, Loran, collision avoidance, inert gas systems and sewage treatment facilities are just a few of these features," he added.

"Not only are our ships well outfitted, but the crews who man them are equally well trained. Atlantic Richfield Company took a leadership role in training

The Arco Juneau *on her first trip to get oil from Alaska*

50 industry captains and pilots aboard the *Arco Fairbanks* during tanker trials in Prince William Sound in April 1977," Captain Lynch said.

The Atlantic Richfield company passed its 50th anniversary in 1966 and issued a special publication recording its first half century. At that point its largest tanker was the *Atlantic Heritage,* of 53,288 deadweight tons. Between 1916 and 1966 it had built 60 vessels. The first was the 10,200 deadweight ton vessel named *H.C. Folger,* which served for 24 years.

AUSTRAL ENTENTE

FARRELL Lines expanded its area of operation from Africa to include Australia and New Zealand. It regularly restocked its fleet of cargo ships and in 1972-73 added four new, specially-designed container vessels to the run between United States East and Gulf Coast ports and the other side of the world, or "down under." They proved so efficient and the trade grew so unexpectedly that it was decided to "jumboize" two of this new quartette. Picked for this strange operation were the *Austral Entente,* shown here, and the *Austral Envoy.* Jumboizing means cutting a ship in half and adding a new middle section. It was a drastic and

The Austral Entente *being lengthened in a shipyard*

expensive operation, but it was quicker than building a new ship. Major ship surgery of this kind was by no means rare, and dated back to early in the 20th Century. The most interesting case had been the enlarging of four Hamburg American Line passenger ships, the *Albert Ballin* class, an operation that increased their speed and cargo capacity but gave them an awkward bow-heavy look. At this writing a major Norwegian passenger liner serving on cruises out of Miami was being cut in half and enlarged to nearly double her passenger capacity.

The sketch above of the *Austral Entente* shows her at Bethlehem Steel Company's Sparrows Point, Maryland plant, during the operation. The 144-foot midbody, which has been welded into place, can be identified by the lighter hull shading just forward of the high superstructure far aft. The ship's length was increased from 669 feet to 813.3 feet and her container capacity was nearly doubled. Instead of carrying 974, maximum, she could take 1,708. A paper presented before the Society of Naval Architects and Marine Engineers by Farrell's marine superintendent, Thomas J. Sartor, Jr., noted also that the conversion had one other advantage. Instead of a crew of 39 the rebuilt vessel could be operated with a complement of only 37. She still had elegant space for 12 passengers. No luxury liner could provide more comfortable and spacious quarters for passengers than this Farrell Lines ship or her sister ships. Eight cabins on the Sun Deck, a card room with bar and pantry, a library and a large lounge are available for the dozen fortunate voyagers. They eat at a large dining saloon with the ship's officers. Although only 12 are ever carried at one time, the cabins offer space for 16 to permit greater booking flexibility. Seven cabins have private toilets and showers, while the eighth has a toilet and tub/shower.

The cost of the jumboizing was $14,000,000 and the designing was done by George C. Sharp, Inc., the company which designed the nuclear passenger/cargo liner *Savannah*. The work was performed at the Bethlehem Steel Company's yard at Sparrows Point, Maryland. It was a complex structural assignment, involving putting the vessel in drydock and ballasting the drydock up and down to move the new section into place. The operation increased the ship's displacement from 30,490 to 42,350 tons. The added bulk meant only a slight reduction of the vessel's 22-knot service speed. Also jumboized was the *Austral Envoy*. The two other 1972-73 class Farrell ships not jumboized are the *Austral Endurance* and the *Austral Ensign*. A unique feature of the jumboizing was the increasing of the depth of each of the six refrigerated holds by approximately 20 feet. This was done by extending the original holds upwards above the main deck. These extensions, called "cocoons", increased the depth of the hold so that it could accommodate eight 20-foot containers stowed on top of each other instead of only six. The accompanying sketch shows the raised cargo holds amidships.

The Delta Norte *and the skyline of New Orleans*

DELTA NORTE

THE EVOLUTION of cargo ships has been a slow process. In the days of St. Paul, the cargo carrier was loaded with slings and cargo nets much the same as was done for the next almost two thousand years. As recently as a decade ago this was still the chief way of doing things, and there remain many old-style cargo ships still in service. But the new frontier, both with the container ship and the LASH (*L*ighter *A*board *SH*ip) is very different. These are the future in the movement of cargo across the oceans of the world, and both forms were American-born.

The *Delta Norte* is an example of the LASH ship under the American flag. She is in a sense 89 small ships in one big one. Her lighters (or barges as they are more commonly called), may be loaded a thousand miles away from their LASH mother ship. And they can be sealed far up river and the seal won't be broken until they have been unloaded in some foreign port and towed by tug to their final point of destination. The obvious advantages from the security standpoint are tremendous. The LASH ship, in its basic design, is a huge floating shell, with a bottom, sides and bow. Sixteen hatches and two on-deck areas could accommodate up to 89 lighters (if operated as a full barge vessel). Between the twin smokestacks, which are located on port and starboard sides of the vessel, the lighters are stacked securely in the open areas above the engine-room. A massive crane straddling the width of the vessel and capable of moving back and forth on tracks running the full length of the vessel aft of the quarters area and navigational bridge lifts the barges either from their stowage position in the vessel for deposit in the water at the stern of the vessel or lifts them from the water at the stern for transfer to a predetermined stowage position on the vessel. It has a 500 short ton capacity.

Forward of the barge carrying hatches is a hatch for containers only. On the average the vessels have been carrying approximately 300 20-foot containers or their 40-foot equivalent, on their present trade route. The container crane is just aft of the forward bridge and pilot house structure, and can lift 33.6 short tons. If only containers are carried, a maximum of 1,728 could be accommodated.

The *Delta Norte* is 893 feet long and has a beam of 100 feet. Her maximum load draft is 38 feet 1½ inches and her total deadweight is 40,710 tons. Of steam propulsion, she has a shaft horsepower of 32,000 and can make a maximum design speed of 22 knots. She has just one propeller.

The two sister ships to this modern *Flying Cloud* are called *Delta Mar* and *Delta Sud*. All three were built in 1973. They link the U.S. Gulf with Guatemala, Honduras, Venezuela, Brazil, Uruguay and Argentina with sailings every two weeks.

A Delta Line statement summarizes their place in the sun in this succinct way:

"These LASH/container vessels constitute a technological breakthrough. They utilize advanced techniques in vessel construction, cargo handling, scheduling, tonnage accommodation and performance reliability. Their flexibility embraces every transportation need, from interport shipping of cargo in bulk to sophisticated intermodalism of cargo under refrigeration."

LASH ATLANTICO

IN THE continuing evolution of ships, the LASH type vessel represents a major evolutionary step in the mechanization of world commerce. The next LASH described in this volume is Prudential's *LASH Atlantico,* one of a fleet of four, *LASH Turkiye, LASH Pacifico* and *LASH Italia,* being the sister vessels. The *Atlantico* is 820 ft. long with a beam of 100 feet and a dead weight of 39,564 tons. This vessel has the capability of carrying 77 450-ton barges, or 1,832 20-foot containers. With a maximum draft of 40 feet and a speed of 22½ knots, she is as fast as most liners and much faster than the traditional cargo vessels of only a few years ago.

The LASH being such a new and revolutionary vessel, requires that a proper description begin from the stem to the stern. The clipper stem and bulbous bow add class to the vessel, and a rounded 360 degree visibility pilot house streamlines the forward superstructure.

An air view of Prudential's Lash Atlantico

The twin stacks are painted blue with a large gold "P" on the outboard side. Their location outboard on either side of the vessel allows the huge lighter crane to pass between them.

The stern of a LASH ship is unlike any other stern on any ship ever built. It consists of two huge protruding arms extending 50 feet out over the water beyond the transom. The arms are sturdy and can withstand the worst pounding of the ocean waves. High over the water they provide tracks on which the giant gantry crane can move out over the water to lift up the 450-ton lighters.

Straddling the cargo area of the vessel, two large cranes can move fore and aft on a rail system located to port and starboard of center line. One crane has a capacity of 30 tons and handles containers. The large crane, with a large decal of the American flag port and starboard, has a capacity of 500 tons and handles barges.

The barges handled by the LASH vessel have a cargo capacity of 20,000 cubic feet and have a draft of only 8 feet 7 inches with a full load. This draft characteristic allows the barges to be towed into most shallow inland areas to receive the cargo or to unload.

The fact that the *LASH Atlantico* and her sister ships can be loaded or unloaded out in the stream means tremendous savings of not only time but pier rentals. Time is of the essence for ships of such great size and high original cost. The massive 500-ton lighter crane, for example, can load four loaded lighters of 1,400 tons in one hour. Compared with the old-fashioned sling method of loading, this represents a leap into the future that could not have been imagined a generation ago.

TILLIE LYKES

SOMETHING even newer than the "LASH"–type cargo ship was devised by the famous old New Orleans steamship company–Lykes Lines. It was called the *Seabee*, and three of these huge craft have been put into service since 1972. The one selected for this volume is the *Tillie Lykes*. The other two are the *Doctor Lykes* and the *Almeria Lykes*. Each is 875 feet long, has a speed of 20 knots and can carry 38 specially-designed barges or 1,368 of the 20-foot containers.

The barges of the *Tillie Lykes* were especially designed to serve on the inland waterway system of the United States. They are one-half the length and the same width as the typical "jumbo" barges of the vast Mississippi River system. Each is 97½ feet long, with a width of 35 feet and a depth of 12½ feet. Lykes has also designed special "flat deck" barges to go with their *Seabee* ships. Slightly longer than the regular barges, they can be brought bow-in to the shore to permit the loading of heavy objects where no shore cranes are available. With a deck load capacity of 8,000 lbs. per square foot, they can take objects as heavy as 750 long tons.

The *Seabee* herself is a vessel of 37,461 tons, deadweight with 36,000 horse-power. She can make 20 knots. Her beam of 106 feet makes her just able to go through the Panama Canal.

Lykes Lines operates out of New Orleans and links the Gulf with Europe, the Black Sea and the Middle East, the Mediterranean, Africa, South America and the Orient.

The sketch of the *Tillie Lykes* shows her unusual stern which features its 2,000-ton capacity submersible elevator. With this elevator the *Seabee* carrier has the greatest heavy lift capacity of any liner afloat. Two tall stacks on either side of the hull at the midpoint between bow and stern may be seen. The forward bridge structure with crew accommodations, pilot house and mast carry the familiar white "L" in its blue diamond design, for Lykes Lines.

On deck may be seen 20-foot and 40-foot containers as well as standard *Seabee* barges. The ability to stow both containers and barges with equal facility is a design achievement of note. The barges are so large that it is astonishing what they can carry. One barge can hold 300,000 board feet of lumber, 442 tons. A typical *Seabee* barge is as long as, and one-third wider than the steamship *Savannah*, of 1819, first steam powered vessel to cross any ocean.

Lykes Lines is one of the oldest and most respected of American steamship companies.

The new Lykes barge carrier Tillie Lykes

The Sea-Land Resource *at her berth next to giant loading cranes*

S.S. SEA-LAND RESOURCE

THIS MASSIVE and speedy container ship is one of eight sister ships built for the Sea-Land Service, Inc. They are among the largest and fastest container ships in the world. With a cruising speed of 33 knots they are, in fact, faster than even the fastest passenger liners, with the exception of the three *Queens*, the *France* and the *United States*. Their dimensions are equally amazing: length—946 feet overall; beam—105½ feet; design draft—30 feet; displacement—51,439 long tons. And yet they are operated with a crew of only 49 men per ship. Their capacity is breathtaking: 896 containers of the 35-foot style plus 200 more of the 40-foot type.

The eight new Sea-Land container ships were added to the company's already large fleet of container vessels in 1972 and 1973. They immediately began setting new speed records on all the runs on which they were placed. The first, named the *Sea-Land Galloway*, broke the cargo ship record from Bishop's Rock to Ambrose Light with a passage of 4 days, 9 hours and 8 minutes. She averaged 31.07 knots on this 3,210-mile crossing. She was followed only six months later by the *Sea-Land McLean* which proceeded to cut more than 12 hours from this record. She took only 3 days, 21 hours and 5 minutes to make the trans-Atlantic crossing, steaming at an average speed of 32.71 knots. On her very next voyage, the *Sea-Land McLean* broke her own record, averaging 33.005 knots on the return passage from Ambrose to Bishop's Rock. She did the trip in 3 days, 20 hours and 30 minutes. Making the same crossing a year later, the still newer *Sea-Land Exchange* established an even faster speed record of 33.21 knots on an eastbound crossing.

Trans-Pacific speed records were made by the new Sea-Land container ships placed on that run. The *Sea-Land Commerce* averaged 32.62 between Yokohama and Seattle in June 1973, taking 5 days and 9 hours to make the run. The next month she averaged an amazing 33.27 knots between Yokohama and Long Beach, for a passage that took 6 days, 1 hour and 30 minutes. Such huge ships make speed essential, for time means money with ships so costly to build.

The power plant in the *Sea-Land Resource* and her seven graceful sister ships consists of two cross compound steam turbines. Each has a shaft horsepower of 60,000. The combined total of 120,000 shaft horsepower is greater than the engine which powered the famous liner *Leviathan,* largest ship in the world in her day. The new Sea-Land ships, which are known as SL-7 class, each have twin propellers made of cunial bronze and weighing 45 tons. They can maintain an average speed of 33 knots with 135 revolutions per minute.

The *Sea-Land Resource* is shown at her Elizabeth, New Jersey terminal. At her right may be seen the eight-story-high shoreside crane device which lifts the containers aboard. The sketch does not do justice to the length of the big vessel, and only a suggestion of her huge main superstructure aft can be seen. Her twin stacks, set athwartships, do not even show at all. I chose this view to draw, however, because it shows the sleek bow lines and fine forward Bridge better than any other angle. These amazing vessels are the Clipper ships of today, and will be so remembered in the years to come.

The little passenger ship Independence

INDEPENDENCE

A NEW BEGINNING for America's passenger fleet may be seen in this sturdy little vessel. The *Independence*, she is operated by the American Cruise Lines, Inc. of Haddam, Conn. along with a slightly smaller companion vessel, named the *American Eagle*. America lost its coastwise passenger liner fleet in the period just before and just after the second great war. Labor troubles, the war itself and a combination of the automobile and the truck caused the ending of this once proud and extensive part of the nation's merchant marine. It was a sad thing to have it go, and most people today don't even remember the many famous lines that served on the Great Lakes, on our Pacific Coast, on the Gulf and up and down the Atlantic coast. The Clyde Line, with all its ships named after Indian tribes, was nearly 100 year old when it died. The Morgan Line, with its slogan— "100 golden hours at sea", linked New York and New Orleans. The Merchants and Miners Line, with ships named after each letter of the alphabet (*Allegheny, Berkshire, Chatham, Dorchester, Essex, Fairfax* etc.), gave up without a struggle after turning its fleet over to war duties. The famed Panama Pacific Line, which in 1929 put into service the three largest liners ever built for American flag service up to then, linked the West and the East coasts. The famed H.F. Alexander company with its west coast liners immortalized in so many early moving pictures lost its fleet to the war and never came back. Books could be written on each of these companies, not to mention the Fall River Line and the famed Old Bay Line—both of which have been immortalized in several good volumes.

The *Independence* and her sister operate on short cruises in New England waters, up the Hudson, in the Chesapeake Bay, along the Carolinas, and as far south as Florida. Serving out of Haddam, they carry small passenger lists in great comfort. Each stateroom has its own toilet and shower. A large Nantucket Lounge forward on each ship offers a good place to view the scenery in bad weather. A good-sized dining saloon on main deck aft provides a happy place for meals, which "are served family style". The brochure put out describing these vessels noted that "no effort or expense is spared in providing you with excellent meals prepared by a truly professional kitchen staff and served with pride".

A number of the cruises visit the South Street Seaport Museum in New York City, and cruise passengers have the opportunity to tour that rapidly growing restoration project and its fleet of ancient sail and steam vessels. The *Independence*, newer of the two, has 37 double staterooms, 4 singles and 2 triple cabins.

It is hoped that these two little coastal liners are only the beginning of a fleet of larger and more commodious passenger vessels that will once again provide overnight cruise service along our four coasts. They are a form of mass-transit, although a very luxurious one, and should prosper in this age of oil shortage and a new awareness of the importance of conservation of fuel. May the American Cruise Lines be the start of a new era in coastwise shipping!

A SELECTED BIBLIOGRAPHY

Adamson, Hans C., *Keepers of the Lights*, Greenberg, N. Y., 1955

Albion, R. G., *Maritime and Naval History: An Annotated Bibliography*. The Marine Historical Association, Mystic, Conn., 1955

Albion, R. G., *Sea Lanes in Wartime*, Norton, N. Y., 1942

Albion, R. G., *The Rise of New York Port*, Scribners, N. Y., 1939

American Bureau of Shipping et al., *The American Merchant Marine*, N. Y., 1933

Angas, Comdr. W. Mack, *Rivalry on the Atlantic, 1839-1939*. Lee Furman, N. Y., 1939

Atlantic Mutual Insurance Company. *The Private War of the C.S.S. SHENANDOAH*, privately printed, N. Y., 1955

Babcock, F. L., *Spanning the Atlantic*, Knopf, N. Y., 1931

Balison, Howard J., *Newport News Ships*, Mariners Museum, Newport News, Va., 1954

Baughman, James P., *The Mallorys of Mystic*, Wesleyan Univ. Press, Middletown, Conn., 1972

Beck, Stuart E., *The Ship, How She Works*, Adlard Coles, Ltd., Southampton, 1955

Belgian Nautical Research Association, *The Belgian Shiplover*, magazine, Bruxelles

Birkeland, Capt. Torger, *Echoes of Puget Sound*, Caxton Printers, Caldwell, Idaho, 1960

Bone, David W., *The Lookoutman*, Harcourt, Brace, N.Y., 1923

Bonsor, N. R. P., *North Atlantic Seaway*, T. Stephenson Prescot, 1955

Bowen, Dana T., *Lore of the Lakes*, Dana Thomas Bowen, Publisher, Daytona Beach, Fla., 1940

Bowen, Dana T., *Memories of the Lakes*, Dana Thomas Bowen, Publisher, Daytona Beach, Fla., 1948

Bowen, Frank C., *A Century of Atlantic Travel*, Little, Brown, Boston, 1930

Bowen, F. C., *From Carrack to Clipper*, Halton, London, 1948

Bowen, F. C., *Men of the Wooden Walls*, Staples, London, 1952

Bowen, F. C., *Port of London*, Dryden Pub. Co., London, 1948

Bowen, F. C., *Ships for All*, Ward Lock, London, 1952

Bowen, F. C., *The Sea, Its History and Romance*, Part 16, Halton & Truscott Smith, London

Bowen, F. C., *Wooden Walls In Action*, Halton, London, 1951

Boyer, Dwight, *Great Stories of the Great Lakes*, Dodd, Mead & Co., N. Y., 1966

Bradlee, F. B. C., *Blockade Runners During the Civil War*, Essex Institute, Salem, 1925

Bradlee, F. B. C., *Some Account of Steam Navigation In New England*, Essex Institute, Salem, 1920

Brady, Edward M., *Tugs, Towboats and Towing*, Cornell Mar Press, Cambridge, Md., 1967

Brassey's Naval and Shipping Annual, William Clowes and Sons, London, various issues used

Braynard, Frank O., *Leviathan, The World's Greatest Ship*, Vol. I, II, III, South Street Seaport Museum, N. Y., 1972-76; Vol. IV, Mariners' Museum, Newport News, Va., 1978

Braynard, Frank O., *Lives of the Liners*, Cornell Maritime Press, N. Y., 1947

Braynard, Frank O., *S.S. SAVANNAH, The Elegant Steam Ship*, Univ. of Ga. Press, Athens, Ga., 1963

Brewington, M. V., *Chesapeake Bay, A Pictorial Maritime History*, Cornell Maritime Press, Cambridge, Md., 1953

Brewington, M. V., *Shipcarvers of North America*, Barre Publishing, Barre, Mass., 1962

Brittain, W. M., *Bibliography of Maritime Literature*, American Steamship Assn., N. Y., 1918

Britten, Sir Edgar T., *A Million Ocean Miles*, Hutchinson, London, 1936

Bross, S. R., *Shipping Nomenclature*, Alcoa Steamship Co., N. Y., 1952

Brown, Alexander C., *The Old Bay Line*, Dietz Press, Richmond, Va., 1940

Brown, Alexander Crosby, *Women and Children Last*, G.P. Putnam, N. Y., 1961

Brown, Giles T., *Ships That Sail No More*, Univ. of Kentucky Press, Lexington, 1966

Bundy, C. Lynn, *The Maritime Association of the Port of N. Y.*, privately printed, 1923

Burgess, Robert H., *This Was Chesapeake Bay*, Cornell Maritime Press, Cambridge, Md., 1963

Burton, Hal, *The Morro Castle*, Viking Press, N. Y., 1973

Carse, Robert, *A Cold Corner of Hell*, Doubleday, Garden City, N. Y., 1969

Carse, Robert, *The Twilight of Sailing Ships*, Grosset & Dunlap, N. Y., 1965

Carse, Robert, *Your Place in the Merchant Marine*, Macmillan, N. Y., 1964

Cary, Alan L., *Famous Liners and Their Stories*, Appleton-Century, London, 1937

Cary, Alan L., *Giant Liners of the World*, Appleton-Century, London, 1937

Cary, Alan L., *Liners of the Ocean Highway*, Appleton-Century, London, 1938

Cary, Alan L., *Mail Liners of the World*, Appleton-Century, London, 1937

Chadwick, F. E. et al., *Ocean Steamships*, Scribners, N. Y., 1891

Charles, Roland W., *Troopships of World War II*, Army Transportation Association, Washington, 1947

Chatterton, E. K., *The Merchant Marine*, Little, Brown, Boston, 1923

Chatterton, E. K., *Steamship Models*, T. Werner Laurie, Ltd., London, 1924

Chatterton, E. K., *The Romance of the Ship*, Seeley, London, 1913

Choules, Rev. J. O., *The Cruise of the Steam Yacht NORTH STAR*, Gould and Livingston, Boston, 1854

Church, A. C., *Whale Ships and Whaling*, Norton, N. Y., 1938

Clark, A. H., *The Clipper Ship Era*, Putnam's, N. Y., 1910

Coleman, Terry, *The Liners*, G.P. Putnam's Sons, N. Y., 1977, First American Edition

Colcord, Joanna C., *Roll and Go*, Bobbs-Merrill Co., Indianapolis, 1924

Coman, Edwin T., Jr., & Gibbs, Helen M., *Time, Tide and Timber*, Stanford University Press, Cal., 1949

Covell, William Wing, *A Short History of the Fall River Line*, A. H. G. Ward, Newport, R. I., 1947

Cramp, C. R., *Commercial Supremacy and Other Papers*, Mover & Lesher, Philadelphia, 1894

Croil, James, *Steam Navigation*, Briggs, Toronto, 1898

Culver, H. B., *The Book of Old Ships*, Garden City Publishing Co., Garden City, 1935

Curwood, James O., *The Great Lakes, The Vessels That Plough Them; Their Owners, Their Sailors, and Their Cargoes*, Putnam's, N. Y., 1909

Cutler, Carl, *A Descriptive Catalogue of The Marine Collection To Be Found at India House*, India House, N. Y., 1935

Dayton, Fred E., *Steamboat Days*, Tudor, N. Y., 1939

Devine, Eric, *Blow the Man Down*, Doubleday, Doran, N. Y., 1937

Dickerman, Marion, *The Story of the Last of the Old Whalers*, Marine Museum of the Marine Historical Assn., Mystic, Conn., 1949

Diggle, Capt. E. G., *The Romance of A Modern Liner*, Sampson Low, London, around 1923

Dollar, Robert, *Memoirs of Robert Dollar*, W. S. Van Cott, San Francisco, 1918

Dow, G. F., *Whale Ships and Whaling*, Marine Research Society, Salem, 1925

Dowling, Rev. Edward J., editor, *Ships That Never Die*. Publication No. 1, The Marine Historical Society of Detroit, 1952

Dugan, James, *The Great Iron Ship*, Harpers, N. Y., 1953

Dugan, James, *The Saga of Hans Isbrandtsen and His Shipping Empire—American Viking*, Harper & Row, N. Y., 1963

Dunbar, Seymour, *A History of Travel in America*, Tudor, N. Y., 1937

Durant, John & Alice, *Pictorial History of American Ships*, A. S. Barnes, N. Y., 1953

Elliott, Richard V., *Last of the Steamboats*, Tidewater Publishers, Cambridge, Md., 1970

Ewen, William H., *Days of the Steamboats*, Parents Magazine Press, N. Y., 1967

Farrington, S. Kip, Jr., *Ships of the U. S. Merchant Marine*, Dutton, N. Y., 1947

Fay, C. E., *Mary Celeste, The Odyssey of an Abandoned Ship*, Peabody Museum, Salem, 1942

Fletcher, R. A., *Steam-Ships, The Story of Their Development*, Lippincott, London, 1910

Fletcher, R. A., *Traveling Palaces*, Pitman, London, 1913

Flexner, James T., *Steamboats Come True*, Viking Press, N. Y., 1944

Forbes, Allan, & Eastman, R. M., *Yankee Ship Sailing Cards*, State Street Trust Co., Boston, 1948

Fortune Magazine, *Our Ships*, Oxford Press, N. Y., 1938

Fraser-Macdonald, A., *Our Ocean Railways*, Chapman and Hall, London, 1893

Fry, Henry, *The History of North Atlantic Steam Navigation*, Sampson Low, London, 1896

Gibbs, James A., Jr., *Pacific Graveyard*, Binfords & Mort, Portland, Ore., 1950

Gibson, C. E., *The Story of the Ship*, Schuman, N. Y., 1948

Gleaves, Albert, *A History of The Transport Service*, Doran, N. Y., 1921

Golding, Harry, editor, *The Wonder Book of Ships*, Ward, Lock & Co., London, about 1927

Graham, Charles, *Ships of the Seven Seas*, Ian Allan, London, 1947

Graham, Philip, *Showboats, The History of an American Institution*, Univ. of Texas Press, Austin, Tex., 2nd printing, 1969

Great Lakes Historical Society, *Inland Seas*, quarterly journal, Cleveland

Grolier Club, The, *The United States Navy, 1776 to 1815*, N. Y., 1942

Hain, John A., *Side Wheel Steamers on the Chesapeake Bay, 1880-1947*, Glendale Press, Glen Burnie, Md., 1947

Hanson, Joseph M., *The Conquest of the Missouri*, Murray Hill, N. Y., 1946

Harlan, George H., & Fisher, Clement, J., *Of Walking Beams and Paddle Wheels*, Bay Books, San Francisco, 1951

Hartley, Herbert, *Home is the Sailor*, Vulcan, Birmingham, Ala., 1955

Hathaway, F. R., *Yale and Harvard*, Marine News, N. Y., March, 1947

Hennessy, M. W., *The Sewall Ships of Steel*, Kennebeck Journal Press, Augusta, Me., 1937

Heyl, Erik, *Early American Steamers*, Buffalo, N. Y., 1953

Hill, Max, *Exchange Ship*, Farrar & Rinehart, N. Y., 1942

Hill, Ralph N., *Sidewheeler Saga*, Rinehart, N. Y., 1952

Hilton, George W., *The Night Boat*, Howell-North Books, Berkeley, Cal., 1968

Holand, H. R., *America 1355-1364*, Duell, Sloan & Pearce, N. Y., 1946

Holly, H. H., *Sparrow-Hawk, A Seventeenth-Century Vessel in Twentieth-Century America*, Pilgrim Society reprint from *The American Neptune*, Salem, Mass., 1953

Holt, Robert B., *History of the USS HARRISBURG*, Brooklyn Eagle Press, around 1920

Howe, O. T., & Matthews, F. C., *American Clipper Ships, 1833-1858*, Vol. II, Marine Research Society, Salem, 1927

Hunter, H. C., *How England Got Its Merchant Marine, 1066-1776*, National Council of American Shipbuilders, N. Y., 1935

Hunter, L. C., *Steamboats on the Western Rivers*, Harvard University Press, Cambridge, 1949

Huntington, Gale, *Songs The Whalemen Sang*, Barre Publishers, Barre, Mass., 1964.

Jackson, G. G., *The Book of the Ship*, Appleton-Century, London, 1938

Johnson, Alfred, translator, *Ships and Shipping, A Collection of Pictures by Antoine Roux and His Sons*, Marine Research Society, Salem, 1925

Johnson, E. R., *Ocean and Inland Water Transportation*, D. Appleton, N. Y., 1909

Kemble, John H., *A Hundred Years of the Pacific Mail*, Mariners' Museum Reprint from *The American Neptune*, Salem, Mass., 1950

Kemble, John H., *The Panama Route, 1848-1869*, University of California Publications in History, Vol. 29, 1943

Kerchove, Rene de, *International Maritime Dictionary*, D. Van Nostrand, N. Y., 1948

Klein, Benjamin & Eleanor, *The Ohio River Handbook and Picture Album*, Young and Klein, Cincinnati, 1954

LaDage, John H., *Merchant Ships: A Pictorial Study*, Revised 2nd Ed., Cornell Maritime Press, Cambridge, Md., 1968

Lawrence, Jack, *When The Ships Come In*, Farrar & Rinehart, N. Y., 1940

Lawson, Will, *Pacific Steamers*, Brown & Ferguson, Glasgow, 1927

LEVIATHAN, History of the, Compiled from the Ship's Log and Data Gathered by the History Committee on Board the Ship, Brooklyn, about 1920

Lubbock, Basil, *Sail,* Blue Peter Publishing Co., London, 1927

Lubbock, Basil, *The Western Ocean Packets,* Lauriat, Boston, 1925

Lyman, John, *Log Chips,* magazine of sailing ship history, Washington, D. C.

Lytle, W. M., Holdcamper, F. R., editor, *Merchant Steam Vessels of the U. S., 1807-1868,* Pub. No. 6, Steamship Historical Society of America, Mystic, Conn., 1952

MacGregor, D. R., *The Tea Clippers,* Marshall, London, 1952

MacMullen, Jerry, *Paddle-Wheel Days in California,* Stanford Univ. Press, 1944

Maginnis, A. J., *The Atlantic Ferry,* Whittaker, London, 1892

Marine Historical Society of Detroit, *The Detroit Marine Historian,* magazine, Detroit, Mich.

Martin, Christopher, *The Amistad Affair,* Abelard-Schuman, N. Y., 1970

Marvin, W. L., *The American Merchant Marine,* Scribner's, N. Y., 1916

Maxtone-Graham, John, *The Only Way To Cross,* Macmillan, N. Y., 1972

McAdam, Roger W., *Priscilla of Fall River,* Stephen Daye, N. Y., 1947

McAdam, Roger W., *The Old Fall River Line,* Stephen Daye, N. Y., 1955—revised edition of original 1937 publication

McCoy, Samuel D., *Nor Death Dismay,* Collins Doan, Jersey City, 1948

McDonald, P. B., *A Saga of the Seas,* Wilson-Erickson, N. Y., 1937

McDowell, Carl E., & Gibbs, H. M., *Ocean Transportation,* McGraw-Hill, N. Y., 1954

McDowell, William, *The Shape of Ships,* Hutchinson House, London, 1950

Melville, John H., *The Great White Fleet,* Vantage Press, N. Y., 1976

Merchant Vessels of the U. S., Department of Commerce, various annual issues used

Meyer, H. H. B., *List of References on Shipping and Shipbuilding,* Library of Congress, Washington, 1919

Mills, James Cooke, *Our Inland Seas,* A. C. McClurg, Chicago, 1910

Mitchell, C. B., *Have Served, The National Cargo Bureau's First Quarter-Century,* NCB, N. Y., 1977

Mitchell, C. Bradford, *We'll Deliver, Early History of the U. S. Merchant Marine Academy,* USMMA Alumni Ass'n., 1977

Morison, Samuel E., *Maritime History of Massachusetts, 1783-1860,* Houghton Mifflin, Boston, 1941

Morrison, John H., *Iron and Steel Hull Steam Navigation,* W. F. Samtz, N. Y., 1903

Morrison, John H., *Iron and Steel Hull Steam Vessels of the United States, 1825-1905.* Reprint Series No. 3, Steamship Historical Society of America, Salem, Mass., 1945

Mott, G. F., *A Survey of U. S. Ports,* Arco Publishing Co., N. Y., 1951

Nevins, Allan, *Sail On,* privately published by United States Lines, 1946

Newell, Gordon R., *Ships of the Inland Sea,* Binfords & Mort, Portland, Ore., 1951

Newell, Gordon and Williamson, Joe, *Pacific Steamboats,* Superior Pub. Co., Seattle, Wash., 1958

Outhwaite, Leonard, *The Atlantic, A History of an Ocean,* Coward-McCann, N. Y., 1957

Peabody Museum, *The American Neptune,* quarterly journal, Salem, Mass.

Perry, John, *American Ferryboats,* Wilfred Funk, Inc., N. Y., 1957

Plowden, David, *Farewell to Steam,* Stephen Greene Press, Brattleboro, Vt., 1966

Pohn, F. J., *Amerigo Vespucci Pilot Major,* Columbia Univ. Press, N. Y., 1944

Pohl, F. J., *The Lost Discovery,* Norton, N. Y., 1952

Pohl, Frederick J., *The Viking Explorers,* Thomas Y. Crowell, N. Y., 1966

Port of N. Y. Authority, *The Port of New York From Colonial Days to the Twentieth Century,* reprints from "Via Port of New York," about 1952.

Prager, Hans Georg, *Blohm & Voss, Ships and Machinery for the World* (English edition translated by F. A. Bishop), Koehler, Hamburg, Germany, 1977

Quick, Herbert & Edward, *Mississippi Steamboatin',* Henry Holt, N. Y., 1926

Rattray, Jeannette Edwards, *The Perils of the Port of New York,* Dodd, Mead, N. Y., 1973

Rattray, Jeannette Edwards, *Ship Ashore!,* Coward-McCann, N. Y., 1955

Remington, Critchell, *Merchant Fleets,* Dodd, Mead, N. Y., 1944

Richardson, John M., *Steamboat Lore of the Penobscot,* Kennebec Journal Print Shop, Augusta, Me., 1941

Riesenberg, Felix, Jr., *Great Men of the Sea,* Putnam, N. Y., 1955

Riesenberg, Felix, Jr., *Currier & Ives Prints—Early Steamships*, Herbert Reiach, Ltd., London, 1933

Ringwald, Donald C., *The MARY POWELL*, Howell-North Books, Berkeley, Cal., 1972

Rosskam, Edwin & Louise, *Towboat River*, Duell, Sloan and Pearce, N. Y., 1948

Russell, Maud, *Men Along the Shore, The I.L.A. and Its History*, Brussel & Brussel, N. Y., 1966

Russell, W. Clark, *The Ship, Her Story*, Stokes, N. Y., 1899

Samuel, Ray; Huber, L. V., & Ogden, W. C., *Tales of the Mississippi*, Hastings House, N. Y., 1955

Sawyer, L. A., and Mitchell, W. H., *The Liberty Ships*, Cornell Maritime Press, Cambridge, Md., 1970

Sea Breezes, The Ship Lovers' Digest, published by Charles Birchall, Liverpool

Seamen's Bank for Savings, *One Hundred Fifteen Years of Service, 1829-1944*, Muir & Co., N. Y., 1944

Schmitt, Frederick P., *Mark Well the Whale*, Kennikat Press, Port Wash., N. Y., 1971

Shipmaster's Club, *Year Book With Illustrations and Stories*, N. Y., 1917

Ships and the Sea, Kalmbach Publishing Co., Milwaukee, various issues used

Slocum, Victor, *Capt. Joshua Slocum*, Sheridan House, N. Y., 1950

Smith, A. D. H., *Commodore Vanderbilt, An Epic of American Achievement*, McBride, N. Y., 1927

Smith, Eugene W., *Trans-Atlantic Passenger Ships Past and Present*, Dean, Boston, 1947

Smith, Eugene W., *Trans-Pacific Passenger Ships*, Dean, Boston, 1953

Spratt, H. P., *Outline History of Trans-Atlantic Steam Navigation*, His Majesty's Stationery Office, London, 1950

Spratt, H. P., *Transatlantic Paddle Steamers*, Brown, Son & Ferguson, Glasgow, 1951

Stackpole, Edouard A., *The Wreck of the Steamer San Francisco*, Marine Historical Association, Mystic, Conn., 1954

Stanton, Samuel W., *Steam Navigation on the Carolina Sounds and the Chesapeake in 1892*, Reprint Series No. 4, Steamship Historical Society of America, Salem, Mass., 1947

State Street Trust Co., *Some Ships of the Clipper Ship Era*, Boston, 1913

Steamship Historical Society of America, *Steamboat Bill of Facts*, quarterly journal, West Barrington, R. I.

Stone, H. L., *The America's Cup Races*, Macmillan, N. Y., 1930

Swan, O. G., *Deep Water Days*, Macrae-Smith, Philadelphia, 1929

Swann, Leonard A., Jr., *John Roach—Maritime Entrepreneur*, U. S. Naval Inst., Annapolis, Md., 1965

Talbot, F. A., *Steamship Conquest of the World*, Lippincott, Phila., 1912

Talbot-Booth, E. C., *A Cruising Companion—Ships and the Sea*, D. Appleton-Century, London, 1937

Tod, Giles M. S., *The Last Sail Down East*, Barre Publishers, Barre, Mass., 1965

Trogoff, J., *La Course au Ruban Bleu*, Societe D'Editions Geographiques, Maritimes et Coloniales, Paris, 1945

Tyler, David B., *Steam Conquers the Atlantic*, D. Appleton-Century, N. Y., 1939

U. S. Merchant Marine Cadet Corps, *Americans Who Have Contributed to the History and Traditions of the U. S. Merchant Marine*, Kings Point, N. Y., 1943

Van Loon, H. W., *Ships and How They Sailed the Seven Seas*, Simon & Schuster, N. Y., 1935

Van Metre, T. W., *Tramps and Liners*, Doubleday, Doran, Garden City, 1931

Vocino, Michele, *Ships Through the Ages*, Luigi Alfieri, Milano, 1951

Way, Frederick, Jr., *The Saga of the Delta Queen*, Picture Marine, Cincinnati, 1951

Weiss, George, *America's Maritime Progress*, Marine News Co., N. Y., 1920

White, A. G. H., *Ships of the North Atlantic*, Sampson, Low, Marston, London, 1940

Williamson, W. M., editor, *The Eternal Sea*, Coward-McCann, N. Y., 1946

Wolfe, Reese, *Yankee Ships, An Informal History of the American Merchant Marine*, Bobbs-Merrill, Indianapolis, 1953

Woon, Basil, *The Frantic Atlantic*, Knopf, N. Y., 1927

Work Projects Administration, *A Maritime History of New York*, Doubleday, Doran, Garden City

INDEX

231